From Periphery to Centre

This book studies the multi-dimensional development and landscapes of the internationalization of China's higher education throughout the past four decades, illustrating its trajectory from the periphery to the centre of the global higher education system.

Combining solid theoretical elucidation and rich empirical studies, the author systematically reviews the key relevant concepts and examines policies and practices of higher education internationalization in China based on rich data gathered from interviews and surveys on overseas Chinese scholars, academic returnees, and international students. With a focus on "internationalization at home" and "transnational academic mobility", the book analyzes the core topics and phenomena of China's internationalizing higher education, including Chinese students studying abroad, overseas academics returning to China, international students in China, Sino-foreign cooperative education, and internationalization of higher education in Hong Kong, Singapore, and Shanghai.

Seeking to offer valuable experience, reflections, and policy reference, this book will be of great value for researchers, policymakers, and university administrators interested in the internationalization of higher education and especially China's successful cases.

Mei Li is Professor of Higher Education at the Institute of Higher Education, Faculty of Education, East China Normal University, China. She specializes in internationalization of higher education, comparative and international higher education, and higher education policy in China.

From Periphery to Centre

The Road of Internationalization of Higher Education in China

Mei Li

LONDON AND NEW YORK

This work is supported by Fundamental Research Funds for the Central Universities of ECNU's project of International Publication of Humanities and Social Sciences (Translation Project, 2021ECNU-HWCBFBWY002).

First published in English 2024
by Routledge
4 Park Square, Milton Park, Abingdon, Oxon OX14 4RN

and by Routledge
605 Third Avenue, New York, NY 10158

Routledge is an imprint of the Taylor & Francis Group, an informa business

© 2024 Mei Li

Translated by Mei Li, Jie Zheng, Ying Yue, Qiongqiong Chen

The right of Mei Li to be identified as author of this work has been asserted in accordance with sections 77 and 78 of the Copyright, Designs and Patents Act 1988.

All rights reserved. No part of this book may be reprinted or reproduced or utilised in any form or by any electronic, mechanical, or other means, now known or hereafter invented, including photocopying and recording, or in any information storage or retrieval system, without permission in writing from the publishers.

Trademark notice: Product or corporate names may be trademarks or registered trademarks, and are used only for identification and explanation without intent to infringe.

English Version by permission of East China Normal University Press Ltd.

British Library Cataloguing-in-Publication Data
A catalogue record for this book is available from the British Library

ISBN: 978-1-032-54382-6 (hbk)
ISBN: 978-1-032-54383-3 (pbk)
ISBN: 978-1-003-42461-1 (ebk)

DOI: 10.4324/9781003424611

Typeset in Times New Roman
by Deanta Global Publishing Services, Chennai, India

Contents

	List of figures	vi
	List of tables	vii
	Foreword by Ruth Hayhoe	x
	Foreword to the Chinese Edition by Rui Yang	xii
	Preface	xv
	Acknowledgements	xix
	Abbreviations	xx
1	Moving from periphery to centre: China's higher education internationalization in the era of globalization	1
2	Theoretical perspectives on international academic mobility	26
3	From brain drain to brain circulation: International mobility of Chinese students and academics	42
4	From luring back to taking advantage of talent: Overseas academic talent policies and their implementation	79
5	From returning to taking root: Institutional environment and patterns of professional development of overseas academic returnees	102
6	From a peripheral player to a major hosting country: Policies and practices on international students in China	145
7	From expansion to quality enhancement: Sino-foreign joint venture institutions and programmes	178
8	A comparative study on internationalization of higher education in international Asian metropolitan cities	213
	Index	231

Figures

3.1	Influencing factors and flow process of Chinese academic talent in the US	55
3.2	Intentions for returning to China ($n = 68$)	59
3.3	Forms of contribution Chinese scholars in the US made for China	72
3.4	Satisfactory levels of collaborative partnership with Mainland Chinese counterparts ($n = 65$)	73
4.1	Classification of policies for Thousand Youth Talent Program awardees	89
5.1	An analytical framework for the career development of the Thousand Youth Talent Program Scholars	124
6.1	The number of international students in China between 1996 and 2018	148
6.2	Number of international degree-seeking students in China, 2000–2018 (unit: Thousands)	152
7.1	XJTLU's external quality governance and internal quality assurance systems	191

Tables

3.1	Number of Chinese students studying abroad from 2000 to 2018	46
3.2	Return rate of Chinese overseas students between 1978 and 2018	48
3.3	Number of Chinese overseas students in the main recipient countries from 1998 to 2017	49
3.4	Scientific and engineering PhDs holding foreign nationality and temporary passport while staying in the US 4–5 years after graduation from 1992 to 2005	50
3.5	Return rate of PhDs who studied in American universities by country and region from 1980 to 2010	51
3.6	Top 20 universities hosting international students in the US in 2018	52
3.7	Chinese students and scholars in the US	53
3.8	Interviewees' information	58
3.9	Level of degree obtained by Chinese scholars staying in the US	59
3.10	Negative factors affecting US Chinese scholars' willingness of returning to China	61
3.11	Favourable factors attracting Chinese scholars in the US to return home	65
3.12	Scholars' comparison of the academic career between China and the US	68
3.13	Collaborative object of Chinese scholars in the US	71
3.14	Major problems in cooperation with Chinese academic colleagues ($n = 65$)	72
4.1	Number of TYTP awardees (2011–2018)	91
4.2	Institutional distribution of TYTP awardees by cohort (2011–2018)	93
4.3	Number of shortlisted Thousand Youth Talent Program awardees at top 20 institutions (2011–2018)	95
5.1	The impact of overseas study and work on individuals	109
5.2	Basic information of the interviewees	122
5.3	TYTPS' higher education and training background	126
5.4	TYTP scholars' research teams	128
5.5	Analysis of three types of career development of the TYTP scholars	132

6.1	Top 5 countries of origin of international students in China, 1998–2018	149
6.2	Proportions of Korean, American, and Japanese students to international students in China, 2004–2018	150
6.3	Types of international students in China, 1998–2018	151
6.4	Distribution of disciplines for international students in China, 2002–2016	152
6.5	The number and proportion of self-financed international students in China, 1999–2018	153
6.6	Tuition fees for international students in Shanghai universities by degree level, 2018	156
6.7	The institutional distribution of international students in Shanghai, 2004–2016	158
6.8	The number of international students in Shanghai's HEIs by place of origin, 2005–2016	159
6.9	The proportion of various types of international students in HEIs in Shanghai	159
6.10	Enrolment of international students in Shanghai's HEIs by funding source, 2006–2016	160
6.11	Sample information of international students from FU, SJTU, and ECNU ($N = 307$)	162
6.12	Reasons for international students to study in China (mean values)	164
6.13	Reasons for international students from FU, SJTU, and ECNU to study in Shanghai	165
6.14	Plans of international students upon graduation from Shanghai (%)	166
6.15	Factors influencing international students' choice of FU, SJTU, and ECNU	167
6.16	Adaptation of international students at FU, SJTU, and ECNU	167
7.1	The leadership of the Sino-foreign joint venture institutions	183
7.2	Academic levels of teachers in Sino-foreign joint venture education programmes in 2016	200
7.3	The professional title structure of the teachers in Sino-foreign joint venture education programmes in 2016	201
7.4	Disciplinary distribution of the teachers in Sino-foreign joint venture programmes in 2016	201
7.5	The number of overseas faculty members by level of educational programme in 2016	203
7.6	Academic degree distribution of overseas teachers in Sino-foreign joint venture education programmes by level of programme in 2016	203
7.7	Distribution of overseas teacher's professional titles in Sino-foreign joint venture education programmes by level of programme in 2016	204
7.8	Qualifications of the overseas teachers in Sino-foreign joint venture education programmes in 2016	205
7.9	Disciplinary distribution for overseas teachers in Sino-foreign joint venture education programmes in 2016	205

7.10	Distribution of overseas teachers in Sino-foreign joint venture education programmes by province/municipality in 2016	206
8.1	The number and proportion of international (non-local) students at the six research universities in 2016 QS Ranking	215
8.2	Number and proportion of international (non-local) faculty at the six research universities in the 2016 QS Rankings	217
8.3	Selected international cooperative institutions/programmes of six research universities	219

Foreword

By Ruth Hayhoe

We are all used to definitions, analyses, discussions, and reflections on the internationalization of higher education from a Western perspective. The pathbreaking work of scholars such as Jane Knight, Philip Altbach, Hans de Wit, and many others has had a huge influence. This book offers insights from a seasoned scholar on the other side of the world in a study that is both theoretically sophisticated and empirically rich on China's experience of the internationalization of higher education in recent decades. The author, Professor Li Mei, has a PhD from the University of Hong Kong (2006), and is based at the East China Normal University in Shanghai, China's most cosmopolitan city. From rich and extensive research done in China and East Asia, as well as at the University of California in Los Angeles, she unfolds an Asian perspective on theories such as world system, human capital, and cosmopolitanism, then presents findings from the Chinese context that are both challenging and instructive.

Concepts such as brain drain, brain circulation, brain gain, and transnationalism take on new meaning as the Chinese experience is presented in remarkable, indeed breath-taking, detail. This includes profound insights from extensive interviews with outstanding Chinese scholars who have chosen to build their careers in the United States rather than returning, parallel interviews with those who decided to return, and an analysis of the policies on the Chinese side that shaped such decisions. Further exploration is made into the ways in which the returnees adapted, and their teaching and research took root in their own society while connecting their colleagues and students to the wider world, including an extensive Chinese diaspora. Of particular interest is the case study of young returnees who were participants in the prestigious "Thousand Youth Talent Program", and were given unique recognition and advantages as they settled into positions in leading research universities on return. There are significant lessons here for other countries in Asia and Africa that are facing similar concerns over the impact of brain drain and are looking to develop policies that will encourage such forms of brain circulation and transnational cooperation.

The final three chapters turn to other fascinating dimensions of China's higher education internationalization process. Most striking has been China's rapid move to a balancing of inward and outward oriented movement with the dramatic rise in international students attracted to study in China, from around 40,000 in 1991 to 490,000 in 2018, giving it third place in the world. This has been clear evidence of the move from periphery to centre highlighted in the book's title and details on the students' origins and the changing profile of the programme and area of study indicate the rising academic standing of China's universities. A survey of international students in three top Shanghai universities presented in Chapter 6 gives many insights into their motivations, the degree of satisfaction they have towards their study experience, and the problems and barriers that need attention. The creation of international joint campuses and programmes is another significant dimension with nine joint venture universities that have independent legal status, as well as a multitude of programmes throughout the country. The comparative case study of one Sino-British and another Sino-American institution opens up many contrasting dimensions with a discussion of the quality assurance system of a third showing the diversity of type. Altogether close to 7,000 faculty members from dozens of countries around the world, more than half holding doctoral degrees, are resident in China, making possible a remarkable degree of "internationalization at home". The final chapter moves to a comparative reflection on higher education and internationalization in three Asian metropolises – Singapore, Hong Kong, and Shanghai – and their global resonance.

In concluding this foreword, I cannot resist expressing the hope that the internationalization models and processes presented in this book will serve as a bridge to bring the richness of China's classical culture to the global higher education community. I look back on the first World Congress of Comparative Education to be held in China in 2017 and note that it met at Beijing Normal University, a sister institution to Shanghai's East China Normal University where Professor Li Mei is based. While education has tended to have a low status as an inter-disciplinary and applied field in the European university, the Confucian scholarly heritage gives it highest status. No wonder the normal school, founded by the French to challenge the traditional university after their Revolution and to nurture teachers who would ensure every child was educated to become a republican citizen, has had such resonance in East Asia, though forgotten in the English-speaking world. The concept of the teacher as a model, *shifan*, the Chinese translation of the French word *normal*, may be the most valuable gift China's universities can bring to the global research university through the dynamic and expanding processes of internationalization analyzed in this groundbreaking book.

Reference

Hayhoe, R. (2017). China in the centre: What will it mean for global education? *Frontiers of Education in China*, *12*(1), 3–28.

Foreword to the Chinese Edition

By Rui Yang

Educational research in different times exhibits diverse characteristics due to the different political, economic, and cultural situations at home and abroad. These features are manifested not only in what is to be researched and how it is researched, but also in who undertakes the research. Since these characteristics and their manifestations occur so quietly in our daily lives, and in the details of our work and life that not every researcher pays attention to, even fewer people observe them as research objects. However, such phenomena are extremely worthy of our in-depth thinking. The status quo is that among various scholars in this contemporary era, some create the era, some adapt to the era, while others reject to adapt to the era. The attitudes and pathways we adopted are diversified, naturally leaving different traces and influences.

A few years ago, I invited an influential scholar from Mainland China to visit the University of Hong Kong. In his presentation, he claimed that in recent years, he went abroad frequently on purpose to see how the education systems in foreign countries were not superior to ours. In my opinion, this attitude is somewhat inappropriate. Confucius instructs us that "If three of us walking together, one of them is bound to be good enough to be my teacher".

Such an attitude for learning confounds the inter-relationship between contemporary Chinese and Western knowledge. It should be noted that since the beginning of the Opium War (1840), we have been working assiduously to learn from the West to improve ourselves. Today, Western knowledge has become an important part of China's modern knowledge system. Simply rejecting Western knowledge is seriously unwise in research, and this is infeasible and even misleading in practice. The development of our country requires us to convert the Western knowledge into nutrients that we can absorb, and cultivate our ability to blend Western and Eastern knowledge. This urges Chinese scholars to have a deep understanding of the advantages and disadvantages of Western academic development, rather than continuing to engage in monologue and divorce from practice. The application of Western methods does not necessarily hinder our academic growth, and reading Western literature is a necessity for contemporary scholarship in China. Ignorance of others leads to mistakes and deficiencies.

Nowadays, the work of the current academic staff in China is under multiple influences, presenting a multifaceted and multi-layered integration. This mixed feature is shown in the way and content of work, as well as in individual scholars and the academic system as a whole. Among them, a successful integration will lead to greater achievements, reaching the realm of "learning without discriminating China and the West, learning without discriminating the old and new" (we should have a compatible attitude towards academic achievements of all times and all countries), as proposed by a prominent modern Chinese scholar – Wang Guowei. We also need to integrate Chinese and Western knowledge like Qian Zhongshu, another modern Chinese scholar, who tapped resources from home and abroad; we shall also learn from Fei Xiaotong, a modern Chinese academic master, who ferried and absorbed knowledge between China and the West. Every form of beauty has its uniqueness, it is precious to appreciate other forms of beauty with openness; if beauty represents itself with diversity and integrity, the world will be blessed with harmony and unity. Keeping on complaining about the inequality of the international knowledge system cannot solve practical problems, even worse, it demonstrates our laziness. We should realize that people who are in a dominant position in the international knowledge system will not be concerned about our disengagement from this system.

Since the Reform and Opening-up, and after more than four decades of continuous development and construction, China has grown into a large country renowned for its higher education, ranking first in the world in terms of scale and volume. However, compared with higher education in developed countries in Europe and the US, gaps exist in terms of investment, quality, management, system, etc. In the process of successive accumulation and stable development of China's higher education, internationalization, marketization, massification, and even popularization of higher education are its main properties and trends. Internationalization is the cardinal strategy and development pathway for China's higher education to integrate into the world's higher education system, and academic system, to raise its quality and global influence. As such, it is necessary to comprehensively sort out the successful experience and existing problems of the internationalization of China's higher education in the past 40 years, so as to provide experience and theoretical support for forging a strong and influential higher education system in China. This book attempts to systematically investigate how China's higher education has moved from the "periphery" of the world's higher education system to the semi-centre and finally to the centre through internationalization policy and practices, displaying the process of its integration into the international higher education system and the development characteristics of each dimension of internationalization.

In the 21st century, China will be more comprehensively open to the outside world. China is a critical participant in the process of world history and plays an increasingly notable role in the world system. The research on the internationalization of China's higher education is particularly indispensable. However, due to its complexity, wide coverage, and rapid changes, the current research on China's internationalization of higher education at home and abroad is still scarce. The domestic research on the internationalization of China's higher education is mainly published as journal articles and degree dissertations, with only a few monographs. Most of the existing studies are confined to "self-monologue", lacking the combination of international research and familiarity with domestic policies and practices, thus failing to effectively absorb international research outputs, to engage in equal dialogues and exchanges, to contribute to China's practical experience, and to tell Chinese stories to international counterparts. "Thinking globally, acting locally" in the field of comparative education has a practical guiding role in the internationalization of China's higher education. This book is stemmed from Dr Li Mei's years of effort on study of the internationalization of higher education, and is an attempt to contribute to the dialogue between China's researchers and foreign colleagues.

To recapitulate, after reading this monograph, what impressed me most is the type of research it represents. Today, human society is experiencing an unprecedented space-time compression in history. One of the keys to responding to globalization is to properly handle the relationship between the local and the global in search of the right way to deal with it. This book closely combines China with the world, and the local with the global from beginning to end, reflecting a conspicuous international perspective, which is embodied in the content and analysis, as well as in the literature review. This is very crucial, as it is what researchers in the new era should do, and is also an urgent requirement for improving our knowledge system. Scholars in China urgently need to establish a global vision and "enter the world" with a more positive attitude. We should pay attention to international educational research, participate in topics of common concern in the international academic community, and interpret China's outlook and theory from the perspective of the world for research in the premise of China's national conditions.

On a personal level, Dr Li Mei and I were predestined to meet and know each other. Although I am seven years older than her, we still call each other brother and sister. The reason is that Professor Mark Bray, my supervisor during study at the University of Hong Kong from late June 1996 to early March 1997, was also her supervisor when she was studying for her doctorate at the University of Hong Kong. The first time we met was when she came to the City University of Hong Kong to attend my academic seminar in April 2002. Since then, we have maintained academic contact. She is well-prepared to become an excellent scholar by having a foundation in English as an undergraduate, being nurtured by Professor Ding Gang in the history of education during her master's degree and being rigorously trained in international and comparative education by Professor Bray during her doctoral project. Dr Li Mei never fails to live up to everyone's expectations. In bustling Shanghai, she insists on studying intently and diligently, and has published high-quality Chinese and English journal articles. I would like to extend my sincere congratulations to her and expect her to contribute more outstanding achievements to the academic community at home and abroad.

Preface

Background of the book and the meaning of the title

Since I commenced my doctorate study, I have always been interested in the process and unique pathway of internationalizing China's higher education in the context of globalization and in the world community. This book continues and expands my research on the internationalization of Chinese higher education since the publication of *International Markets for Higher Education: The Global Flows of Chinese Students* in 2008. While the first book focuses on the globally mobile Chinese students in the international markets of higher education, this book delves into the multi-dimensional policies and practices of the internationalization of higher education, bespeaking the new landscape, new trends, new issues, and new impetus of the international development of China's higher education in the 21st century. This book focuses on the education of overseas students studying in China, international flows of Chinese academic talent, the academic career development of overseas returnees, Sino-foreign cooperative universities and programmes, and the international development of higher education in Asian metropolises. The internationalization of China's higher education in the new era has presented thriving changes, but the theoretical research fails to provide forward-looking, comprehensive, and basic guidance; the policy system has been constantly improved, and the policy implementation was also promoted, but it is still difficult to adapt to the rapid and complex realities of development. This book is a potent brew of the author's exploration and reflections in this field over the past years, in an attempt to provide foundation and inspiration for academic peers to conduct relevant research.

The title of the book, *From Periphery to Centre: The Road of Internationalization of Higher Education in China*, has two layers of meaning. First, it signifies the historical on-going process of China's higher education transforming from a "gigantic periphery" to a semi-central or even a central country of the world's higher education system through the internationalization strategy of the past 40 years. It does not mean that China's higher education institutions have already been at the centre of world's higher education arena. In other words, this book presents the development process, experiences, and features of the main dimensions of the internationalization of higher education (IHE) in China within the world higher education system, instead of the status of China's higher education in the "Centre-periphery" structure of the world's higher education community. The second meaning of *From Periphery to Centre: The Road of Internationalization of Higher Education in China* refers to the fact that the significance of the internationalization strategy in China's higher education has been shifting from periphery to centre over the past four decades. The role of internationalization strategy has been gradually transformed from the marginal position and local practice of China's higher education development to becoming its core strategy and key feature. The wave of internationalizing higher education in China has progressed from the internationalization of some institutions to the extensive internationalization of the whole higher education sector. Within colleges and universities, it has gradually evolved from partial internationalization into a more comprehensive internationalization. At present, the internationalization of China's higher education is still at a stage of rapid development. Looking ahead, against the backdrop of the ethos of globalization and de-globalization, anti-globalization, China's further reintegration into the world community is going to be strengthened yet will face greater, more complex challenges; the research on internationalization of higher education at home and abroad is now more critically needed than ever before. More in-depth and systematic research needs to be conducted to provide thoughtful guidance and theoretical resources for China's higher education development.

Purpose and significance of this book

Since the Reform and Opening-up, after 40 years of continuous development and construction, China has become an advanced country in terms of its higher education. China has realized the massification of higher education and is proceeding into the stage of the popularization of higher education. Although its scale and volume of higher education rank the first in the world, China is still lagging behind European countries and the US in terms of higher education development. In the process of continuous accumulation and stable development, internationalization, marketization, diversification, and massification are its main properties and trends. Among them, the internationalization of higher education and opening-up are the cardinal strategies and development pathways for China's higher education to integrate into the world's higher education system. IHE has led to a comprehensive and profound transformation of higher education at the macro, the meso, and the micro levels, and has also provided intellectual support, talent resources, and scientific research bases for social and economic development in China. On the whole, the integration of international, cross-cultural, and global dimensions into China's talent cultivation, scientific research, and management services of higher education institutions has been increasingly deepened and strengthened.

However, few studies have integrated theoretical investigation, policy analysis, and practical exploration to outline the multi-dimensional landscapes and development status of higher education internationalization in China. It is necessary to comprehensively analyze experiences and existing problems of China's higher education internationalization development over the past four decades.

This book attempts to investigate how China's higher education is moving from the periphery of the world's higher education system to a more central position with international educational policies and practices. It aims to elaborate the development experience, characteristics, mode, and pathway of higher education internationalization in China.

The research is of significance for understanding China's fast-changing modernization of higher education. The IHE in China also has an increasingly important impact on the overall development of the world. Against the backdrop of global tensions and knotty issues and crises facing the world, as an emerging power, a non-Western Asian socialist country with a long history of civilization, China plays an irreplaceable role in the world's development in general and Asian progress in particular. The particular development pathway and experience of higher education internationalization in China has implications for other developing countries. This book attempts to provide policy reflection for the government and university administrators engaged in the management of international higher education, to trigger theoretical dialogues and reflection for researchers regarding the internationalization of higher education.

Content and structure of the book

This book aims to reveal the policy evolution and practical features of the internationalization of China's higher education in the past 40 years. Due to the limited space and energy of the author, this book does not intend to portray the internationalization of China's higher education in an all-round way. Some aspects of internationalization, such as internationalization of curricula and teaching, internationalization of scientific research, education hubs, Confucius Institutes, and the "Belt and Road" Initiative and the "Belt and Road" *Educational Action Plan*, will not be discussed in detail. This book highlights two aspects of internationalization, namely "Internationalization at Home" and "Transnational Academic Mobility". In terms of theoretical interpretations, this book teases out concepts of globalization, internationalization of higher education, international flows of academic talent, transnational capital, and academic career development of Chinese academic returnees. As for policy analysis, it describes the policy system and its development changes of different dimensions of higher education (overseas students studying in China, international flows of Chinese academic talent, attracting of overseas talent, Sino-foreign joint venture universities, internationalization of higher education in Asian metropolises). This book is based on rich empirical investigations and analysis of both qualitative and quantitative data on the aforementioned aspects of internationalization of higher education in China.

The book consists of eight chapters. Chapter 1 offers a broad overview of higher education internationalization and China's experiences, and the next seven chapters unfold different dimensions of internationalization of higher education in China. Chapter 1 outlines the background, theoretical basis, historical stage, model evolution, and prospects of the internationalization of China's higher education. Chapters 2, 3, 4, and 5 focus on the international flows of academic talents. Chapter 2 summarizes the theoretical narratives of the international flows of academic talent, providing a theoretical perspective for explaining the policies and practices of academic talent flows in Chapters 3, 4, and 5. Chapter 3 details the international flows of Chinese students and academic talent, including its trends, characteristics, and impact. Meanwhile, through the survey of Chinese scholars staying in the US, it also reveals the reasons for their choices, their intention to return home, and career development status. Chapter 4 highlights the policy of overseas academic talent and its implementation, particularly the changes of overseas talent policy and the implementation of the policy of the "Thousand Youth Talent Program". Chapter 5 depicts and summarizes the academic career development features and development environment of overseas returnees through the field survey of ordinary overseas returning teachers and those young scientists selected in the "Thousand Youth Talent Program". Chapter 6 investigates international students in China, tracing the evolution of education policy for overseas students, the current situation, and the problems and countermeasures of international student education. Chapter 7 takes three Sino-foreign joint venture universities as cases and reveals their development features, management system, and quality assurance system, before statistically analyzing the features of teachers and the situation of overseas teachers in Sino-foreign joint venture programmes. Chapter 8 makes a comparative study of the internationalization of higher education in Singapore, Hong Kong, and Shanghai, three Asian international metropolises.

Changes of the English version of this book

This book is translated from the original Chinese version, which was published in 2019, before the pandemic crisis. At that time, the author saw the future of China's higher education internationalization in a more optimistic light than now. The English version has been modestly modified from the Chinese version. The changes are as follows. First, for reasons of length, some unimportant tables and figures and outdated data in Chapters 3, 6, 7, as well as the afterword, have been omitted. Second, some detailed descriptions about policies and practices have been condensed in Chapters 3, 4, 6, 7, 8 so that the text is more concise. Third, a foreword by professor Ruth Hayhoe and acknowledgements by the author have been added. Fourth, the preface has been revised. In addition, some new publications have been added to the references (particularly in Chapter 1), and some literature of the translated articles have been replaced by the original English articles as references. I hope through the English version of this book, international readers can open a window for observing the landscapes of internationalization of higher education in China.

Acknowledgements

This is the English version of my Chinese book, titled as "Moving from Periphery to Centre: The Road of Internationalization of Higher Education in China". The Chinese version was written based on a research project entitled "Relationship between Construction of Professional Space of Academic Returnees and the Disciplinary Development in Universities" (16YJA880020), funded by the Ministry of Education (MOE) of the People's Republic of China – Humanities and Social Science Research Foundation. The Chinese version was well-received and was conferred a national award as an outstanding educational research work by the MOE in 2021. Hopefully, the English version can also be popular with the international research community.

I owe a special debt of gratitude to Professor Ruth Hayhoe and Professor Rui Yang, not only because of their remarkable forewords to the English and Chinese versions of the book, but also for their unfailing support and guidance on my academic career for decades. I would like to express my great gratitude to three young scholars – Dr Zheng Jie, Dr Chen Qiongqiong, and Dr Yue Ying – for their efforts in translating the book. I would like to acknowledge the contribution made to the book by Dr Janette Ryan, Dr Xu Wen, Li Weijun, and Chen Anan who proofread some parts of the translation.

My appreciation also goes to Professor Simon Marginson, Professor Mark Bray, and Professor Qiang Zha, who have supported my research on internationalization of higher education. Particularly, I would like to express my gratitude to my colleagues and students from the Institute of Higher Education, East China Normal University. A big thank you also goes to my participants; it would have been impossible to complete the book without their support in my field work. I am also indebted to Mr Chong Daoyang and Ms Sun Juan at the ECNU Press, who collaboratively managing the publication of my book bilingually. The translated version was supported by ECNU's project of International Publication of Humanities and Social Sciences (Translation Project, 2021ECNU-HWCBFBWY002).

Abbreviations

BRI	Belt and Road Initiative
CAS	Chinese Academy of Sciences
CPC	Chinese Communist Party
CSC	China Scholarship Council
CSCSE	Chinese Service Center for Scholarly Exchange
ECNU	East China Normal University
FU	Fudan University
HEIs	Higher Education Institutions
HKU	University of Hong Kong
HKUST	Hong Kong University of Science and Technology
IHE	Internationalization of Higher Education
MoE	Ministry of Education (China)
NSF	National Natural Science Foundation (China)
NTU	Nanyang Technological University
NUS	National University of Singapore
NYUS	New York University Shanghai
QAA	Quality Assurance Agency (for Higher Education)
RMB	Renminbi
SCI	Science Citation Index
SJTU	Shanghai Jiao Tong University
SSCI	Social Science Citation Index
TYTP	The Thousand Youth Talent Program
TYTPS	The Thousand Youth Talent Program Scholar
UK	The United Kingdom
UNNC	University of Nottingham Ningbo China
US	The United States
WTO	World Trade Organization
XJTLU	Xi'an Jiaotong-Liverpool University

1 Moving from periphery to centre

China's higher education internationalization in the era of globalization

1.1 Higher education internationalization in the era of globalization

1.1.1 The challenges facing higher education

Since the 1980s, the ideology of the free-market economy advocated by neo-liberalism has swept across the world and multinational enterprises and groups have been expanding globally. Consequently, international and regional organizations have been increasing in number. And with this, the transportation and communication-related technology sectors have grown rapidly. Under the influence of this ideology, globalization has exerted a far-reaching impact on the world's politics, economy, population, and culture. Globalization and market globalism are thus reshaping the structure of worldwide higher education. In response to the challenges of globalization, research-oriented universities across all nations are speeding up the process of their internationalization in order to realize the coordinated development of university and regional internationalization. Therefore, researchers have raised the need for a systematic study of the comprehensive and profound impact that globalization has exerted on education, especially on higher education.

First of all, globalization poses a challenge to the status and governance functions of nation states. The "nation state" is not a concept or entity that has evolved naturally with human society. Throughout the history of human development, the existence and prominence of the nation state's status is a phenomenon of more modern times. Originally, "state" and "nation" were two separate concepts, but more recently these two words are often used collectively to refer to the same entity. In the era of globalization, with the nation state being the major institutional form that handles all domestic and international affairs, its role has become more and more complex. Globalization pushes cross-border mobility in the areas of business capital, information, goods and services, and people and technology in an increasingly accelerated way. The mobile and communication network sectors are seeing rapid development. Compressing time and space, these industries have allowed individuals to interact instantaneously. Whether it be geopolitically or in the minds of individuals, the concept of territory is growing weaker. People carry various capital flows around the world and live and work together with different ethnic groups, different nation states, different belief systems, cohabitating and collaborating in this global village. When crossing national borders becomes commonplace and when the inherent powers of nation states are transferred to international organizations, and multinational enterprises, they compete with local industries, local trade, and local societies. Will this be when nation states play more of a supportive role, will they just simply become more sophisticated figureheads so that the nation is more adaptive in the state of globalization? Leading on from this viewpoint, as national boundaries are crossed and characterized by all kinds of flows and behaviours, nation states are no longer separate governing units. In other words, it is harder for one government to completely handle all of its affairs within its own territory. Furthermore, there appear to be more and more affairs that are outside the control of the nation, on issues such as global warming, epidemics, organized crime, terrorism, the global financial crisis, world organizations, provision of universal education – the list goes on. Various mechanisms and connections have transformed the world into a connected but unbalanced whole, with neither inseparable from the other.

Globalization has brought with it a multitude of educational problems and phenomena beyond the territory of one nation state. It poses various challenges to ways of thinking in regard to the nation state as being the controlling unit of analysis and governance. Education is categorized as one of the free trade services stipulated by the World Trade Organization (hereinafter abbreviated as WTO). There are four forms of educational trade services, namely cross-border supply, consumption abroad, commercial presence, and human resources. These services are not only hot topics of governmental negotiations, but they are also the modes of educational consumption by people from WTO countries. Ever since China became a member of the WTO in 2001, it has moved gradually from the semi-periphery to the central arena of the world system. Not only is it a passive recipient, China has been actively involved in the rule-making of global governance systems, taking part as one of the leading players and stakeholders. Therefore, in a certain sense, China is a beneficiary of the globalization wave. Since being admitted into the WTO, China has established varying forms of agreements surrounding educational trade services. As for services of consumption abroad (such as studying abroad), there are no regulatory restrictions. For cross-border supply (of distance and virtual education), China has no commitment to open the market. When it comes to attracting personnel (educators and professionals), specific qualifications are required. For the commercial presence (of internationally recognized schools and award-winning projects), strict regulations and approval procedures are stipulated.

Globalization has brought an unprecedented wave of Chinese individuals studying abroad. With the growing number of middle-class families in China and their soaring demand for the diversification, differentiation, and internationalization of their children's educational experience, the domestic higher education sector has been unable to meet their demands in this regard. Studying abroad has, therefore, become common practice among junior and senior secondary school students. Some students have even given up sitting for the high school entrance exams and the National Entrance Exam to study abroad. China has become the world's largest exporter of students studying abroad. Overseas study agencies have sprung up across China and the international education industry is booming. And with it, forgeries and scams have become hard to prevent. There are also other concerning issues, such as overseas students' safety, racial discrimination, interpersonal conflict, and adaptation to local surroundings. Some irresponsible behaviours by students, such as excessive conspicuous consumption and/or the display of wealth have left many negative impressions on local populations. The most serious problem is the phenomenon of "Studying abroad fever" whereby China has been consistently sending its own talented individuals to more developed countries, causing a large loss of high-calibre students and consequently impacting the development of domestic higher education. In recent years, the number of internationally recognized high schools has been slowly creeping up, some of which are set up under government supervision while others are not. These kinds of schools are sometimes integrated into the higher education system of developed countries, which is how top students are sometimes retained in those countries.

Globalization has not only enabled the worldwide flow of Chinese students and scholars, but also increased the number of international students studying within China. In 2016, China became the world's third largest recipient of international students and the top-ranking destination in Asia. With the increase in the number of students from different countries and with different cultural backgrounds, the internationalization of China's higher education has become more pronounced. To enhance the educational level of international students and meet the requirements of international development, an increasing number of English language medium courses, and a number of English language classes and programmes, have been introduced in a growing number of universities. When different cultures are integrated and different values are exchanged on campus, problems can arise that include resource allocation between domestic and international students. Different staff management modes, teaching styles, and cultural mindsets can bring about not only communication problems and misunderstandings but also conflicts and turmoil.

As agents of globalization, all kinds of profit or non-profit educational institutions and online courses are crossing national borders. On the one hand, they have satisfied the diversified and internationalized demand of educational consumers, but on the other, they have presented a series of challenges relating to quality assurance and over-commercialization. To be specific, more attention should be paid to the quality and suitability of curriculum and teaching for the changing population, paying particular attention to their influence on national educational sovereignty and values, commercialization in the local market, and supervisory mechanisms to ensure standards. English is the lingua franca in the education, science, and business fields, and it has become increasingly important with globalization. This places higher education organizations in a dilemma about the suitable choice of teaching language. When faced with competition for international students, and in the era of increasingly competitive markets for education and research, higher education organizations are finding it hard to decide whether to teach in English or Chinese.

As the international competition for scientific research intensifies, Chinese universities have been paying close attention to international publication. But what does this mean for each discipline? Does this bring about a new form of academic and cultural colonization? Would it affect the national identities of the humanities disciplines for example? In terms of the principal functions of teaching, scientific research, and social service, how will universities keep a balance between internationalization and indigenization? A growing number of new practices and phenomena – such as college ranking systems, internationally based courses, English-only classes, the presence of world-class universities, managerialism, the emphasis on SSCI/SCI publication, and "publish or perish" policies – have been cutting into the daily lives of decision makers, managers, and teachers and have severely influenced their style of teaching, academic discipline, and managerial behaviours.

To sum up, globalization has brought many challenges and opportunities for higher education. At the same time higher education internationalization means strategies and activities that are carried out by higher education organizations and departments have had to adapt in response to the previously mentioned challenges. In the 21st century, we have witnessed increasingly complex internationally based dilemmas and constant political and other international realignments. The global order of "one overarching superpower and many smaller powers" is facing an increasingly unstable transition. The competition between countries for education, human talent, finance, and research has become more and more intense. Within such a complicated and constantly changing environment, the development of higher education internationalization has developed the following characteristics: It is complex, multifaceted, dynamic, and influential. It is a pity that the theoretical and empirical knowledge in this regard appears to be so lacking that it is unable to respond to the rapidly changing global situation in order to solve various problems and issues that arise. The paucity and shortcomings of academic research in the field of internationalization have meant that there is a lack of useful guidance in the development of policy due to a limited number of theoretical studies and sound models of analysis. Given the importance of higher education internationalization in the era of globalization, and the transformation of higher education internationalization through the improvement of China's national strength and political and economic status, this book offers a thorough investigation and analysis of some salient aspects of higher education internationalization in China.

1.1.2 Concepts and characteristics of globalization

1.1.2.1 Concepts of globalization

Globalization is the outcome of the global expansion of capitalism. Since the 1980s, world economic integration has deepened. With information and communication technologies closely linking all parts of the world, every nation has entered into a developmental stage where mutual influence and relationships have deepened and expanded. This is the so-called era of globalization. Globalization is not only the unavoidable outcome of capitalist expansion, but it is also an inevitable result of the development in communications, transport, and research. But globalization is not just about markets and the spread of neo-liberal capitalism. In terms of its influence on higher education, globalization has varying impacts on different nations, different educational institutions, varying disciplines, and academic talent.

Different authors have presented varying definitions of globalization. Held et al. (1999) argue that globalization denotes the growing magnitude, expansion, and deepening of relations around the world that affect politics, economy, culture, and military dimensions. In Anthony Giddens' (1990) opinion, the essence of globalization is the "modernity of flow" – what is encompassed by different "flows" in the modern world – with flows referring to the trans-spatial and temporal movement of material products, people, signs, symbols, capital, knowledge, technology, and trade. Globalization reflects characteristics of the capitalist mode of production which is constantly expanding, breaking the constraints of time and space (Xue & Cao, 2005). Globalization has manipulated time and space allowing for instantaneous interaction, and long-distance manipulation and influence.

Philip Altbach (2004) regards globalization as the intensification of political, cultural and academic ties, interdependence, control, and penetration. It is impossible for any nation or organization to prevent, stop, or even ignore globalization, they can only adapt to its realities regarding the global penetration and mutual impact of information technologies, utilization of the English language, and the emergence of the private sector and higher education commercialization

Not only have Marginson and Rhoades (2002) highlighted the growing intensity and expansion of globalization's influence, they have also clarified its three interlinking domains, emphasizing the simultaneous significance of global, national, and local agencies and their respective forces. They elaborated that the abovementioned relationships coexist and have an impact on one another. These interlinked relationships create both contradictory and synergistic effects that affect development within various fields. There is not only the reification and localization of global power, but also the globalization and internationalization of local power.

1.1.2.2 Characteristics of globalization

Globalization is an integrated process of imbalanced and dynamic development, which has various meanings for different nations and organizations. In the global system as a whole, there are three types that these nations, organizations, and individuals can be categorized into: The dominating class; the integrated class; and the isolated class. Globalization is not an objective and neutral process, but a historical process shaped by both subjective and objective forces. It is an enormously complex historical process, filled with uncertainties. Globalization consists of both loyal supporters and opponents. In developed, capitalist societies such as in Europe and the US, the ideology of globalization once held a dominant position, and neoliberalism and free trade ideologies guided policy development and organizational structuring for various nations. However, in recent years, there has been a rise in the occurrence of anti-globalization sentiment, nationalism, and populism, such as, for example, the advent of the Brexit movement in Britain. After becoming president, Donald Trump reconstructed his diplomatic agenda, foreign economic, and trade policies, setting off a global trade war and trade protectionism. Recently, the

Sino-US trade war has intensified and their relations have become more strained. The clash between the world's most important nations as they compete, negotiate, and collaborate, means that there are significant impacts not just on China and the US but perhaps even globally on higher education exchange, as well as student mobility and talent migration. In 2018, the growing trend of Chinese students studying in America reversed, and work opportunities for talented Chinese scholars in America became more uncertain.

Globalization has brought about the proliferation of multinational organizations and institutions, which calls for the enhancement of global governance. A growing number of multinational organizations, regional organizations, multilateral organizations, civil societies worldwide, and environmental protection groups have emerged and participated in global governance and globalization development. In the 21st century, as China enters the world market and integrates into the world hierarchy, the country on the one hand plays an increasingly important role in contemporary education, on the other hand, it participates and leads the establishment of new multinational education institutions, and is assuming its responsibility as a major global power driver.

1.1.3 Internationalization of higher education: Concepts and rationales

As a dynamic historical process, internationalization is accompanied by globalization. The word "international" describes the relationship between countries, while internationalization refers to the specific policies and activities initiated by governments, departments, and institutions worldwide that pursue global development. Internationalization requires countries and their own institutions to take structured measures and spontaneously respond to globalization, while higher education institutions (HEIs) can determine whether and how to participate in the global academic system. Internationalization of higher education involves, first and foremost, the conceptualization of internationalization. In academia, scholars and researchers often use the "activity-based approach", the "competency approach", the "rationale/ethos approach", and the "process-based approach" to define IHE (Chen, 2002). The "activity-based approach" describes IHE by focusing on specific dimensions such as curriculum, talent mobility into a country, joint research activities, and research-related areas. The "competency approach" highlights the internationally oriented development of knowledge, skills, and attitudes of its students, faculty, and staff. The "rational/ethos approach" puts an emphasis on the development of an intercultural and international ethos. Focusing upon policies and programmes, Altbach (2004) defines internationalization as a certain group of policies and programmes that are approved procedures of governments, educational systems and institutions, and even individual departments to respond to globalization. Jane Knight (2006) underlines the "process approach" and frames internationalization as "the process of integrating an international, intercultural or global dimension into the purpose, functions or delivery of post-secondary education" (p. 214). She describes international, intercultural, and global features in terms of purpose, functions, and delivery for post-secondary education by integrating the three dimensions of HEIs, focusing closely on departments and procedural processes. Her conceptualization has been widely used in academia. Nonetheless, only by taking all of the above four approaches into consideration can the dimensions of IHE be completely explored. Given that the internationalization process is facilitated by varied activities, a further study on internationalization will help to enhance understanding of the international drivers of talent flows in higher education and shed light on the international culture of institutions and policies.

The rationales underpinning IHE can explain why there is a push for IHE, i.e. what rationales motivate each country and what kind of internationalization strategies should be implemented. Four rationales for IHE have been categorized internationally, which include political, economic, socio-cultural, and academic rationales (Knight, 2006, p. 216). Zha (2003) considers that such categorizations can offer a conceptual framework for debates on the rationales for internationalization. Zha (2003) further illustrates the features of the four rationales that drive countries to promote IHE activities. He argues that a political rationale is crucial for a country's status and role as a nation in the world, more specifically a country's impact on the world's security, prosperity, and ideology. To give an example, the recruitment of international students in Japan in the post-war period was driven by the country's political rationales as Japan expected to become a political power. Economic rationales consider long-term economic benefits and direct economic benefits. Long-term economic benefits of IHE are the training of talent with international competitiveness. International graduates are key to a nation's trade relationship. Direct benefits of IHE include tuition fees and living expenses brought by international students. Towards the end of the 1980s, the UK implemented a full-fee paying policy for international students. Australia regards higher education as the country's largest source of export trade and international students account for more than a quarter of the student population in Australia. As such, higher education has become a main service export industry of the two nations. The recruitment of international students is dominated by short-term economic rationales of generating financial income. The US has adopted different policies in terms of recruiting international students for those who are self-financed or those who are post-doctoral researchers. Recruiting international self-financed students is mainly driven by economic interests, while recruiting post-doctoral students in science and engineering is aimed at achieving long-term economic goals, gaining high-quality human resources through visa application and immigration avenues, as well as contributing to the social and economic development of the US. The academic rationale refers to the academic purposes and functions of HEIs, such as implementing international standards for teaching and learning, in addition to research. HEIs regard enhancement of institutional branding, academic reputation, and profile-status as their main goals. Other dominant rationales such as the recruitment of graduate students on scholarships, collaborative work with foreign HEIs, and hosting international events that contribute to a country's capacity building, collaborative scientific research, as well as collaborative knowledge and technology innovation, belong in the academic rationale category. The socio-cultural rationale reflects the importance of the role, position, and promotion of a country's language and culture, combined with the importance of understanding foreign languages and cultures. To give an example, in order to promote mutual understanding and integration among EU member states for establishing a European educational community and to enhance the competitiveness and international influence of EU higher education, the bloc has developed objectives for facilitating students' and faculty's mobility among EU countries. The four categories of rationale described above can be used for examining the driving forces and intentions of different institutions and actors in carrying out international activities.

1.1.4 Types of internationalization of higher education

1.1.4.1 Forced/spontaneous IHE

Internationalization can be categorized into forced IHE and spontaneous IHE in terms of whether the institutions or systems of IHE spontaneously adopt internationalization strategies or whether they are mandated to undertake them. The latter is often threatened or coerced by external forces. Spontaneous IHE means that in order to meet national and institutional development needs, nation states and institutions control the power to carry out international expansion, independently formulate strategic guidelines, and identify rationales focusing on policy measures, key points, models, and approaches to use in relation to internationalization. In the 19th century, the US sent a large number of students and scholars to Germany for a study tour, whereby at the end of it they borrowed the German higher education development model. The returned American scholars and students assisted in the setting up of the nation's research universities and teaching culture. This was a good example of spontaneous IHE. Another good example is when EU countries implemented European integration in education using the Bologna process. Forced internationalization refers to internationalization carried out under the coercion or control of external forces. For instance, colonies were forced to adopt their colonial master's education model for their teaching materials and the languages used.

1.1.4.2 Inward- and outward-oriented IHE

IHE has been differentiated by inward-oriented and outward-oriented internationalization depending on the direction of resource movement (Wu & Zha, 2018; Wu, 2021). Inward-oriented IHE refers to the form and type of international activities of importable HE resources (of projects, institutions, and courses) as well as the exportation of talent and consumers; while outward-oriented IHE refers to the international activities of export resources (outsourcing projects offshore and to institutions that are externally managed, and educators and faculty members outflow) combined with the recruitment of international students. Given that inward-oriented internationalization manifests in sending students and scholars abroad while attracting high-quality foreign professors and resource-rich educational materials, it is also known as imported internationalization and is often displayed in developing countries. Such countries have been peripheral or semi-peripheral in the global higher education system. Outward-oriented internationalization, also known as exported internationalization, refers to the export of academic and educational resources through cross-border delivery or delivery of education abroad. Developed countries such as European and American countries which are the pillars of world higher education largely facilitate outward-oriented internationalization. The third model is communicative internationalization, which is a combination of the inward-oriented and outward-oriented internationalization models. Countries like Japan, Singapore, and some European countries, which are located between the centre and the inner borderline of the global higher education and knowledge system, adopt this particular model. Their tactical model involves sending quite a large number of students and faculty members abroad, which allows them to bring in externally sourced educational assets, for example curricula, promoting the import of educational resources while also accepting a large cohort of international students, and at the same time promoting the exportation of their own educational resources. Both outward-oriented and inward-oriented internationalization are considered as unilateral internationalization (Bi & Zhang, 2006).

Wu and Zha (2018) believe the direction of higher education internationalization revolves around innovations and proliferation. In terms of an inward-oriented higher education internationalization, the "recipients" [the recipient being the countries and/or regions] proactively take knowledge and culture from the outside world and adapt them to their own education models, taking up their academic standards of norms and academic nomenclatures to attain "expansion diffusion", but also to promote "relocation diffusion" through facilitating studying abroad, bringing in cooperative educational partners and joint programmes. In terms of outward-oriented higher education internationalization, "expansion diffusion" originates with the "providers" [the originating countries/regions of innovations] in that their innovations, culture, higher education models, and norms are spontaneously followed by the "recipients". Furthermore, "relocation diffusion" occurs when the "providers" actively introduce innovations, culture, higher education service models, and norms to the world through international student recruitment, sending of experts abroad, establishing foreign campuses, and other outreach measures.

China's IHE used to be inward-oriented, the recent decade has witnessed the transformation to a balance of both inward- and outward-oriented development models, featuring the mobility of people, programmes, and institutions. Inward-oriented IHE includes an outbound flow of people to foreign countries and inbound flow of course programmes and institutions into China. Outward-oriented IHE includes an inbound flow of people to China and the outbound flow of programmes and institutions to foreign countries (Ye & Wang, 2018). China should take both inward-oriented and outward-oriented models in a collaborative way to enhance the country's soft power and international influence.

1.1.5 New forms and trends of internationalization of higher education

1.1.5.1 New forms

Higher education hubs – Some emerging countries and regions regard higher education as an important industry and propose the establishment of regional higher education hubs. An education hub is an organized education centre initiated by a government, a reputed centre for higher education excellence, and a cluster of top educational institutions and colleges. It is able to attract high-quality international academics and a larger cohort of quality international students, directing the areas of innovation in a series of disciplines, and preserving infrastructures to meet the challenges brought on by the ever-changing international environment (Song, 2015). Singapore, Hong Kong SAR, and Malaysia have formulated policies and approaches for establishing similar education hubs. Knight (2011) identified three kinds of education hubs, i.e. the international student hub, the skilled workforce hub, and the knowledge/innovation hub.

Global campuses – Driven by globalization, developed countries began establishing schools abroad and their own global campuses. As of April 2018, more than 30 countries, mainly in Europe and America, have established 263 campuses in seven countries through an "outreach" strategy (Merola, 2018). As of June 2016, the numbers of overseas campuses of certain countries are 89 campuses in the US, 45 campuses in the UK, 22 in Russia, and 9 in India (Hawawini, 2016). In recent years, Chinese universities have been called-to-action to establish campuses abroad. For example, Suzhou University founded Lao Soochow University in Laos in 2011. Zhejiang University commenced its establishment of the Imperial College of Science, Technology and Medicine in Britain in 2013, and Xiamen University established Xiamen University Malaysia in 2014. Tongji University also established an overseas campus in Florence, Italy in 2014. Moreover, the "Belt and Road" *Educational Action Plan* encourages universities in China to go abroad and establish educational cooperation with other nations.

1.1.5.2 New trends

Western nations have been the dominating countries driving the IHE process for a long time. However, many countries in Asia, more economically developed nations and emerging countries have started to play an increasingly important role in IHE from the beginning of the 21st century. The rationales for IHE were once dominated by external assistance grants for political purposes during the Cold War. While in the post-1980s period, seizing economic benefits became the dominant rationale for recruiting international students and building global campuses abroad. Education has become a trade commodity and a commercialized industry. However, entering the 21st century, the emphasis on academic rationales along with social and cultural rationales has become more apparent. Academic rationales are manifested in the establishment of world-class universities combined with global academic influence through internationalization initiatives. The social and cultural rationales are reflected in the focus on the improvement of a nation's flexibility and the global exchange of its culture. It is important to recognize that internationalization has advanced and expanded globally. The quantity, scale, scope, and impact of the flow of international academic talent starting from the second half of the 20th century is unprecedented.

1.1.6 The centre-periphery model in the global academia and higher education sector

The global academic and higher education system is a hierarchical structure similar to that of a pyramid. The status of academic institutions in each country is unequal largely because of each nation's uneven advancement. The "centre-periphery" structure in the higher education sector existed in the past, and it is also with us at present, and will continue to exist for long into the future. The ranking of HEIs in countries in the global academic and higher education system is not unchangeable, it frequently moves in a dynamic pattern. Academia and HEIs in developed countries take varied mechanisms to constantly reshape and reinforce their position in the global higher education system. One of their usual means is to attract the world's leading and brightest professionals by changing the nation's policies. Another crucial strategy is managing the diverse academic production and tools available (e.g. publication, journals, access to publishers). In addition, many academic centres and famous universities in developed countries are responsible for academic ranking, academic appraisals, and setting academic standards. The unilateral academic ranking system has a far-reaching negative impact on developing and marginalized countries in the academic world. It grants stakeholders and governments the right to make academic appraisals and resource allocations based on those indicators, resulting in missed opportunities for local talent training and scientific research that are deemed irrelevant to the cause. Institutions blindly pursue these globally recognized performance indicators of so-called international academic rankings.

English as a lingua franca for teaching, research, and exchange programmes further highlights its position in academic institutions and HEIs in English-speaking countries such as Britain, the US, Australia, and Canada in the global academic system. In addition, programmes and courses instructed in English are being increasingly offered by HEIs in China and European countries such as the Netherlands, which aim to attract international students and improve their international exchange and competitiveness. In the long run, the globalization of education needs to break through the limitations of the "centre-periphery" model and build more systematically balanced higher education.

Globalization has led to a lack of localization in the development of higher education, weakening the cultural roots and local autonomy of HEIs. Academic appraisals in developing countries follow Western standards where the humanities and social sciences imitate the evaluation model of natural science disciplines and research. Furthermore, the international rankings conducted by participating universities and research institutions foster the convergent development of global universities.

1.2 Changing from the periphery: Process, modes, and approaches and prospects of higher education internationalization in China

Since the 1950s, there has been a significant improvement in Asia's national and regional socio-economic development and its role in the international system. As the major power driver of Asia and the largest developing country in the world, China has created a new environment for higher education development along with its unceasing evolution and increasing role in global politics and economy. The opening-up of China's higher education sector is key, coupled with the driving force of China's national open agenda. Internationalization and the opening of higher education are not only connected but also distinctly related. The internationalization of higher education refers to the process, academic ranking, and characteristics of a globalized system for higher education, colleges, and institutes. However, the opening-up of higher education is a component of a wider national initiative. It refers specifically to the procedures and strategic direction of the Chinese government which is managing the local economic Open Access strategy. It has also been fostering international relationships and facilitating two-way exchange with regard to higher education under the respective principles and frameworks issued by the World Trade Organization (WTO). Several initiatives have been adopted to accomplish these call-for-action plans, which include deploying Chinese scholars offshore and promoting and introducing Chinese institutions to the world, as well as bringing international scholars and educational resources into the country. Whether it be openness to the outside world or internationalization itself, the content and characteristics of internationalization are integrated into the main functions of higher education.

1.2.1 The history of China's higher education internationalization

Influenced by the open-door policy of 1978, the internationalization and opening-up of higher education in China has been reflected in a number of aspects. From one angle, China has progressively and continually improved management of its own policies. The influence and roles of China have become increasingly more significant. From another perspective, the concept of internationalization has progressed from process to content. In the areas of staff training, research generation, and operational measures, higher education institutions now integrate a greater degree of internationalism, intercultural experience, and global elements into their education portfolios. The internationalization aspects have developed gradually from a slow and steady progression to now influencing the entire education system. It has influenced the top-ranking universities and now affects other higher education institutions. Due to historic events and past policy making experiences, there have been a number of stages in China's opening-up process in higher education.

Chen and Fan (2018) have interpreted the changing policies of China's education becoming more internationally open. They note that from 1978 to the 1990s, China was an "internal developer" and took the strategy of "bringing in" more during the initial opening-up period. From the late 1990s to the beginning of the 21st century, as the regional power geared up, China incorporated the strategies of "sending out" and "bringing in" more from the outside. Since the 2020s, China has taken a role as a "leader" and puts more effort into its involvement in global education governance.

1.2.1.1 Stage one 1978–1991: The initial stage of reforms and opening-up

Following the national reforms and the opening-up from 1978 to 1991, the opening-up of education originated from Chinese political ideas. Before the reform and opening-up, China was affected by political ideology and educational opening-up was very much reliant on the need for political development. The internationalization of higher education in China began from the 1980s, when, in 1983, Deng Xiaoping proposed that educational development should embrace modernization, the world, and the future. In 1985, the *Decision on the Reform of the Education System* clarified the rights of higher education institutions in carrying out international education and academic exchange. At this stage, internationalization was characterized by being partial, unidirectional, internal, and small scale. Specific policies also came out at that time. Leading on from that, China began to cooperate with socialist countries and a small number of Western countries with developed economies. Some students and scholars went abroad and pursued overseas study, while a small number of international students were invited to visit China, bringing in foreign educational resources, management styles, and the latest educational theories.

1.2.1.2 Stage two 1992–2000: The deepening opening-up of education within the market-oriented economy

Based on Deng Xiaoping's Southern Talks in 1992, China's reform and opening-up entered into a new historical era: Establishing a socialist market-oriented economy with a focus on economic construction and development. Higher education became more globally open and the market mechanism was integrated into the operation and management of the higher education system, where the market economy played an important role in the internationalization process. Furthermore, China enlarged the scope of the opening-up, and expanded its inbound and outbound education. In 1996, the establishment of the China Scholarship Council (CSC) marked the transformation of the management of the official opening-up of higher education, where professional educational institutions (or agents) took over the organization's management from the government. In January 1995, transnational education began as dictated by state policy. In 1998, the Higher Education Policy stipulated that "higher education institutions are to have exchange and cooperation with overseas universities and colleges in science, technology and culture". In the year 2000, the Ministry of Education (MoE) published a series of policies relating to international students coming to China, which aimed to promote the sustainable development of China's international education. By this time, the meaning of higher education internationalization was mainly about sending Chinese students overseas, and importing foreign educational resources and technologies, so as to meet the needs of local demand and to attract international talent.

1.2.1.3 Stage three: Integration into the international system after joining the WTO

China entered into the crucial phase of opening-up together with its entry into the WTO in 2001. The development strategy in this stage was to expand areas for opening-up, to transform, and to align the national systems with the world rules (Li, 2007).

The internationalization of higher education in China was at the stage of comprehensive, bidirectional, and both outward and inward development. In order to conform to the rules of the WTO, China opened the space for educational providers such as consumption abroad (overseas education), presence of personnel (inbound academics and professionals), and commercial presence (transnational education). A growing number of people, projects, and institutions arrived in China, which shifted the direction of development from quantity expansion to a quality-focused orientation. Furthermore, high-quality educational materials, concepts, and management styles were brought in from overseas. In 2003 and 2004, the national government launched the *Rules for Sino-Foreign Joint Venture Education in China* and the *Measures for Implementing the Rules for Sino-Foreign Joint Venture Education in China*, respectively, which effectively facilitated the development of this front.

Meanwhile, an increasing number of Chinese international students returned to China which helped to balance the ratio of inbound and outbound travellers. Be that as it may, the government continued to drive the immigration of foreign talent. High-level Chinese returnees and international talent played increasingly significant roles in universities and other institutions.

Additionally, the government and universities again emphasized their strategies for "going out" in relation to higher education and culturally specific resources. Since 2004, universities have started to establish Confucian Institutes abroad to spread Chinese language and culture. However, the main aims at that stage were still around the mobility of staff, importation of resources, and growing staff capability in higher education.

1.2.1.4 Stage four post-2012: The comprehensive stage in the global open-up

China's socialist economy development has entered a new era since 2012. Motivated by the growing trend of massification, China has become one of the leading countries offering higher education. By 2018, there were 2663 higher education institutions, with a student population of 38.83 million. The gross enrolment rate has reached 48.1%, which implies that higher education in China has entered the stage of massification (MoE, 2019). As the second largest economy in the world, China plays a significant role in global politics and economics with its demanding needs and requirements, such as transferring from a scale-oriented country of higher education to a powerful nation, and, from a large country of human resources to a powerful and research-driven nation. Meanwhile, the international community has indicated its high expectations of China, which is to take greater global responsibility. China has witnessed the transformation of its developmental stages and confronted the new era of opening-up, which has been monumental in that the Chinese government has carefully considered the situation and formulated comprehensive, wide-scale, and multi-functional educational policies of the open-up process.

In 2012, President Xi and the leadership group carried out a more active opening-up policy in terms of the internationalization of higher education, which encouraged China to take initiatives to participate in global rule-making policy and governance responsibilities. In 2016, the State Council published *Notable Suggestions on the Opening-up of Education in the New Era*, and in that same year, the MoE formulated the *Education Initiatives in Advancing the Joint Construction of the "Belt and Road"*, which has promoted higher education internationalization in a new era and improved the quality, efficacy, and transformation of the open-up process as a whole. The concept of internationalization has been engaged in the formulation of strategies, management, teaching, and research in higher education. The state has attached more importance to its meaning, quality, structure, and efficacy. Universities have highlighted outbound internationalization strategies, and started to establish overseas university campuses (e.g. Xiamen University has set up campus and research institutions in Malaysia), plus the establishment of 51 Confucius Institutes overseas. In 2016, China became one of the main destinations for international students as the third largest country with international students in the world, with many universities and institutions setting up English curricula and disciplines.

In January 2017, the State Council issued the *13th Five-Year Plan for the Development of National Education*, and projected targets in terms of education opening-up planning, the level of opening-up, and global governance. In 2019, the central government launched *China's Education Modernization 2035 Blueprint*, which facilitated the stages of internationalization planning, and promoted the idea and value of "going out" in terms of the national quality of educational resources, to construct a community for the shared future of mankind, as well as to promote the Belt and Road Initiative (BRI). In education, the policies included exchange and collaboration with the 65 countries along the "Belt and Road" to allow for talent training, cultural exchange, think tank construction, and scholarship, in order to establish people-to-people connections, develop the regional economy, and support mutual learning among nations. The "Belt and Road" *Educational Action Plan* made a difference to the collaboration modes among institutions and created zonal and regional models of cooperation with higher education institutions. This stage emphasized the harmonious interactions between the opening-up of higher education and the development of the economy, society, and culture, so as to strengthen the capacity of higher education internationalization in terms of national strategies and the educational situation. For instance, internationalization of higher education can play a role in public diplomacy, which will increase soft power and the power of Chinese education to flow out to the world.

1.2.2 The development modes and paths of China's higher education internationalization

1.2.2.1 Government-led progressive mode of internationalization

During the last 40 years, the "overseas internationalization", "internationalization at home", "going out", or "bringing in" internationalization initiatives have all followed the government-led progressive model. With the enhancement of universities' autonomy and the improvement of the market mechanism, the governance and management of government has returned to legal construction, policy optimization, and administration regulation at the macro level. Universities and markets play increasingly important roles in the development of higher education. Universities, professional/vocational institutions, and markets, as providers, users, and subjects of higher education, independently promote and practice internationalization strategies and approaches with Chinese characteristics. The mobility of personnel (studying abroad, studying in China, import of foreign talent), projects, and institutional mobility (transnational education, establishment of Confucius Institutes), the "Double First-Class" construction project, and the "Belt and Road" *Educational Action Plan* of China's higher education internationalization, all indicate the increased deepening of higher education internationalization.

1.2.2.2 The evolutionary development of the "Internationalization of Personnel", the "Internationalization of Projects", and "Regional Internationalization"

Opening-up in China followed a path that took the experience of one unit and popularized it to a whole region, from the coastal areas to inland China, from a fragmented model to a holistic one, and from east to west. The internationalization of higher education followed a similar path, from a single example travelling to the regional areas and then ultimately applying to the whole sector, from one dimension within an institution to other dimensions of internationalization. There are three stages of internationalization of higher education in the world. The first stage is about the "Internationalization of Personnel", which is mainly focused on student and talent mobility: The booming market of international students, and the movement of academics. It starts with an individual being spontaneous, having the freedom for mobility and slowly evolves into a larger scale consisting of movements of groups, which has resulted in brain drain, the return of talent who had travelled overseas, and brain circulation. The second stage included the "Internationalization of Projects and Institutions", which is about the movement of educational projects and institutions, as well as transnational higher education. The third stage refers to "hubs of regional internationalization" which has focused on the construction of regional hubs and higher education centres of internationalization. These three stages were not discrete but rather overlapped each other.

The internationalization of higher education in China conformed with the policy on "personnel internationalization", "project and institutional internationalization", and "regional internationalization". There has been an in-depth, extensive spread and influential exchange among students and teachers during the earlier stages, with internationalization of curricula, transnational education, research collaborations, and the "Belt and Road" regional development all emerging at this time.

1.2.2.3 From the unidirectional mode of inward-oriented internationalization towards two-way inward- and outward-oriented internationalization

There are three modes of internationalization of higher education depending on the different types of knowledge transferral: Inward, Outward, and Synthesized. During the past 50 years, the US has "exported" its education through outwards internationalization while China was on the path of internalized ("imported") internationalization. Whether it be the outward-oriented or inward-oriented approach, both countries underwent unidirectional internationalization (Bi & Zhang, 2006). There have been underlying structural concerns due to the unbalanced development of the export and import and unidirectional nature of internationalization. For China, inward-oriented internationalization resulted in talent drain and the reliance on the import of foreign education, while outward development conducted by the US has caused a bias in teaching where internationalization was equivalent to Americanization.

Since 2012, the Chinese government has balanced inward-oriented and outward-oriented internationalization of higher education, adopting moving out strategies, proposing the concept of a "Community for the Shared Future of Mankind" and the "Belt and Road" *Educational Action Plan* which have signified the transformation of internationalization in higher education from an extensive design concept to its practical uses, which can potentially change unidirectional internationalization into bidirectional internationalization.

1.2.2.4 Moving from "an adopter to an innovator"

For a long time, and to some extent, the standards and modes followed in higher education led to diversified patterns but also reduced its academic independence. The research universities in the US were regarded as the model for first-class universities which made it difficult to integrate the university system of the West into local teaching styles (Yang, 2011). However, in recent years, China has paid more attention to moving beyond the imitation of the American research university model, and suggested that it is necessary to establish Chinese universities that have solid foundations in the history and culture of the local area. Marginson (2018) and Zha et al. (2016) characterized the Chinese university model as a "strong state-led development model" where a close bond exists between universities and government. The government continues to explore a unique development model for China's education and research. Meanwhile, the Confucian tradition brings in family traditions and the values of the whole society which recognize the importance of education and the significance of political philosophy, as well as the synergistic role of domestic and international factors. However, these characteristics have not been an area of expertise for Chinese universities, and thus require further research by them. Yang (2017, 2022) has been committed to examining the area of civilization and spiritual connections of Chinese universities, attempting to answer how we can integrate Chinese and Western higher education, and how to reconstruct Chinese university culture. Wang (2018) has noted that China's first-class universities have overemphasized internationalization in a narrow way as they have focused more on international standards and ranking but ignored the realities and institutional and cultural development of internationalization.

1.2.3 Has China's higher education moved to the centre of the world stage?

The policy and practice of China's internationalization of higher education should be examined within the context of China's internationalization and the reform and opening-up of the nation. Since the 1960s, the global situation has changed dramatically, from the bipolarity of the US and the Soviet Union, to the multi-polarity that is characterized by American dominance. At the same time, China has moved from being the socialist "brother" of the Soviet Union to a socialist country with a market economy that has opened its borders to the whole world. After 50 years of reform and openness, China has become an independent market-oriented country. It is on its way to being the centre of internationalization. With globalization and the opening of China to the world, especially after entering into the WTO and engaging in the international system, it is no longer a geographically isolated country, but a country within the global economy. This is an unprecedented change for China which has existed as it is for the last 3,000 years.

From the end of the 20th century, China has actively involved itself in the world's economic system as a developing country and has played an important role in the world. There is an abundance of research related to China's decades of economic development, which attempts to explain the drivers and underlying factors behind these developments. Meanwhile, the "China-is-a-threat Philosophy" and the "Toppling-of-China Theory" have long existed in the West. However, it is noteworthy that both predictions have failed to be accurate.

Since the 1980s, China has followed the path of peaceful development through reforms and opening-up and has been deeply engaged in the world system (Hayhoe, 1996, 1999). After 2001, China achieved comprehensive opening-up to be involved in the world economic system, including the import of foreign investment, opening-up of the market, enlarging trade, adjusting the economic system, transforming the system, and in company management. Reform of the economy and society accelerated its development, increased incomes, and improved the living conditions of the Chinese people, and facilitated the urbanization and modernization of its infrastructure. Higher education research has also experienced a move into the world system, which requires a global perspective of knowledge and understanding.

In the last 40 years of the reform and opening-up, China's higher education has moved from the world periphery to that of a centre position; however, China is still only a large system of higher education but not yet a strong nation. The strategies and practices of internationalization have permeated into all aspects of universities, including outward exchange, external flow of curriculum and teaching style, research conducted overseas and outward knowledge production and management, and the constructive data management of higher education. All these have moved from partial concept to an entire framework, applying from one institution to a large majority of institutions, from the top universities rolling out to the low-tier universities. Internationalization has gone deep into the internal systems of training and research, and the management of international, intercultural, and global dimensions. The number of international publications and citations of Chinese researchers has increased significantly. In international university rankings, the continued rise of Chinese universities' rankings has been obvious. For instance, in 2003, there were only nine universities that made it into the top 500 universities in the world; however, by 2017, there was a staggering 45 universities (Yang & Li, 2017). Starting as early as 2016, China has become the third most popular and the highest ranking of all Asian countries in accepting international students. The aim of the Chinese government is for the nation to become the major driving force of higher education and become the first choice for international students by the mid-21st century.

Considering the position and role of higher education in China from a global perspective, there are various verdicts and issues for discussion. China has now become one of the leading countries, gradually assuming international responsibilities and actively taking part in the role of internationalized governance. According to an interview by Li Shengbing (Li, 2018), Altbach believes that in the next 20 years, if this rate of development is maintained, China's top-ranking universities will have the potential to become leading research institutions. However, China may not become the research-based superpower it envisions itself to be if it continues to compete only with a few countries, but with that said, China still has the potential to be one of the main scientific research and journal article-generating countries. China and India were once giant peripheral countries in terms of their positions in the world's higher education system (Altbach, 1998). However, with decades of reform and the opening-up, there have been great improvements in higher education and research in China. Relatively speaking, however, there have only been a few Indian universities that have been highly ranked. Higher education in China is described as being a transparent "glass ceiling" which is supported by "clay feet" (Li, 2018). The glass ceiling means there are top universities but the lower sections that uphold this ceiling are made of clay due to their poor standards (Li, 2018). Gao (2017) predicted that Beijing and Shanghai would become influential education centres worldwide by 2030. Hayhoe (2017) believes that China is on its way to approaching the world's centre, as it seeks external assistance, education management, and staff training, which positively influences the development of other countries around the world, in particular those that are well developed in terms of economics.

Notably, it is impossible for China to become the centre of global higher education and research in a short period of time. However, China could potentially become the centre in Asia after continuing its trajectory over a longer period. Singapore, Hong Kong, and Malaysia are all devoted to the construction of higher education regional hubs (Song, 2015). Beijing and Shanghai could soon take the example of their internationalization strategies. As Asia moves to being the main student provider for global higher education, there is potential for a huge demand for international higher education within the region. It is a realistic goal that some major cities of China will become the centre of higher education for all of Asia.

1.2.4 Reflections and prospects of higher education internationalization in China

1.2.4.1 The limitations

The internationalization of higher education in China has been heavily reliant on government opening-up policies. The development approach is to follow government guidance and to mobilize the principal roles of institutions. However, such an over-reliance on this policy is a double-edged sword, which may constrain the dynamics and creativity of HEIs, imposing restrictions on the development of higher education and its global involvement in the world higher education system. There are disadvantages both within the driving of the system and its operating mechanisms.

First, the strategic targets and concepts of higher education internationalization cannot meet the demand for what is to come in the future. The unitary development mode and approach, in the service of politics or the economy, has dominated the internationalization of higher education, which has been largely influenced by instrumentalism and utilitarian goals in China. The internationalization of higher education lacks consideration of values and ignores academic values, teaching standards, and the cultural mission of education. There is no long-term strategy or setting of targets; the short-term interests are overwhelming.

Second, universities cannot play a major role in the opening-up and internationalization. Reliance on government policies limits their advancement and creativity. Meanwhile, there are similar strategies among universities, which lack their own characteristics. The lack of participation and supervision and the restrictive mechanisms on the relevant professional institutions, society, and markets, disconnect them from communication with the governance system of international activities for international higher education.

Third, China's internationalization of higher education is still at the stage of pursuing quantity and scale, rather than focusing on quality, efficacy, construction of systems, and the improvement of legal frameworks.

1.2.4.2 The prospects for higher education internationalization in China

Since the reform and opening-up, the Chinese government has established various internationalization strategies for higher education from the perspectives of politics, economy, education, culture, and diplomacy. Developments in recent years have been signified by trends in strategic transformation, which can be identified as follows:

1. Proposing new concepts for the creation of a new landscape in the opening-up of higher education

In recent years, China has maintained its path of peaceful development, and proposed new ideas for the opening-up of higher education. The first is to maintain harmony and diversity, that is, for each country to live in peace and achieve a cordial coexistence. The second is to construct a community for the shared future of mankind. The Chinese government has advocated the value of international education exchange based on that community. It tries to promote education exchange and cooperation between China and other countries through equality, democracy, and mutual benefits. It thus launched the "Belt and Road" *Educational Action Plan* and established the community for regional higher education development. The third is to establish educational concepts of soft power enhancement and knowledge diplomacy.

Zheng (2018) highlights the need for the rise of China to be supported by soft power, which comprises four aspects, namely, the rebuilding of China's social and moral system, the construction of contemporary Chinese ideology in the context of globalization, how China can enhance its international discourse power, and whether China can provide another cultural choice for the world. He notes that in recent years, regardless of where the diplomacy came from, whether it be from large nations or from neighbouring countries, great changes have taken place in China, from "keeping a low profile" to "making a difference". The core of any civilization is the cultural system. Without a strong cultural system, it is hard to say there is a strong civilization. The key to revitalization of Chinese civilization is to create a Chinese cultural system.

2. Cultivating high-level international talent

Whether it be China's international education or transnational education, they are both highly successful in cultivating international talent. The targets of China's international education are foreign students, while transnational higher education is for local Chinese students. Only a few transnational institutions and projects are attracting international students (for example, 49% of students in New York University Shanghai are international students). Yanching Academy in Peking University and Schwarzman Scholars in Tsinghua University are top-notch institutions for elite Chinese cultural studies (Han, 2017).

China cultivates social elites and managers who "know China" (*zhihua*), "become friends of China" (*youhua*), and "become intimate with China" (*qinhua*) through its international education. China's international education provision is a part of its participation in the international higher education market in order to be involved in the fierce competition between providers of international education. It is used to meeting the excessive demands and diverse needs for higher education in the global market. China's contribution to international education is to provide diversification and quality and competitive education to meet these needs.

3. Actively carrying out mutual exchange and two-way learning among civilizations

In order for Chinese development models and experiences to be understood by foreign universities and academia, China has interpreted and emphasized the construction of knowledge and theoretical innovation in the humanities and social sciences in the context of China's philosophical and social discourse system. China puts an emphasis on international exchange and cultural consciousness and rebuilding in its international cooperations. Universities in China are the inheritors of Chinese culture and human development, they need to rebuild local academic traditions and cultural conceptualizations. Top-tier universities should take special responsibility for the cultural inheritance and innovation of Chinese culture (Yang & Li, 2017).

4. Improving the quality and level of Sino-foreign Joint Venture higher education

Sino-foreign joint venture higher education, as one of the main parts of higher education internationalization, requires further improvement in terms of its quality and level. Sino-foreign joint venture higher education, from the perspective of the supply side of reform, meets the requirements of excess and diversified needs in the domestic higher education context, which addresses the problem of the unbalanced and inadequate development of higher education. These ventures develop in parallel with local agents, which improves the competency of local internationalization, and offers an alternative to overseas study for children from middle-class families. However, there are differences in terms of Chinese and foreign educational concepts. Influenced by neo-liberalism, some Chinese institutions and a majority of foreign institutions are driven by economic interests, which in turn affects education quality and sustainability. The over-commercialization of Sino-foreign joint venture higher education has affected the quality of education.

5. Improving policies and regulations to enhance the establishment of campuses overseas

It is important that China further improves policy and regulations, and encourages high-level universities to go out and establish overseas schools in order to maintain a mutual exchange of high-quality resources and education, both in terms of their exportation and importation. Since the beginning of the 21st century, Chinese universities have started to establish Confucius Institutes abroad where people can learn Chinese language and culture. In 2018, there were a total of 51 Confucius Institutes in 140 countries (Hayhoe, 2017). China has also encouraged high-level universities to establish branches and research centres abroad.

6. Optimizing opening-up policies

The internationalization of higher education needs to be institutionalized, including the improvement of legislation, the establishment of professional organizations, and the augmentation of financial support. We cannot rely on one single administrative instrument to manage the internationalization of higher education. There is no current legislation which focuses on the opening-up and internationalization of higher education in a holistic way.

The implementation of the internationalization of higher education needs a synthesis of "bottom-up" and "top-down" strategies, so as to facilitate the agency of various authorities with the sector, including government, non-government institutions, foundations, intermediary institutions, higher education institutions, research centres, and private agents. Professional institutions and non-government institutions should be encouraged to launch projects and research centres for the internationalization of education. Moreover, China should encourage institutions to establish sound information tracking systems to monitor the development of internationalization of higher education in their annual reports, which can help stakeholders to be informed about internationalization development and features.

To conclude, if China wants to become a strong provider of higher education and increase its international impact on global politics, economy, society, and culture, it is important for government and universities to follow multiple strategies, including encouraging two-way exchange, internationalizing academic curricula, developing a strategy for transnational higher education, establishing collaborative research schemes, and spreading the Chinese language and culture around the world.

References

Altbach, P. G. (1998). Gigantic peripheries: India and China in the world knowledge system. In P. G. Altbach (Ed.), *Comparative higher education: Knowledge, the university, and development* (pp. 133–146). Ablex Pub. Corp.

Altbach, P. G. (2004). Globalization and the universities: Myths and realities in an unequal world. *Tertiary Education and Management*, *10*(1), 3–25.

Bi, X. Y., & Zhang, X. M. (2006). Neixiangxing yu waixiangxing: Zhongmei gaodeng jiaoyu guojihua fazhan moshi Fenxi [Imported and exported: A comparison of the model of higher education internationalization between the United States and China]. *Xiandai Daxue Jiaoyu [Modern University Education]*, *1*, 84–88.

Chen, J., & Fan, G. R. (2018). Gaige kaifang 40 nianlai woguo jiaoyu duiwaikaifang zhengce bianqian yanjiu:jiyu guojia juese guannian shijiao [Research on the changes of China's educational opening policy in the past 40 years of reform and opening-up: Based on the perspective of national role concept]. *Zhongguo Gaojiao Yanjiu [China Higher Education Research]*, *9*, 20–24, 30.

Chen, X. F. (2002). *Gaodeng jiaoyu guojihua:kuashiji de daqushi [Internationalization of higher education: A cross-century trend]*. Fujian jiaoyu chubanshe.

Gao, S. G. (2017). 2030 zhongguo jiang huigui shijie jiaoyu zhongxin diwei [By 2030, China will return to its status as the world's education center]. *Zhonguo Jiaoyuxuekan [Journal of the Chinese Society of Education]*, *4*, 1–6.

Giddens, A. (1990). *Consequences of modernity*. Polity Press Ltd.

Han, Y. F. (2017). Zhongguo gaoxiao guojihua fazhan xindongxiang: Jiyu Beijing daxue Yanjing xuetang,qinghua daxue sushimin shuyuan anli de Fenxi [The new trend of Internationalization development of Chinese universities: based on the case analysis of Yenching School of Peking University and Schwarzman College of Tsinghua University]. *Jiaoyu Xueshu Yuekan [Education Research Monthly]*, *5*, 14–19.

Hawawini, G. (2016, October 28). Multicampus internationalisation of higher education institutions. SSRN. Retrieved June 20, 2018, from http://ssrn.com/abstract=2860633

Hayhoe, R. (1996). *China's universities 1895–1995: A century of cultural conflict*. Garland.

Hayhoe, R. (1999). *China's universities and the open door*. M.E. Sharpe, Inc.

Hayhoe, R. (2017). China in the centre: What will it mean for global education? *Frontiers of Education in China*, *12*(1), 3–28.

Held, D., McGrew, A., Goldblat, D., & Peraton, J. (1999). *Global transformations: Politics, economics and culture*. Polity Press.

Knight, J. (2006). Internationalisation: Concepts, complexities and challenges. In J. J. F. Forest & P. G. Altbach (Eds.), *International handbook of higher education* (pp. 207–227). Springer.

Knight, J. (2011). Education hubs: A fad, a brand, an innovation? *Journal of Studies in International Education*, *15*(3), 221–240.

Li, A. F. (2007). Tansuo duiwaikaifang de zhanluechuangxin: "xinkaifangguan"yanjiu de Lishi Beijing yu lilunneihan [Explore the strategic innovation of opening to the outside world: The historical background and theoretical connotation of the study of "new opening concept"]. *Shijie Jingji Yanjiu [World Economy Studies]*, *3*, 13–18, 87.

Li, S. B. (2018). Zhongguo Chengwei Shijie jiaoyu zhongxin bawen:yu feilipuatebahe jiaoshou de duihua [China as the world center for education: A dialogue with professor Philip Altbach]. *Jiaoyu Fazhan Yanjiu [Research in Education Development]*, *38*(17), 1–5.

Marginson, S. (2018). National/global synergy in the development of higher education and science in china since1978. *Frontiers of Education in China*, *13*(4), 486–512.

Marginson, S., & Rhoades, G. (2002). Beyond national states, markets, and systems of higher education: Glonacal agency heuristic. *Higher Education*, *43*(3), 281–309.

Merola, R. (2018, May 4). Tracking down student outcomes at international branch campuses: The observatory of borderless higher education. Retrieved June 20, 2019, from http://www.obhe.ac.uk/documents/view_details?id=1085

Ministry of Education China. (2019, July 24). The 2018 national statistical bulletin on education development. Retrieved August 10, 2019, from http://www.moe.gov.cn/jyb_sjzl/sjzl_fztjgb/201907/t20190724_392041.html

Song, J. (2015). Yazhou gaodeng jiaoyu shuniu zhizheng: Lujing, zhengce he tiaozhan [The rivalry for higher education hub in Asia: Path-dependent, policies and challenges]. *Waiguo Jiaoyu Yanjiu [Studies in Foreign Education]*, *42*(12), 79–91.

Wang, Y. (2018). Guangyi guojihua yu shijie yiliu daxue jianshe [The internationalization of broad sense and the construction of world-class university]. *Bijiao Jiaoyu Yanjiu [Comparative Education Review]*, *40*(7), 3–10, 86.

Wu, H. T. (2021). *China's outward-oriented higher education internationalization: A new typology and reflections from international students*. Springer Nature Singapore.

Wu, H. T., & Zha, Q. (2018). A new typology for analyzing the direction of movement in higher education internationalization. *Journal of Studies in International Education*, *22*(3), 259–277.

Xue, X. Y., & Cao, R. X. (2005). *Quanqiuhua Yu Wenhuaziben [Globalization and cultural capital]*. Social Sciences Academic Press.

Yang, R. (2011). Zhongguo gaodengjiaoyu yanhua de ruogan qishi: Jiyu wenhuabijiao de shijiao [Implications of China's higher education development: From the perspective of comparative culture]. (Q. Zhang, Trans). *Gaodeng Jiaoyu Yanjiu [Journal of Higher Education]*, *32*(7), 9–17.

Yang, R. (2017). The cultural mission of China's elite universities: Examples from Peking and Tsinghua. *Studies in Higher Education*, *42*(10), 1825–1838.

Yang, R. (2022). *The Chinese idea of a university: Phoenix reborn*. Hong Kong University Press.

Yang, R., & Li, M. Y. (2017, November 28). Zhongguo dingjian daxue de wenhua shiming [The cultural mission of China's top universities]. *Guangming Ribao [Guang Ming Daily]*, 13A.

Ye, L., & Wang, Z. T. (2018). Zhongguo gaodeng jiaoyu guojihua: Yige leixing kuangjia yu pingjia [China higher education internationalisation: A stock take of current activity]. *Bijiao Jiaoyu Yanjiu [Comparative Education Review]*, *40*(5), 43–52.

Zha, Q. (2003). Internationalisation of higher education: Towards a conceptual framework. *Policy Futures in Education*, *1*(2), 248–270.

Zha, Q., Shi, J. H., & Wang, X. Y. (2016). Is there an alternative university model? The debate around the Chinese model of the university. In J. Côté & A. Furlong (Eds.), *Routledge handbook of the sociology of higher education* (pp. 273–285). Routledge.

Zheng, Y. N. (2018). *Zhongguo de Wenming Fuxing [The revival of Chinese civilization]*. Oriental Press.

2 Theoretical perspectives on international academic mobility

Since the 1990s, with the acceleration of globalization and further development of the idea of the "knowledge economy", ways of conceptualizing the international flow of academic and intellectual expertise have emerged and changed. Terms such as brain circulation, knowledge diaspora, international competition, migration of technical talent, talent grabs, and transnational capital are often used. As the flow of knowledge becomes increasingly diversified, complicated, and globalized, competition for academic talent is also becoming more international and market-oriented. The competition for talent in higher education and scientific research has become an important part of the competition among countries in science and technology, economic development, and comprehensive national strength. The "Matthew effect" (the rich get richer and the poor get poorer) of this global market competition, and the essentially zero-sum game, do coexist to some degree with mutual benefit and a win-win scenario – transferring technology for building a shared future for mankind, and promoting global cooperation and assistance. Within the general study of globalization, the international flow of academic talent is an important issue in higher education research.

2.1 Concepts related to international academic mobility

This book defines "high-level academic talent" as professional and skilled personnel who hold doctoral degrees and engage in teaching, research, and other work related to the development and dissemination of knowledge and technology for higher education institutions and/or scientific research institutes. International academic mobility refers to the flow of academic talent across national borders. The domestic mobility of academic talent is beyond the research scope of this book. Terms and concepts related to talent mobility include brain outflow, talent inflow, the overflow of talent, brain drain, and brain gain. These ideas are, at the same time, both related and different. The Canadian International Development Agency defines brain outflow as "scientists, scholars, doctors, engineers, and other highly educated people moving from one country to another" (Chen, 1996, p. 13). Brain overflow refers to the phenomenon of a country's talent, for various reasons, outgrowing the country's economic and social development, so idle or unemployed professionals emigrate and find work opportunities abroad

(Chen, 1996, p. 19). Brain drain is seen from the perspective of the source country of talent. It means the obvious fact of losing talent to other countries, with the concept's focus on the impact on the country where the talent initially came from. Brain drains from developing countries cause negative impacts upon, and damage to, the development of knowledge, technological progress, and socio-economic development in these countries. Brain gain, conversely, refers to the phenomenon in which experts who have left for other countries return to the home country for social, economic, or various other reasons. Brain circulation or migration of human capital refers to free migration of talent around the world, moving from one country to another, or from one's homeland to another country, and then back to their own country. Circulating talent may have more than one nationality and identity.

Another concept that is closely related to, but actually different from, talent mobility is migration. Migration includes both immigration and emigration. The difference between talent mobility and migration is that the former may only involve a change of residence or temporary residence while the latter means a change of nationality, that is, changing the citizenship from the country of origin to the receiving country so as to enjoy the political rights and social welfare of the receiving country. The two are connected in that talent mobility may ultimately point to emigration, which means that migration may become one of the important reasons for international academic mobility.

Researchers use the term diaspora, or knowledge diaspora, to refer to academics who have travelled from one country to various parts of the world, and who have a continuing relationship with their home country as well as the receiving country. The word "diaspora" originates from Greek and means settling on a new land, like spreading seeds to make them first take root and then germinate. It was later used to refer to the Jewish people's exile from Israel to the Kingdom of Babylon in the sixth century BC – so those who have lost their homeland but still have a fond memory of it, and have a desire to one day return to their ancestral homeland (Yang & Welch, 2010).

According to different classification standards, international academic mobility can be categorized in the following ways:

By the migrant's identity, they are identified as international students, full-time teachers, researchers, technical personnel, and management talent.
By the period for which they maintained this position, they are categorized as long term or short term, with long-term mobility usually being longer than one year.
By the identity and nationality (whether changed or unchanged) of the migrant, whether they are simply current residents or immigrants.
By the dominant driving force, whether it's internal or external, in that there are active flows and passive flows. If the migrant is basically self-motivated, it is active flow; otherwise, it is passive flow. For the former, the typical example is skilled talent migration and investment immigration, and the latter refers to knowledge diaspora incurred by war.

According to the direction of the flow and the relationship between the origin country and the receiving country, international academic mobility can also be classified as follows:

First, by the degree of development of the country of origin and the receiving country, there are talent flows from developing countries and emerging countries to developed countries, flow between developing and emerging countries, and flow between developed countries.

Second, by the scope of mobility and relevant geopolitical relations, there are flows within and across regions.

Third, by whether there is a historical relationship between the suzerain and the colony, there are flows from the original colony to the original suzerain and other types of flows. Although the world has already entered the post-colonial era, the influence of colonial history can still be seen in all sorts of places, and the flow of academic talent is also affected by this historical factor.

Fourth, according to the similarity between languages and cultures, there are flows within the same language and culture circle, and between different language and culture circles. The former is represented by the flow of academic talent between English-speaking countries, and the latter is represented by, for example, the flow of Chinese academic talent to the US.

2.2 Theoretical perspectives on international academic mobility

Since the 1980s, researchers have studied the phenomenon of transnational mobility of academic talent from a variety of theoretical perspectives. Early studies looked into the mobility of talent from a macro perspective of political economy, as represented by the world system theory, human resource competitiveness and push-pull factors model. In recent years, researchers have focused on the investigation of the dynamic mechanism and change of academic talent flow from the cultural, post-colonial, and transnationalism perspectives. The world system theory still has a macro-level explanatory power while brain circulation, ideas of knowledge diaspora and associated networks, as well as transnationalism, have expanded the theoretical horizon and imagination space of international academic mobility. The international flow of talent is an interdisciplinary field, and it is necessary to examine this complex social phenomenon from a multidisciplinary theoretical perspective. The following section will further elaborate on the four major theoretical perspectives on the international flow of talent, namely, the world system theory, the brain drain, brain gain, and brain circulation theories from the perspective of human capital, the knowledge diaspora and transnational space constructed from the perspective of networks, and the accumulation and transfer of transnational capital from the perspective of transnationalism.

2.2.1 World system theory

The world system theory is a crucial theory for investigating the cross-border flow of international students and talent. Immanuel Wallerstein (2004) proposed the world system theory to explain the position and influence of various countries in the global system. This theory divides the world into countries that are centrally located in the system, semi-peripheral or intermediate countries, and peripheral countries according to their political and economic status (Wallerstein, 2004). When matched by the social system, there are capitalist countries and socialist countries; whereas if it is matched by the degree of economic development, there are developed countries, developing countries, and least-developed countries. Developed countries dominate globalization while developing countries are being globalized and the least-developed countries are on the periphery of the globalization system. The central-peripheral systems of the international students and academic talent flow network are consistent with the political and economic systems. The world system theory that manifests from economic determinism originates from the neo-Marxist political economy which emerged from South American countries. Wallerstein (2004) believed that the countries' relative position in the world system was not fixed since there were still chances of peripheral or semi-peripheral countries to be able to move towards the centre.

Altbach (2004) applied the world system theory to higher education research, emphasizing that the relationship between the centre and the periphery of the global higher education system is caused by the uneven development of countries. The rich and powerful countries are at the centre where they have excellent infrastructure, such as libraries and laboratories, state-of-the-art academic platforms, and traditions, values, and regulations that support academic freedom (Altbach, 2004). Academic centres are in a leading position in the development of world sciences, academic research studies, and knowledge systems. There are also some universities that play sophisticated roles which serve as regional or national centres. They not only function as the academic centre of the region – at times for an entire country whereby they are the centre of knowledge development and technological progress, social and economic growth, and talent training of that country – but also as the intermediary and bridge between the world and the local system (Altbach, 2004). The marginal academic institutions, academic systems of developing countries, and some small developed countries rely on the world centre for knowledge exchange and talent training.

Considering higher education institutions in developing countries are at the periphery and semi-periphery of the world's knowledge production system, academics in these countries look to, and have a dependence on, the scientific research methods, knowledge discourse, fields of research, and learning systems of the major institutions in developed countries. Scholars and students from developing countries establish their capabilities of mobility and professional development in the global knowledge system through degrees and experience gained from the core institutions in dominant countries. These major institutions in developed countries are eager to attract talent from developing countries, which is the key reason for the brain drain from developing countries. Being in such an uneven relationship of talent exchange, the higher education institutions of developed countries can easily benefit by taking advantage of attracting academics from developing countries.

Altbach (2004) used world system theory and neocolonialism theory to explain the unequal relationship and unbalanced development of higher education systems between developing and developed countries. This relationship determines the developed countries' dominance of the division of the international higher education market. Developed countries have become the main exporters of education and the main importers of talent while emerging countries (such as Singapore and South Korea) and developing countries (such as China and India) are the main importers of education, knowledge, and technology and the main exporters of talent. The US, the UK, Germany, France, Japan, Canada, Australia, and other countries occupy a major resource share of the global higher education market. The global higher education system and hierarchical power fully reflect the uneven progress of politics, economy, education, and culture.

Chen and Barnet (2000) used this theory to analyze the international student mobility network from a macro perspective. They analyzed the situation of international students in the top 64 countries in terms of the number of international students in 1985, 1989, and 1995. These research results showed that the US and other developed countries maintained their status at the centre of the network during that period. Eastern European and Asian countries are moving from the periphery to the centre while countries in Africa and the Middle East are still on the margins (Chen & Barnet, 2000). This shows that the higher a country is in the hierarchy, the more likely it will have the privilege of maintaining its economy and higher education system (Chen & Barnet, 2000).

Is it likely that the world system will change? Will there ever be any opportunities for developing countries and small developed countries to establish a top-ranking university, so as to improve their status within the world's knowledge system? Altbach (1998) believes that the cost of establishing world-class universities is becoming increasingly high, and the requirements for knowledge, technology, and talent are getting higher as well. It is becoming increasingly difficult for developing countries to build world-class universities. China and India are two massive countries who sit on the sidelines, with only a few elite educational institutions participating in international competition and becoming a part of the world-class university cohort, which function as the sole platform of knowledge transfer within that country and act as a bridge for understanding and sharing world knowledge and scientific research results (Altbach, 1998).

The core-periphery characteristic of higher education describes the unequal structure of the global academic network and the dependence of peripheral countries and organizations on the central countries and organizations. While this theory explains the flow of international academic personnel and the structural relationship between importers and exporters of education at a macro level, its structuralism epistemology ignores the dynamic relationship between importers and exporters of talent and the status transformation mechanism of core-periphery countries. Therefore, it has its historical limitations. Given the nature of contemporary globalization and rapid development of the world market, any form of general structure of a system cannot be permanent. Higher education researchers should pay more attention to understanding the roles of different stakeholders in a developing market. The world system theory fails to explain the influence of market relations and the supply and demand sides in the global system, that is, the influence of institutions and talent, the changes in asymmetric relations as well as the factors and micro-level forces that may affect or even deconstruct the existing system and order. Moreover, it also pays inadequate attention to the dynamic and interactive processes of global, regional, national, and local organizations and mechanisms.

The world system theory mainly focuses on the existing relationships and structures between different countries and institutions as a whole, as well as the causes of these relationships and structures. Some scholars emphasize the relative stability or even super-stability of the structures and relationships, ignoring the bottom-up, periphery-centre, local and global deconstructive forces, more specifically the market drivers and the drivers of peripheral countries. The global system and order are not fixed, but undergo continuous deconstruction and reconstruction along with the change in the relative strength of the central and peripheral countries. In the long run, quantitative changes cause qualitative changes. Quantitative changes at the micro level and the accumulation of power will inevitably lead to qualitative change and adjustment of the relationship at the macro level. Part of the old centre may move to the periphery for a variety of reasons; and peripheral countries may become semi-peripheral and then ultimately become the new centre. In the 21st-century world, this change is moving much faster and becoming more unpredictable and complicated than in the past.

2.2.2 Brain drain, brain gain, and brain circulation: From the perspective of human capital

Brain drain, brain gain, and brain circulation all focus on the impact of talent flow on both source and receiving countries against the background of the global talent competition brought about by economic globalization and the development of the knowledge economy. In the 1960s, some UK talent flowed to the US and subsequently scholars regarded the outflow of talent from a country as the loss of human capital (Huang, 2017). Since the 1990s, the flow of human resources has been seen from brain drain, brain gain, and circulation perspectives. Brain drain is simply talent flow from an economic perspective and that outflow is seen as permanent loss and displacement. But it does not address the phenomenon of talent circulation (Gao, 2010). Talent flow in the 21st century has changed from one-way and one-off flows to multi-directional and frequent flow. At the same time, academics can have multiple identities and contribute to their home country even though they live in other countries. The original concept of brain drain fails to explain the brain gain, brain circulation, and transnational cyberspace construction and practice of academic talent. Those who have gone abroad still feel a sense of national identity for their ancestral home and work in service for that "distant homeland". Their remote participation in home domestic affairs leads to transfer of social capital, cultural capital, and knowledge and technology. Therefore, existing studies using the framework of a single country to reflect on the transnational talent flow as well as its role and significance show limitations. Given the frequent large-scale talent circulation and the growing integration and development of the international academic labour market in the new conditions, it is difficult to explain the circulation of talent from a single nation-state perspective. In fact, overseas Chinese influence both China and the country where they live through transnational space construction and transnational practice and networking, and constitute the international talent community living in the transnational space.

The trend of international academic mobility in recent decades shows that talent flow has changed from one-way brain drain or brain gain to the coexistence of brain drain, brain gain, and brain circulation. Changes in the direction and mechanism of international talent mobility have influenced the formulation of policies around the world to promote the circulation of talent. Human capital theory often dominates government policy documents and relevant academic literature on technology development and international talent flow, in both source and talent receiving countries. Seeing the international flow of academic talent purely within the framework of skilled migration policy provides only an economic perspective, fully reflecting the significant impact of economic concepts upon policy formulation and implementation. The human capital theory holds that in the production chain of these academic talents, China exports raw materials or semi-finished products which go through the processing and reproduction of (for example) American higher education before becoming highly competent intellectual talent. Under the impact of neoliberalism, the changes in the international talent market push various countries to adopt skilled migration and visa policies as policy tools for international competition for knowledge and technology talent.

If a high number of world-class universities is taken as a defining indicator of a global academic centre, and with the current academic centres being mainly located in developed countries, this encourages global academics from the periphery or semi-periphery to move to the centre of the academic system. However, developing countries and emerging economies, like China, India, South Korea, Singapore, and other countries have joined the international talent competition by rolling out policies that attract international talent. These countries have shifted their international education and talent policies from focusing on enabling the backflow of overseas talent to improving their domestic policy and institutional environment to encourage both the return of their own talent from overseas, and attracting academics from around the world to serve these countries in various ways.

2.2.3 Knowledge diaspora and its transnational space construction: From the perspective of network relationship

In the age of globalization, the development of information technology brings about global networking, space-time compression, and instant interaction. Some scholars use diaspora to describe and analyze groups of people living or emigrating abroad (Shuval, 2000). Diaspora in the modern sense refers to the fact that people who have moved overseas maintain strong emotional, physical, and social ties to the home country. The elements affecting the connections of a diaspora include the historical basis of that diaspora, their memory and imagination of the home country, alienation from the receiving country, the desire to eventually return to the home country, the provision of continuous support for the original homeland, and a sense of common identity shared by a community based on the above relationships. Diaspora discourse reflects that the groups living abroad are part of a continuing transnational network of which the home country is an integral part. The people in a diaspora are distinctive and interested in the source country. The policy of open borders, the presence of an international job market, international standard of job responsibilities, and rapidly advancing transportation and communication all make it easier to communicate and connect with one's home country as well as the rest of the world on a continual basis. The deterritorialization of social identity challenges the traditional definition of the sense of common identity of people and communities within the single nation-state concept and has made loyalty to the one country give way to multiple citizenship (Shuval, 2000).

The increasing portability of information technology within highly developed transnational network connectivity means that the concept of a traditional community, based on daily communication in a physical space and geographical location, has evolved into an abstract community connected only through a sense of common identity in language and culture as well as common interests. Benedict Anderson (1983) discussed how boundaries operate in the creation of a community in *Imagined Communities: Reflections on the Origin and Spread of Nationalism.* Communities now involve people no longer limited to close neighbours or to relationships based on the daily face-to-face contact of the traditional physical and geographical communities. Instead, a broader and more abstract community where people have a sense of common identity based on interconnectedness and communication has emerged. It requires that the relationship between individuals, between physical space, and cross-culture locations should all be regulated by common values or a sense of shared interests. Physical space is now replaced by virtual relationships. The theory on diaspora includes three categories of stakeholders: The diaspora, the receiving country, and the homeland. The attitude of the homeland towards the diaspora provides cultural, emotional support and security for the latter. At the same time, the homeland obtains material, knowledge, and other supportive outcomes from the receiving country through the diaspora (Shuval, 2000).

Knowledge diaspora refers to the global diaspora of knowledge and technology communities. Knowledge Diaspora and International Knowledge Networks focus more on the flow of talent and the transnational knowledge and communication networks they bring. They have an impact on the dynamic development of the world knowledge system and the knowledge development of different countries (Welch & Zhang, 2008). China's intellectual diaspora tends to maintain regular association and correspondence with China, thereby contributing to transnational academic cooperation (Yang & Welch, 2010).

International Knowledge Networks are closely related to the concept of knowledge and technology transfer. Diasporic academic personnel constitute a node in the International Knowledge Networks, promoting the transfer of knowledge and technology between their home country and the receiving country (Welch &

Zhang, 2008). China's knowledge diaspora community is growing in scale and on a professional level acquiring specific skill sets, as well as transnational social networks and relations. Some members of the diaspora have become permanent residents or citizens of the receiving country.

Global knowledge networks and knowledge diaspora concepts mainly consider the flow of global academic talent from the perspective of knowledge sociology. In the global knowledge system and the international flow of academic talent, it is difficult to explain new phenomena, problems, and developments by using the nation-state as a framework to investigate and analyze the flow of academic personnel. The scattered intellectual personnel are not only individuals, but also form networks and communities, establishing complex and changeable identities, which has given rise to the transnational social space and contact zone as well as the intermediate zone. As a result, the study of social space, location, knowledge, and power is no longer limited to the nation-state, but extends to the transnational space and the construction of the knowledge-power relationship. On the concepts of intellectual diaspora and the construction of transnational social space, there have been a number of important works published. Especially, Fahey and Kenway (2010) put forward the concepts of geographies of power/knowledge, empires of knowledge, and edges of empires in *Thinking in a "Worldly" Way: Mobility, Knowledge, Power and Geography*. Kim discusses issues about identity capital and transnational capital in *Transnational Academic Mobility, Knowledge and Identity Capital* (Kim, 2010). Chen and Koyama (2013) stress the concept of "flexible identity", highlighting the subjectivity of the diasporic intellectuals and their complex interactive relationship with the macro-environment and the system at the middle level in *Reconceptualizing Diasporic Intellectual Networks: Mobile Scholars in Transnational Space*. Chen (2017) has narrated the experiences of Chinese academic returnees in building up the world-class university.

Diasporic intellectuals exert influence on the construction of transnational social space, individual behaviour, their home country, and the receiving country in multiple ways. The transnational space is divided into four types by Thomas Faist (1999, pp. 36–72) according to the extension and stability of this space: The first type, decentralization and assimilation (with weak synchronous embedding into the source and receiving countries, has a short-term transnational social connection); the second type, transnational exchange and reciprocity (though with strong synchronous embeddedness, remains a short-term transnational social connection); third, transnational networks (with weak embeddedness, but a long-term transnational connection); and fourth, transnational community (with strong embeddedness, and has a long-term transnational connection).

2.2.4 Transnational capital accumulation and transfer of academic talent: From the perspective of transnationalism

2.2.4.1 The perspective of transnationalism

The flow of academic talent developed from initial sporadic and scattered individual movement to a large-scale, systematic, and organized circulation in the late

20th century. In the era of globalization, increased numbers and changes to international frameworks posed new challenges for the flow of talent and also the study of international education. This also provided an opportunity to break with the existing linear one-way thinking. The old paradigm of nationalism research was challenged by the paradigm of transnationalism. In the 1990s, scholars such as Basch, Schiller, and Blanc (1994) used the term "Transnationalism" to describe the process of synchronically twisted social relations forged and maintained by immigrants to link their home country with the society of the country of emigration, and thus to establish a social field that transcends geographies, cultures, and politics. Transnationalism focuses on the study of transnational practices with a certain scale of participation, duration, frequency, and depth of progress as well as a conventional and continuous form of transnational social connection. The transnational social space and transnational social networks have become the basis for the study of transnationalism (Ding, 2012). In analyzing the phenomenon of transnationalism, Basch et al. (1994) introduced the field theory of Pierre Bourdieu and put forward the concept of the transnational social field. This kind of field refers to the different types of network systems constructed by immigrants and their groups through information communication, interaction, and occupation of social capital, which facilitate people's transnational migration, and also support the economic, political, and cultural practices of the emigrants. Relatively speaking, once the transnational social field of immigration takes form, it also regulates and restricts the actions of immigrants (Chao, 2007). Though based in one country, these people undertake businesses and work in multiple countries where they live a transnational life with the home country and the receiving country as the axis.

2.2.4.2 Accumulation of transnational capital by academic talent

Scholars define the unique advantages of academic returnees and the capital accumulated during their study abroad as transnational capital (Rosen & Zweig, 2005). There are mainly three types of capital embedded in or carried by transnational talent, namely, human capital, cultural capital, and social capital. Human capital refers to the knowledge and skills accumulated by transnational personnel in the process of transnational flow and practice; cultural capital includes physical published books and cultural resources, institutionalized qualifications, and implicit cultural concepts. Transnational personnel have advantages in that they possess transnational social networks and resources. Social capital refers to the network of social relationships established and maintained in the process of transnational learning, together with the resources, trust, and support embedded in the network. The maintenance of social capital requires constant emotional input and interaction, and the role of social capital that has been established outside the home country will decline after the transnational talent returns home. After returning to China, for example, they would build and accumulate new social capital by taking advantage of the new working environment and their status as returnees.

Jonkers and Tijsen (2008) proposed the concept of scientific social and human capital to study the professional networks, scientific and technological knowledge, and skills possessed by transnational talent. They use this concept to analyze the international communication, cooperation, and scientific research productivity of Chinese returnee scientists (76 highly talented plant molecular biologists). Scientific social capital refers to the size and number of professional contacts and networks that researchers have. Scientific human capital refers to the scientific and technological knowledge and skills possessed by researchers. As the number of scientists with whom these researchers have connections, and the quality and intensity of their relationships slowly increases, the data has shown that their scientific social capital increases correspondingly. The ability and tendency of researchers to cooperate with their foreign counterparts is not only influenced by scientific social capital, but also constrained by scientific human capital (Jonkers & Tijsen, 2008).

Transnational human capital is defined as strengthened human capital that is difficult to acquire at home, which is linked to an individual's overseas study experience, method of learning, and an individuals' connectivity to the local community. At the same time, transnational talents have a dual network of academic social relationships at home and abroad. The transnational capital accumulated through transnational experience exerts a very positive influence upon their career development and scientific research innovation (Lu et al., 2014). Stanley Rosen and David Zweig (2005) have examined the status of the returnee scientists and local scientists. They concluded that the returnee scientists enjoy advantages in many aspects including the fact that when the overseas talent return home, they tend to translate the transnational capital accumulated overseas into career development capital at home.

2.2.4.3 Transfer and the spread of transnational capital

In the process of studying or working abroad, returning home and circulating knowledge, human capital, social capital, and cultural capital are accumulated. Transnational capital has become a comparative advantage for returnees to develop their academic career at home. Such capital is embedded in the academic talent travelling across countries, systems, and institutions. The embedded knowledge, skills, and experience are embodied, and even further developed when they carry out their work. Transnational capital conversion refers to the cross-border transfer of different forms of capital possessed by transnational talent between different fields of activity. This mobile talent maximizes the use of their resources and their own development is enhanced through this conversion of different types of capital.

According to Li Feng (2018), the localization of transnational capital is a process whereby returnees take advantage at home of the human capital they acquire through the transplantation and spread of their transnational capital. We need to evaluate the localization benefits of transnational capital from the three aspects, namely, the transplantation, spread, and appreciation of transnational capital. Transplantation is a process in which returnees take home their transnational human capital and transnational social capital acquired overseas and bring it into play. The spread of transnational capital by a returnee refers to the spillover effect of capital, namely, respected abilities and capacity to share new knowledge, and strong influence upon his/her surrounding coworkers, organizations, and institutions. Returnees often "pass" their transnational capital to their students, partners, and colleagues through teaching, postgraduate training seminars, scientific research cooperation, and academic institution management to ensure that the transnational capital is spread (Li, 2018). Returnees serve as a bridge connecting domestic and international academic networks. They help shorten the distance between domestic and international academic circles, and attain the spread and spillover effect of transnational social capital by sharing their social networks with their peers and students at home. Not only that, they also promote the transfer of knowledge and technology innovation through cooperative research (Yang et al., 2015).

The accumulation and transfer of transnational capital involves the spread of social capital and the transfer of knowledge and technology innovation. Cao and Suttmeier's research on the recipients of the Chinese National Science Fund for Distinguished Young Scholars shows that they have advantages in academic creativity and contribution, where their transnational academic capital plays a critical role (Cao & Suttmeier, 2001). Another study by Chen et al. (2015) discussed aspects of researchers who were selected into the Thousand Youth Talent Program (TYTP), whose professional relationship networks are both international- and home-based. The combined network of domestic and international relationships has a significant impact on the professional promotion and academic productivity of returnees. The foreign embeddedness of returnees affects the quantity and quality of knowledge they share with their domestic peers, and their domestic embeddedness directly affects the ultimate effect of knowledge sharing (Yuan et al., 2017).

2.3 Characteristics of the transnational flow of academic talent and the transnational academic work

Since the 1990s, the international flow of academic talent has been approached by international scholars from the perspectives of academic diaspora, migration options, talent flow, and transnationalism.

2.3.1 Characteristics of the transnational flow of academic talent

The international flow of Chinese academic talent has the following characteristics: First, studying abroad has become one of the most important ways for talent to emigrate to foreign countries. Second, some academics going overseas have obtained citizenship or green cards; having a job, family, assets, and social networks abroad, they find it difficult to give up all of these to return home. Third, most of the emigrants have good education backgrounds, professional knowledge, technology, and international experience. Some of the best and most promising of Chinese academic talent are currently residing abroad. They mostly engage in academic work with institutions of higher education and scientific research in the US and in developed European countries. The higher the academic level of the talented individual, the more likely he/she will emigrate overseas and the more difficult it is for them to return since talent always try to seek "greener pastures". They hope to be at the international forefront of a field, they attach importance to their cooperation and communication with high-ranking peers, and have a desire for easily accessible research resources, as well as a constraint-free and flexible learning environment.

One of the main motivations for transnational academic mobility is the difference between academic occupations and working environments in different countries. These can include different economic returns, academic norms, organizational cultures, and varying resources and status in the international academic system. The academic career environment includes the academic system, academic culture, and organizational environment. It is necessary to compare and analyze the differences between Chinese and foreign academic career environments, and explore the impact of these on the brain circulation of Chinese academic talent, to understand talent flow and perhaps to suggest measures to improve the otherwise unfavourable academic career environment. This can enhance the international competitiveness of the academic career in China and encourage talent inflow.

Government policies and systems have an impact on the flow of talent. There are obvious differences between academic and professional environments at home and abroad. The differences are reflected at the macro, organizational, and disciplinary levels. The policy on migration and recruitment of foreign skilled personnel constitutes the institutional environment at the national level. The knowledge and technology development strategies and innovation programmes of various countries and their talent development programmes complement and promote each other. At the local government level, there are also various development strategic plans and measures for talent attraction. Universities as academic organizations and teaching, research, and service units are the main competitors for talent flow and direct participants in talent wars. The higher-level the universities are, the more they put a premium on these talents and the more vigorously a country will need to compete to attract back its talented worldwide diaspora.

Different discipline cultures have a varying degree of influence on the flow of academic talent. Disciplines differ according to their own culture and attributes. For example, hard science (natural science) study is relatively compatible around the world. The area of humanities and social sciences show more national, ethnic, and regional differences, which contribute to cultural diversity. But even for humanities and social sciences, the dialogue and exchange between countries is more important and convenient than ever before and must be accompanied by the transnational flow of knowledge and scholars, who are in essence the carriers of knowledge and culture.

2.3.2 Characteristics of academic talent's transnational academic work

The transnational flow of academic talent has become increasingly common. Transnationalism theories have been utilized to analyze the flow. High-calibre talent in academia and technology fields with high-level education and corresponding resources, maintain regular interaction and contacts in both their home country and the receiving country. They establish transnational networks through mobility and professional practice in a transnational academic space, conduct transnational academic work, and have a sense of common identity with multiple groups of people. The transnational behaviour of academic talent gives rise to the transnational space, and the frequent flow of academic talent in the new era of technology expands the concept of space that is divided into physical space, institutional space, social cultural space, and interpersonal space. Returnees and diasporic talent produce and publish knowledge works in transnational space to gain academic reputation. The transnational field becomes their space for knowledge creation, knowledge circulation and consumption, and for gaining reputation and recognition.

A fundamental characteristic of mobility is the enhanced development of academic talent. An individual's development comes from their study and work experience with international first-class universities to increase their value in the labour market, and enable them to stay at the forefront of teaching and research in their field. As such, mobility is a necessity for the growth of high-level academic talent and an inherent attribute of academic activities. In addition to being loyal to the organization with which they work, they are also loyal to their discipline and academic circle, also known as the invisible institute. The invisible institutes make the international cooperation, exchange, and mobility of scholars an essential part of academic life. Therefore, it is necessary to make use of domestic academic platforms, and, more importantly, the international academic platform, to promote the training, attraction, and use of top scholars. As the domestic market and the international market are becoming increasingly integrated in the 21st century, we need to have a good understanding of the process of talent flow in the domestic academic labour market, and, more importantly, understand the process of talent flow in the international academic labour market.

Academic personnel connect to both their institution and their discipline. For international talent, their connection to the discipline not only shows recognition of the domestic academic community, but also implies recognition of the global academic community and the invisible institute. The higher-level the talent are, the more likely that their place in the discipline transcends geographical and national boundaries, and they seek academic status and a sense of common identity in the international academic community (Li, 2017). In addition, countries around the world, especially developed countries, are vying for high-level academic and professional talent. They have adopted corresponding competitive and attractive skilled migration policies and connected policies to attract and use talent, so that high-level academic talent easily flows within the global academic community. Developed countries tend to attract the world's best and brightest potential talent by offering them overseas education, and attract global professional talent by issuing work visas, thus building an ever-renewing pool of talent.

In short, theories regarding the international flow of academic talent have been developed through a range of important research works. Studies have been conducted analyzing this process from the political and economic perspective to the sociocultural perspective, from the macro structure to the initiative of agency, from nation-state analysis to transnationalism analysis. The study of the international flow of academic talent has become an interdisciplinary research field with the development of core concepts such as international migration, technological talent, circulation of talent, knowledge diaspora, talent competition, and importance of knowledge and technological innovations.

References

Altbach, P. G. (1998). Gigantic peripheries: India and China in the world knowledge system. In P. G. Altbach (Ed.), *Comparative higher education: Knowledge, the university, and development* (pp. 133–146). Ablex Pub. Corp.

Altbach, P. G. (2004). Globalization and the universities: Myths and realities in an unequal world. *Tertiary Education and Management*, *10*(1), 3–25.

Anderson, B. (1983). *Imagined communities: Reflections on the origin and spread of nationalism*. Verso.

Basch, L., Schiller, N. G., & Blanc, S. C. (1994). *Nations unbound: Transnational projects, postcolonial predicaments, and deterritorialized nation-states*. Gordon and Breach.

Cao, C., & Suttmeier, R. (2001). China's new scientific elite: Distinguished young scientists, the research environment and hopes for Chinese science. *China Quarterly*, *168*, 960–984.

Chao, L. Q. (2007). Yiminshi yanjiu zhong de kuaguo zhuyi lilun [The theory of transnationalism in the study of the history of immigrants]. *Shixue Lilun Yanjiu [Historiography Bimonthly]*, *3*, 52–63, 160.

Chen, C. G. (1996). *Rencai Wailiu yu Huigui [Talent outflow and return]*. Hubei Education Press.

Chen, D. H., Duan, Y. B., & Pan, Z. Y. (2015). Eryuan guanxi wangluo dui haigui kexuejia chanchu de yingxiang: yi zhongguo "qingnian qianren jihua" weili [The impacts of ambidextrous network on returnee scientists' productivity: Evidence from the 1000-youth elite program in China]. *Zhongguo Keji Luntan [Forum on Science and Technology in China]*, *9*, 143–147.

Chen, Q. Q. (2017). *Globalization and transnational academic mobility*. Springer Science Business Media Singapore and Higher Education Press in China.

Chen, Q. Q., & Koyama, J. (2013). Reconceptualising diasporic intellectual networks: Mobile scholars intransnational space. *Globalisation, Societies and Education*, *1*(1), 23–38.

Chen, T., & Barnet, G. (2000). Research on international student flows from a macro perspective: A network analysis of 1985, 1989 and 1995. *Higher Education*, *39*(4), 435–453.

Ding, Y. Y. (2012). Lun kuaguo zhuyi jiqi lilun gongxian [Transnationalism and its theoretical contributions]. *Minzu Yanjiu [Ethno-National Studies]*, *3*, 112, 107.

Fahey, J., & Kenway, J. (2010). Thinking in a "worldly" way: Mobility, knowledge, power and geography. *Discourse: Studies in the Cultural Politics of Education*, *31*(5), 627–640.

Faist, T. (1999). Developing transnational social spaces: The Turkish-German example. In L. Pries (Ed.), *Migration and transnational social spaces* (pp. 36–72). Ashgate.

Gao, Z. P. (2010). Kuaguo rencai liudong; Yanjiu Fanshi de Yanjin yu chongsu [Transnational academic mobility: The evolution and reshaping of research paradigm]. *Tansuo Yu Zhengming [Exploration and Free Views]*, *12*, 106–108.

Huang, H. G. (2017). Cong rencai liushi dao rencai huanliu: Guoji gaoshuiping rencai liudong de zhuanhuan [From brain drain to brain circulation: Paradigm shift to talent mobility]. *Gaodeng jiaoyu yanjiu [Higher Education Research]*, *38*(1), 90–97, 104.

Jonkers, K., & Tijsen, R. (2008). Chinese researchers returning home: Impacts of international mobility on research collaboration and scientific productivity. *Scientometrics, 7*(2), 309–333.

Kim, T. (2010). Transnational academic mobility, knowledge, and identity capital. *Discourse: Studies in the Cultural Politics of Education, 31*(5), 577–591.

Li, F. (2018). Haigui xuezhe de kuaguo ziben bentuhua jiqi xiaoguo pingjia yanjiu [A study on the localization of returnee scholars' transnational capital and its effect evaluation]. *Huaqiao Huaren Lishi Yanjiu [Journal of Overseas Chinese History Studies], 2*, 26–33.

Li, M. (2017). Zhongguo liumei xueshu rencai huiguo yixiang jiqi yingxiang yinsu Fenxi [The willingness of returning to China and the push-pull factors leading to Chinese academics' staying in the United States]. *Fudan Jiaoyu Luntan [Fudan Education Forum], 15*(2), 79–86.

Lu, X., Hong, W., & He, G. X. (2014). Haigui kexuejia de xueshu yu chuangxin: Quanguo keji gongzuozhe diaocha shuju Fenxi [The academic and innovation productivity of overseas returnees: An analysis based on the national survey of science and technology personnel]. *Fudan Gonggong Xingzheng Pinglun [Fudan Public Administration Review], 12*(2), 7–25.

Rosen, S., & Zweig, D. (2005). Transnational capital: Valuing academic returnees in a globalizing China. In C. Li (Ed.), *Bridging mind across the Pacific: US-China educational exchanges 1978–2003* (pp. 111–132). Lexington Books.

Shuval, J. (2000). Diaspora migration: Definitional ambiguities and atheoretical paradigm. *International Migration, 38*(5), 41–57.

Wallerstein, I. (2004). *World-systems analysis: An introduction*. Duke University Press.

Welch, A., & Zhang, Z. (2008). Higher education and global talent flows: Brain drain, overseas Chinese intellectuals, and diasporic knowledge networks. *Higher Education Policy, 21*(4), 1–19.

Yang, R., & Welch, A. (2010). Globalisation, transnational academic mobility and the Chinese knowledge diaspora: An Australian case study. *Discourse: Studies in the Cultural Politics of Education, 31*(5), 593–607.

Yang, Z. B., Gao, S. X., & Liu, X. H. (2015). Jiyu shehui wangluo Fenxi fangfa de guiguozhe kuaguo shehui ziben zhuanyi yanjiu [Keep good men company: A study on transnationalsocial capital transfer of expatriates based on social network analysis model]. *Shehui [Social], 35*(4), 171–198.

Yuan, Q. H., Zhang, Y., Zhang, A. S., & Zhang, Y. M. (2017). Fenxiang haishi yousuo baoliu? Liuxue guiguo renyuan guonei qianru Chengdu yu zhishi fenxiang xingwei [Sharing or pulling any punches? Returnees' home-country embeddedness and knowledge sharing behaviour]. *Kexuexue Yu Kexue Jishu Guanli [Science of Science and Management of S&T], 38*(11), 168–180.

3 From brain drain to brain circulation

International mobility of Chinese students and academics

From the beginning of this century, some countries have committed themselves to building world-class universities and research centres, whereby they are contributing towards the advancement of research and promotion of the internationalization of higher education. Under this phenomenon, the crusade for global talent has been launched. Without a doubt, China has been witnessing the concurrence of academic talent's brain drain, brain gain, and brain circulation, as a country of growing position in the world. The phenomenon of talent mobility has become increasingly complicated. Why is the brain drain of high-level academic talent not so severe in countries like Japan, South Korea, Singapore as that in Mainland China and India? For this reason, the research on the international mobility of Chinese academic talent is of great significance. This will not only provide a basis for formulating strategies and policies on medium- to long-term study abroad and talent attractions, but it will also inform colleges and universities on reasons why they must participate in international competition and submit this for global knowledge as it has reached a remarkable period and complex setting in the international arena.

As the carrier of knowledge, culture, and technology, as well as the connection between global knowledge networks and the bridge between the international academic community and Chinese community, Chinese scholars around the world are of great importance in knowledge sharing, technological information sharing, and collaboration in higher education and research. Given the situation of unbalanced progress and inequitable competition on the world ranking system, China, a growing powerhouse with a considerable higher education system, is facing serious challenges in competing for global academic talent. In comparison, other developed countries have accumulated desirable policies that attract talent. China has long confronted the problem of academic talent's outflow, or what is known as "brain drain", among Chinese academe, which leads to structural inconsistency between the supply and demand of talented academics and professionals. This has seriously affected China's growing economy in both its structural transformation and industrial progress. It has restricted its efforts in training the next generation of creative endeavours and its move towards being an innovative country. With an enormous population of 1.4 billion, China's human capital pool is relatively insufficient. Despite the considerable number of people who have received higher education, talented individuals are still very much in short supply. Even worse, there are Chinese talent, especially the highly talented academics, who go abroad without

DOI: 10.4324/9781003424611-3

the intention of returning and who decide to emigrate overseas. Undoubtedly, the phenomenon of academic talent's outflow will continue to exist in the long run, but there may still be some new trends and particularities in terms of brain drain, brain gain, and brain circulation, as well as their respective rationales.

Based on the theoretical foundation of academic talent's mobility in Chapter 2, this chapter will focus on the outflow of Chinese students and academic talent leaving China. Section 3.1 makes a comprehensive review of the current situation of the outflow of Chinese students and academic talent and clarifies its characteristics and problems. Section 3.2, based on a research survey of the Chinese scholars staying in the US, examines the reasons why certain Chinese academic scholars are choosing to stay in the US and their status of existing academic development. Section 3.3 summarizes the new trend of international flow of Chinese academic talent.

3.1 Higher education internationalization in the era of globalization

The structural inequality caused by the uneven development from one country to another and from one institution to another on a global basis, as well as the differences between academic environment and policies, are some of the main reasons for talent mobility. Globalization and internationalization are by all standards not a value-neutral concept. Their conceptualizations and definitions vary across different countries, institutions, and individuals. In essence, the global knowledge networks and academic networks are centred on developed countries, especially those Anglo-European countries, whose plunder of talent from developing countries has exacerbated the abovementioned lopsided competition and unevenly distributed development system.

3.1.1 Classification of Chinese academic talent overseas

There are four types of Chinese academic talent overseas: International students, visiting scholars, post-doctoral fellows, and the faculty members and researchers. The international students refer to undergraduates, masters, and doctoral students, whose main purpose is to study for a degree. Aside from this, there is a large number of students who study the local language. After a certain period of learning this language, they are more likely to apply for a degree and become qualified degree-earning students. Ultimately, after completing their studies, some of the overseas students will return to China and become Chinese academic talent, which are important resources for technological, social, and economic development. However, there is a considerable number of them who will choose to study for higher degrees or to work abroad. For example, some elite students tend to stay abroad to engage in research and teaching as a post-doctoral fellow.

Visiting scholars are academic staff whose itineraries are usually organized by the Chinese government bodies or work units. In general, they are often funded by the Chinese government, institution, or third parties to conduct long-term or short-term overseas exchanges and take part in independent or cooperative research and teaching programmes. In some cases, a number of visiting scholars would decide to become staff members and reside abroad.

There are two types of post-doctoral fellows: Those who earned their doctorate degree in China, and those who earned their degree in a foreign country. They are generally employed by foreign universities and scientific institutions for one to three years. After that period, they are confronted with the option of either returning to China or continuing to stay overseas. Compared to full-time faculty members, they are more likely to be influenced by domestic policies and career development opportunities.

The fourth category of Chinese academic talent overseas is the faculty and scientific researchers. They are the ones who have a certain amount of academic and social capital, and are more inclined to develop abroad. The members of this group differ in their intentions of returning to China, because of their varying identities abroad. Depending on whether they have obtained permanent residency or whether they have become foreign nationals, this academic talent can be further divided into two groups: (1) Chinese with green cards and (2) Chinese without foreign nationality and green cards. According to their employment status, they can be divided into full-time and part-time staff. Relative to part-time staff, full-time staff enjoy higher job security.

Among the four major categories of academic talent, the most important avenue for becoming an academic talent overseas are international students and postdoctoral fellows. In this chapter, I will mainly discuss Chinese students studying abroad, as the research data on international students are seen as somewhat, correspondingly, more comprehensive. The field survey in Section 3.2 focused on full-time Chinese academic staff staying in the US, of which this particular set of research is capaciously lacking.

3.1.2 Characteristics of international mobility of Chinese students and academics

3.1.2.1 Studying abroad: The main channel for the outflow of academic talent

The most prominent trend of higher education development in China is to move from elite education to mass education, and then to popularization. During this process, both the supply of, and the demand for, academic talent has not only expanded in quantity, but also improved in quality and developed in wide variety and diversity. For students who are in the demand side of higher education, there coexist a higher education market within Mainland China and an overseas higher education market outside Mainland China, including those in the Hong Kong, Macao, and Taiwan regions, as well as foreign countries. The domestic and overseas higher education markets are complementary to each other, forming an integrated education market system. If students choose the external higher education markets, it means that they expect to fulfil their educational needs there. The main reason for students choosing the external market over the internal market is that the higher education provided by the internal education market cannot satisfy their needs for educational quantity, quality, or category. The so-called disequilibrium of supply and demand in quantity refers to the total amount of demand which exceeds that of supply, leading to the flow of students to the external market. In such circumstances, this demand is called "excess demand". The instability between supply and demand in category means that the education supply in the internal market cannot provide the special quality and category of education that the students intend to pursue, and this demand is called "differentiated demand" (Li, 2008, p. 136). In essence, students studying abroad is caused not only by excess demand, but also by differentiated demand.

Li (2008, p. 116) summarized the reasons of Chinese students for studying overseas: (1) The reform and opening-up policy created a favourable macro environment; (2) the sustainable economic growth became a strong driving force; (3) the economic development of the middle class called for diversified demands for higher education; (4) the mismatch between supply and demand in domestic higher education led to the continuous increase of students' outflow; (5) the one-off college entrance examination system contradicted the diversified needs for talent's development; and (6) the cultural tradition and family aspects induced the pursuit of overseas higher education.

Studying abroad is one of the main reasons leading to brain drain in China. Since the reform and opening-up, especially after the 1990s, the development of Chinese students studying abroad has shown the following characteristics: (1) A large number of people studying abroad as well as returning home; (2) policies and regulations are gradually improved and implemented; and (3) the international market is opened up step-by-step and the international higher education market is integrated gradually.

Table 3.1 shows data from 2000 to 2010 of the increase in number of Chinese students studying overseas with an average annual growth rate of 28.2%. In 2011, the number of Chinese students studying abroad reached 339,700, gaining first place globally. The number of students studying abroad continued to break new records every year, reaching 662,100 in 2018. From 1978 to 2018, China had sent a total of 5,857,100 students to study abroad, among which, 4,323,200 completed their studies. For those who completed their studies, 3,651,400 had returned to China, accounting for 62.34% of the students who had gone abroad (Ministry of Education, 2018). It is estimated that the number will continue to grow in terms of speed and scale for some time.

3.1.2.2 Public and self-funded study abroad, coexistence of brain drain, gain, and circulation

Since the 21st century, a huge number of students go abroad and return home every year. The international mobility of Chinese students and academic talent has the following characteristics: First, the number of students studying abroad and those who decide to return to China has increased on a large scale, with total figures repeatedly reaching new records; second, three forms of studying abroad have concurrently developed, namely funded by the state, work units, and individuals; third, there is a parallel development of three kinds of movement, namely brain drain, brain gain, and brain circulation. Self-funded students have become the mainstream mobility body. For instance, between 2001 and 2018 (with the exception of

Table 3.1 Number of Chinese students studying abroad from 2000 to 2018

Year	Total number of students (10,000 persons)	Number of students sent abroad officially (10,000 persons)	Number of students self-funded (10,000 persons)	Percentage of students self-funded (%)	Total growth rate (%)
2000	3.90	0.70	3.20	82.05	—
2001	8.40	0.80	7.60	90.48	115.38
2002	12.50	0.80	11.70	93.60	48.81
2003	11.73	0.81	10.92	99.09	−6.16
2004	11.47	1.04	10.43	90.93	−2.22
2005	11.85	1.20	10.65	89.87	3.31
2006	13.40	1.33	12.07	90.07	13.08
2007	14.40	1.50	12.90	89.58	7.46
2008	17.98	1.82	16.16	89.88	24.86
2009	22.93	1.92	21.01	91.63	27.53
2010	28.47	2.47	26.00	91.32	24.16
2011	33.97	2.49	31.48	92.67	19.32
2012	39.96	2.51	37.45	93.72	17.63
2013	41.39	2.96	38.43	92.85	3.58
2014	45.98	3.68	42.30	92.00	11.09
2015	52.37	4.19	48.18	92.00	13.90
2016	54.45	4.63	49.82	91.50	3.82
2017	60.84	6.71	54.13	88.97	11.74
2018	66.21	6.58	59.63	90.06	8.83

Source: The author collected data from the official website of the Ministry of Education (http//www.moe.gov.cn/) in January 2019.

Note: "—" refers to missing data.

a year or two), the number of self-funded students studying abroad accounted for more than 90% of the total number. In 2018, the number of self-funded students reached 596,300 (see Table 3.1).

Under the political influence of home and abroad, the 21st century has witnessed a wave of Chinese overseas students returning home. Since 2004, the return rate of overseas students has steadily increased. In 2009, it exceeded 30% of the original figure. In 2018, the total number of overseas students who returned to China reached 519,400, among which, 25,300 were sponsored by the state, 26,500 were publicly funded by their work units, and 467,600 were self-financed. Compared to the statistics in 2017, 2018 saw that the number of students studying abroad increased by 53,700, with a growth rate of 8.83%; the number of overseas students who returned increased by 38,500, with a growth rate of 8%. According to the data released by the Ministry of Education in March 2018, of the students studying abroad from 1978 to 2017, a total of 3,132,000 people have chosen to return to China after completing their studies, which accounts for 83.73% of those who have completed their studies. The percentage in 2011 was only 72.02%.

3.1.2.3 The main reasons for being unwilling to return to China upon graduation

Return rate refers to the ratio of the number of people returning to China against the number of people going abroad in a certain period or years. This is regarded as an important indicator to evaluate the talent gains in academia. Another indicator, the turnover rate, which is equivalent to 100% minus the return rate, is used to examine the degree of brain drain. From a quantitative point of view, the higher the return rate, the higher the talent gain. At the same time, the higher the turnover rate, the more severe the brain drain.

1. Overall return rate

Table 3.2 shows the return rate of Chinese citizens studying abroad during different periods. In the 40-year period of 1978 to 2018, the overall net return rate of people studying abroad showed an upward trend in fluctuations; while the period 1996–2006 showed a downward trend, with the return rate declining from 38.66% in 1996 to 25.09% in 2006. For the period 2008–2018, there was a steady upward trend, with the return rate increasing from 38.54% in 2008 to 78.45% in 2018.

2. Return rate of different finance-scheme students

As presented above, the return rate varied over different periods and years, and the return rate of overseas students differed according to the financial sources as well. From the 1980s onwards, the return rate of state-sponsored overseas students is rated the highest, followed by the institution-sponsored and the self-funded students. From 1978 to 1996, there were 270,000 students studying abroad, and about 90,000 of them returned home, with a return rate of 33%. Among them, 44,000 were sponsored by the state and 37,000 of them returned, with a return rate of 84%. Of the 86,000 work units-sponsored overseas students, 48,000 returned, with a return rate of 56%. Of the 139,000 self-financed overseas students, 4,000 returned, which equates to a return rate of 3% (Chen et al., 2003).

According to statistics from the China Scholarship Council, the total number of publicly funded overseas students in China reached 91,560 between the years 1996 to 2010, with an average return rate of 98.23%. From 1996 to 2008, among a total of 48,605 state- and institution-sponsored students, 36,614 actually returned (Wang, 2009).

3. Return rate of overseas students by host country

The return rate of Chinese overseas students differed significantly by host country. From 1978 to 1998, 160,000 Chinese students went to the US. Among them, 30,000 returned home, with a return rate of 18.8%. During the same period, the average return rate of Chinese overseas students who went to Japan, Canada, Germany, and the UK was 50%, while that of France and Australia was higher than 60% (Ye, 2001).

Table 3.2 Return rate of Chinese overseas students between 1978 and 2018

Year	Number of Chinese citizens studying abroad	Number of Chinese citizens returning home	Return rate (%)
1978	860	248	28.84
1980	2,124	162	7.63
1982	2,326	2,116	90.97
1984	3,073	2,290	74.52
1986	4,676	1,388	29.68
1988	3,786	3,000	79.24
1990	2,950	1,593	54.00
1992	6, 540	3,611	55.21
1994	19, 071	4,230	22.18
1996	20,905	6,570	31.43
1998	17,622	7,379	41.87
2000	38,989	9,121	23.39
2002	125,179	17,945	14.34
2004	114,682	24,726	21.56
2006	134,000	42,000	31.34
2008	179,800	69,300	38.54
2010	284,700	134,800	47.35
2012	399,600	272,900	68.29
2014	459,800	364,800	79.34
2016	544,500	432,500	79.43
2018	662,100	519,400	78.45

Sources:
1. 1978–1998 data source: Cao Cong (2009). Brain Drain, Brain Gain and Brain Circulation. *Science & Culture Review*, 6(1): 13–32.
2. 2000–2016 data source: National Bureau of Statistics of China. (2018) (n.d.). Zhongguo Tongji Nianjian 2018 Jiaoyu: Liuxuesheng he liuxue renyuan qingkuang [China Statistical Yearbook 2018: Education of postgraduate and overseas students]. Retrieved June 28, 2019, from http://www.stats.gov.aVtjsj/ndsj/2018/indexch.htm.
3. 2018 data source: Chinese governmental website. (March 28, 2019). 2018 Woguo chuguo liuxue renyuan qingkuang tongji [Statistics of Chinese overseas students in 2018]. Retrieved June 28, 2019, from http://www.gov.cn/xinwen/2019-03/28/content_5377626.htm.

Note: Return rate equals the proportion of the number of citizens returning to the country compared to the number of citizens going abroad for studying in that year.

3.1.2.4 Developed countries are the main destinations of China's academic mobility

The geographical distribution of Chinese overseas students showed that the developed countries are the main destinations of Chinese student mobility. As shown in Table 3.3, the main recipient countries of Chinese students are industrialized countries such as European countries and the US. Chinese overseas students travel mainly to English-speaking countries and European countries. In 2017, the number of Chinese overseas students in the US was 350,755, Australia had 114,006, the UK had 97,850 and Canada had 90,700 students. The fluctuation of Chinese

Table 3.3 Number of Chinese overseas students in the main recipient countries from 1998 to 2017

Recipient countries	1998	2000	2002	2004	2006	2008	2016	2017
US	46,958	54,466	63,211	61,765	62,582	81,127	328,547	350,755
UK	2,883	6,310	20,710	47,740	50,755	45,355	94,995	97,850
Germany	4,773	6,256	14,070	25,284	27,390	—	30,259	32,268
France	—	2,111	5,477	11,514	17,132	—	28,043	28,760
Australia	5,273	6,191	23,332	41,562	63,543	82,144	97,984	114,006
Japan	22,810	32,297	58,533	77,713	74,292	72,766	74,921	75,262
Canada	3,505	11,059	29,811	39,396	39,845	—	83,990	90,700
New Zealand	139	3,735	18,831	29,881	21,036	—	16,520	17,870

Sources:
1. 1998–2008 Data source: Kemal Gürüz (2011). Higher Education and International Student Mobility in the Global Knowledge Economy. Albany: State University of New York Press. US data (p. 219), UK data (p. 247), German data (p. 253), France data (p. 260), Australia data (p. 266), Japan data (p. 271), Canada data (p. 278), New Zealand data (p. 283).
2. 2016 Data source: Zhongguo Jiaoyu Zaixian (2017). Zhongguo Chuguo Liuxue Fazhan Qushi baogao (2017). Retrieved June 20, 2019, from https://www.eol.cn/html/lx/report2017/yi.shtml.
3. 2017 Data source: Institute of International Education (2017). Project Atlas. Retrieved June 29, 2019, from. https://www.iie.org/Research·and·Insights/Project-Atlas/Explore-Data.

Note: "—" refers to missing data.

students in the major host countries is influenced by the international environment and Sino-foreign relations. For instance, the trade war between China and the US in 2018 has led to a downward trend of Chinese students studying in the US during the past couple of years.

3.1.2.5 The Sino-US educational exchange: US is the biggest beneficiary of China's outflow of academic talent

The educational exchange relationship between China and the US has become the most significant educational exchange to both sides. The Sino–US higher education exchange relationship is crucial in terms of the breadth of educational cooperation, the extent of talent mobility, and the influence of talent mobility in the two countries and higher education institutions. When we look at the international mobility of Chinese academic talent, China has gradually grown to be the largest exporter of students studying in the US and the major source of scientific and engineering qualified PhDs within the US. Table 3.4 shows that the PhD candidates who graduated from American universities in 1987/1988 from Mainland China, while in 1992, 65% still stayed in the US for employment. Following 1992 and around five years after they obtained their PhDs, the Mainland Chinese who stayed in US reached a record high of more than 90%.

Table 3.4 Scientific and engineering PhDs holding foreign nationality and temporary passport while staying in the US 4–5 years after graduation from 1992 to 2005

Origin	1987/88 PhDs who stayed in the US in 1992	1990/91 PhDs who stayed in the US in 1995	1992/93 PhDs who stayed in the US in 1997	1994/95 PhDs who stayed in the US in 1999	1995/96 PhDs who stayed in the US in 2001	1997/98 PhDs who stayed in the US in 2003	1999/2000 PhDs who stayed in the US in 2005
Mainland China	65%	88%	92%	91%	96%	90%	92%
India	72%	79%	83%	87%	86%	86%	85%
UK	—	59%	56%	60%	53%	60%	58%
Canada	32%	46%	48%	55%	62%	58%	56%
Greece	44%	41%	46%	49%	53%	60%	54%
Germany	—	35%	38%	53%	48%	51%	49%
Taiwan (China)	47%	42%	36%	42%	40%	47%	50%
Japan	17%	13%	21%	27%	24%	37%	39%
Brazil	13%	25%	15%	21%	25%	25%	30%
South Korea	17%	11%	9%	15%	21%	34%	42%
Average	41%	47%	53%	51%	56%	61%	65%

Source: Oak Ridge Associated Universities.
Extracted from: Finn M. (2005). Stay rates of foreign doctorate recipients from US universities. Oak Ridge: Oak Ridge Institute for Science and Education.

Note: "—" refers to missing data.

As is shown in Table 3.5, the return rate of Mainland Chinese who obtained a PhD in the US had dropped from 25.9% in the 1980s to 8.3% in the 1990s, and down even further to 7.4% by the 21st century. Only India and China show the similar situation among all Asian countries, but the return rate of the former has been growing steadily in the 1990s and into the 21st century. The average return rates in the 21st century for Asia, Europe, Latin America, and Africa are 50.7%, 25.7%, 45.6%, and 39.5%, respectively. With these data, it can be concluded that the high-level academic talent which were initially attracted by the US were not only from developing countries, but also from developed ones. The US is the biggest beneficiary of the global academic talent flow, which confirms the "centre-periphery" influence of the world academic system for talent flows, as described by Altbach (2004).

3.1.2.6 Research universities in the US have the lion's share of Chinese overseas talent

For a long time, American world-famous universities have always been important host institutions of accepting and training Chinese academic talent due to their advantages in academic reputation, enrolment policy, English teaching language, academic and research platforms, as well as the countries' immigration and visa policies. Table 3.6 shows the top 20 American institutions that accepted international students in 2018. They are largely prestigious universities attracting a large number of international students. In 2017, these universities attracted numerous Chinese students (see Table 3.6).

Table 3.5 Return rate of PhDs who studied in American universities by country and region from 1980 to 2010

Country/Region	1980s	1990s	2000s
Mainland China	25.9%	8.3%	7.4%
India	13.1%	13%	10.3%
Japan	42.1%	49.5%	45.9%
South Korea	38.1%	30.9%	23%
Taiwan (China)	45.1%	47.5%	43.7%
Thailand	78.4%	80%	84.8%
Turkey	36.2%	57.6%	50%
Canada	56.2%	45.8%	37.7%
Mexico	67.8%	73.5%	60.6%
Brazil	85.7%	73.6%	59.9%
Europe	36.9%	33.2%	25.7%
Asia	59.8%	58.2%	50.7%
Latin America	63.6%	54.9%	45.6%
Africa	62.2%	51.2%	39.5%

Source: Kim D., Bankart S., & Isdell L. (2011). International doctorates: Trends and analysis on their decision to stay in US. *Higher Education*, 62(2): 141–161.

Table 3.6 Top 20 universities hosting international students in the US in 2018

Ranking	University	Number of international students in 2018	Number of Chinese international students in 2017
1	New York University	17,552	5,632
2	University of Southern California	16,075	5,480
3	Northeastern University	14,905	3,010
4	Columbia University	14,615	5,228
5	Arizona State University	13,459	3,374
6	University of Illinois at Urbana-Champaign	13,445	6,295
7	University of California, Los Angeles	12,017	3,406
8	Purdue University, West Lafayette	11,044	—
9	University of California, San Diego	9,883	5,227
10	Boston University	9,742	3,802
11	The University of Texas at Dallas	9,713	1,900
12	University of California, Berkeley	9,331	2,909
13	University of Washington	8,902	3,893
14	The Pennsylvania State University	8,636	3,602
15	Carnegie Mellon University	8,604	2,801
16	The University of Michigan	8,442	3,340
17	University of California, Irvine	7,902	4,616
18	Michigan State University	7,624	4,412
19	Indiana University	7,343	2,501
20	University of California, Davis	7,316	4,135

Source: Institute of International Education (IIE) (2018). (n.d.). America's Open Portal Data. The top 20 universities in the US accepting international students in 2018. Retrieved June 21, 2019, from https://www.iie.org/Research-and-Insights/Open-Doors/Data^International-Students?7Leading-Host-Institutions.

3.1.2.7 More than half of American post-doctoral fellows are made up of foreigners

Since the 1980s, the number of foreigners doing post-doctoral fellowships in the US has been growing steadily. According to the National Science Foundation (NSF), post-doctoral fellows holding temporary passports accounted for 35% in 1980. This proportion exceeded 50% for the very first time in 1991, which increased to 55% in 2000, and further rose to 58% in 2007. In 2009, among the 60,000 American post-doctoral fellows, foreigners accounted for 53%. In fact, a considerable proportion of Chinese science and engineering PhD graduates studying in the US chose to stay as post-doctoral fellows for those universities.

Chinese scholars have a preference for American prestigious universities for further study. Therefore, the number of Chinese visiting scholars in the US ranks the highest among all other international visiting scholars. Since the 1990s, the number of teachers from Chinese universities and research institutes who go abroad for further training or as a visiting scholar has gradually increased. Among them, the proportion of young and middle-aged teachers are considerably high, and they are the ones who are largely funded by the China Scholarship Council, provincial and municipal governments, the Chinese universities and institutes they work for, or the American ones they have applied to, or sometimes, other international organizations.

Table 3.7 shows the number of Chinese students and scholars in American universities and their percentage among all the international students and visiting scholars in the US from 1993 to 2015. The number of Chinese students studying in the US has long been ranked either first or second, with 44,380, accounting for 9.9% in 1993 and increased to 328,547 in 2015, accounting for 31.5%. Meanwhile, the number of Chinese visiting scholars in the US increased from 11,156 in 1993, accounting for 18.6%, to 44,490 in 2015, accounting for 33.2%.

To sum up, the main characteristics of the international mobility of Chinese academic talent since the reform and opening-up are as follows: (1) The main channel of mobility is to study abroad; (2) the main reason of brain drain is that the overseas talent do not return after completing their studies; (3) the main trend of mobility shows the coexistence of brain drain, brain gain, and brain circulation; (4) the main directions of international mobility are headed for developed countries, such as the Anglo-European countries and Japan; (5) the main gathering places are those world famous universities in the developed countries; (6) the number of Chinese scholars going abroad for further studies is increasingly growing, and they are largely sponsored by public funds, and its flow direction and concentration in famous universities are similar to those of Chinese overseas students; and (7) foreigners account for half of all the post-doctoral fellows in the US, and a considerable proportion are Chinese and Indian science and engineering post-doctoral fellows. It is foreseeable that as long as the basic structure of the world knowledge

Table 3.7 Chinese students and scholars in the US

Year	Number of Chinese students studying in the US (ranked)	Number of Chinese students studying in the US among all the international students in the US (%)	Number of Chinese visiting scholars in the US	Number of Chinese visiting scholars in the US among all the international visiting scholars in the US (%)
1993	44,380 (1)	9.9	11,156	18.6
1995	39,613	8.7	9,228	15.5
1997	46,958	9.8	10,709	16.4
1999	54,466 (1)	10.6	13,229	17.7
2001	63,211 (2)	10.8	15,624	18.2
2003	61,765 (2)	10.8	14,871	18.0
2005	62,582 (2)	11.1	19,017	19.6
2007	81,127 (2)	13.0	23,779	22.4
2009	127,628 (1)	18.5	29,471	25.6
2011	194,029 (1)	25.4	32,120	27.5
2013	274,439 (1)	31.0	36,409	29.9
2015	328,547 (1)	31.5	44,490	33.2

Source: Institute of International Education (IIE) (n.d.). America's Open Portal Data. Retrieved June 20, 2019, from https://www.iie.org/opendoors.

system remains unchanged, there is no fundamental policy change, and as long as China becomes more integrated into the world system, the abovementioned trends and characteristics will continue to develop in that direction.

3.2 Survey on Chinese academic talent in the US

China is a major exporter of talent, and the US is one of the most important developed countries that is known worldwide for its talent attraction and the primary destination of Chinese academic talent. Hence, this section focuses on Chinese scholars staying in the US as the target of this investigative study. Surveys and interviews were conducted and the data were analyzed to find out the reasons of Chinese students for staying in the US, their intention of returning to China, and their academic cooperation with domestic counterparts, aiming to understand the development pattern of talent outflow and backflow by revealing the influential factors and changing aspects of academic talent's outflow and inflow.

3.2.1 China's brain drain to the US and the push-pull factors

The phenomenon of Chinese academic talent who decide that they will not return to China upon graduation is remarkable for those who have studied in the US. The competition for academic talent between China and the US reflects a competitive state between the largest developing country and most developed country, as well as the competition of higher education and research institutions in the two countries. The flow of academic talent between these two countries is so huge in scale, broad in scope, and has remarkable depth of impact. Hence, it will undoubtedly have a profound impact on the integration of China's higher education into the world system in the 21st century. The educational exchange and talent flow between China and the US is crucial to the development of higher education internationalization. The first choice for many Chinese overseas students is to be able to study in the US. Up until 2014, there have been 1,460,000 Chinese students studying in the US alone (Yang & Liu, 2014). For a long time, it has been worrisome for China that there is a large number of high-level talent who would finish their studies in the US but would choose not to return home. As Cao Cong (2009) discussed, the most outstanding academic talent choose not to return from the US, which has become most problematic.

Among the abundant literature on global mobility of students, scholars, technicians, and immigrants, the "push-pull" model is one of the most widely used theoretical frameworks for explaining the directional trend on the flow of students and talent. Some scholars believe that the flow of students and talent from developing countries to developed countries is mainly caused by the pushing force of the talent's original country and the pulling force of the host country (Zweig & Chen, 1995; Altbach, 1998). In fact, the pushing and pulling forces are two-way. Even in those countries that consist of a large outflow of talent, it is not only the pushing force that drives the loss of talent, but also the pulling force which attracts them back to their country of origin. Similarly, the pull and push factors also exist in the in-flowing countries. In other words, those underlining factors that cause talent to not to return to their motherland include the domestic "push" factor and the foreign countries' "pull" factor, and those factors that attract talent to return include the domestic "pull" factor and the foreign countries' "push" factor. Both the pull and push factors from the home country and the destination country need to be considered in order to reasonably explain the external factors or determining forces influencing Chinese academic talent to stay in the US or return home in the global academic talent market.

Based on interaction between two-way push and pull external factors and internal factors of individuals, a framework for analyzing factors influencing Chinese academic talent staying in the US has been constructed (see Figure 3.1). This figure shows that the factors that affect Chinese academic talent studying in the US who decide to return home or stay abroad are multi-directional, constantly changing, and in two-way stream, with the main and obvious factors being the reality faced by these scholars and its incurring judgement, subjective understanding, and behavioural aspects. These factors can be further divided into seven aspects: Career development, family-related factors, economy and income, social status, cultural identity, living conditions, and political environment. The decision on whether to immigrate to the US or not is made after considering and weighing the abovementioned factors.

After comparing all seven factors in China and the US, these talented individuals usually make three conclusive statements. First, they think that the US is better than China in general (as per Model A); therefore, they will make a choice to stay in the US, either for a long term or temporarily. The second possibility is that they think that China is better than the US in general, they decide to return home in the long run or temporarily (as per Model B). The third possibility is they believe that China and the US both have their own advantages and disadvantages. This would result in them choosing to be simultaneously between China and the US, which presents a continuous back-and-forth circulation phenomenon (Model C).

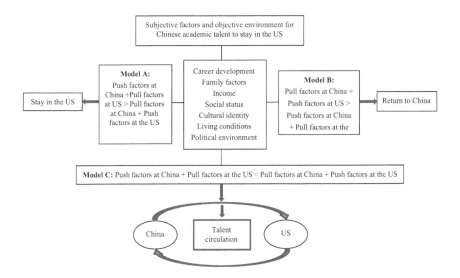

Figure 3.1 Influencing factors and flow process of Chinese academic talent in the US.

3.2.2 Research questions and research methods

For Chinese academics in the US, the choice of leaving or staying in the US is rarely a result of separate analyses of one's individual conditions. It is often considered by combining the mutual relationship between macro-environmental, meso-organizational, and micro-individual factors, in order to have a bigger picture of the situation. The field survey aimed to address the following questions:

(1) What are the attitudes of scholars studying in the US towards returning home?
(2) What are the reasons for them to stay in the US and not to return?
(3) What are some favourable factors that attract them to return China?
(4) What are their thoughts regarding the academic environment and career opportunities in China and the US?
(5) What is the situation between their exchange and collaborative relationship and their counterparts in China?

This study adopts a combined method of quantitative and qualitative surveys, with the questionnaire component being the main data collection method and interviews as supplementary. From April 2011 to April 2012 the author attended the University of California, Los Angeles (UCLA) as a visiting scholar and had plenty of time and opportunity to contact Chinese scholars who were based at UCLA. Drawing data from questionnaire surveys and interviews, the section explored the push and pull factors leading to Chinese academics' choice of staying in the US, exploring their opinions on their academic life and cooperative activities with Mainland Chinese counterparts.

3.2.2.1 Questionnaire survey

In order to gain a deeper understanding of Chinese scholars staying in the US, including their intention of returning to China, reasons for staying in the US, relative working conditions, their cooperation with domestic counterparts, their comparison of academic careers in China versus the US, and their views on domestic governments' policies on attracting overseas academic talent, the author conducted an online questionnaire survey of Chinese scholars working in American universities, mainly at UCLA. The survey was conducted for a period of three months, from November 2011 to February 2012. The questionnaire consisted of five parts, with a total of 53 questions, including the candidate's personal information, reasons for staying in the US, their current work conditions, intentions to return to China, and cooperation with Chinese counterparts. A total of 70 sets of questionnaires were collected. However, some questions were left unanswered by the respondents, leading to some questions with less than 70 responses.

Given the geographical spread of scholars in the US, it was difficult to obtain their contact information. The author selected Mainland Chinese scholars from the 2011 UCLA Directory (Yellow Pages) and sent them individual emails. The content of the emails included the researcher's identity, name of the research project that they will be involved in, the research purpose, the principle of anonymity implemented in this research, and the direct link to the online questionnaire.

Simultaneously, the author made use of the snowball sampling method to recruit "new" acquaintances and other social networks to send survey invitation letters and online questionnaire link to Mainland Chinese scholars working in other American universities. Moreover, this research utilized SurveyMonkey, a network surveying tool, as its data collection platform.

The survey respondents were full-time faculty members, researchers, and post-doctorates working in American universities. Among the 70 respondents, 64 were PhD graduates and were classified as high-level academic talent staying in the US. Among them, 43 (61.4%) were male, and 61 (87.1%) were married. In terms of age, 16 (22.8%) were under the age of 35, 20 (28.6%) were aged 35 to 45 years old, and 27 (38.6%) were aged between 46 and 55 years old. With respect to their academic titles, the number of participants who are a (Research) Professor accounted for 25.7%, Associate Professor accounted for 28.6%, Assistant Professors accounted for 22.9%, and those who hold a post-doctorate accounted for 18.6%. In terms of institution types, most of the respondents either worked in research universities (51.4%) or the teaching and research universities (45.7%). In terms of the specific type of disciplines, science and engineering accounted for 73.9%, social sciences 23.2%, and humanities 2.9%. Their source of funding for studying abroad largely originated from American universities (81.4%). The respondents have lived in the US for an accumulated number of years ranging from 1 to 28.

3.2.2.2 Interviews

Semi-structured interviews were conducted among 14 Chinese scholars working in American universities. Information about them is listed in Table 3.8. Among the interviewees, eight were male, nine had the title of Associate Professor or above, eight had been to the US during 1980 to 1990, and the rest arrived between the period of 1991 to 2002. The content of the interviews largely revolved around their personal experience, reasons for staying in the US, intentions and reasons for returning to China, academic employment, cooperation with Chinese counterparts, and comparison of their academic careers in the US and in China, as well as opinions about Chinese overseas talent policies and so forth.

3.2.3 To return or not to return is a question for scholars staying in the US

3.2.3.1 Close ties with China and a good impression of returning to China in the short term

In this research, the closeness of keeping ties with China and the frequency of returning to China were indicators used to evaluate the strength of the ties between the scholars and their homeland. The survey shows that most scholars staying in the US often kept in touch with China. Half of the respondents returned China at least once, mainly to visit relatives (64.7%), for collaboration and communication with domestic counterparts (29.4%), and to participate in conferences (4.4%), among others. Most of them held comparatively positive impressions on returning to China during their short stay.

58 *From brain drain to brain circulation*

Table 3.8 Interviewees' information

Interviewee	Gender	Year of coming to the US	University at which they obtained their Bachelor degree	Year they obtained their PhD degree	University at which they obtained their PhD degree	Discipline	Academic title
Scholar 1	M	2001	Nanjing University	2008	University of North Carolina	Psychology	Associate Professor
Scholar 2	F	1984	Sun Yat-sen University	1989	SUNY Albany	Sociology	Professor
Scholar 3	F	2002	Xiamen University	2009	University of Maryland	Statistics	Assistant Researcher
Scholar 4	F	1990	Wenzhou University	1996	University of California, Los Angeles	Education	Assistant Researcher
Scholar 5	M	1988	Peking University	1994	Brown University	Psychology	Associate Professor
Scholar 6	M	1991	Nanjing University	1995	Case Western Reserve University	Genetics	Professor
Scholar 7	M	1984	Peking University	1987	University of Utah	Geography	Professor
Scholar 8	F	1989	Binzhou Medical University	1996	Duke University	Medicine	Professor
Scholar 9	M	1984	Fudan University	1989	Harvard University	Math	Professor
Scholar 10	M	2000	University of British Columbia	2008	Michigan University	Anthropology	Assistant Professor
Scholar 11	F	2001	East China Normal University	2007	Michigan State University	Education	Assistant Professor
Scholar 12	F	2000	University of Science and Technology Beijing	2005	University of California, Los Angeles	Psychology	Assistant Professor
Scholar 13	M	1982	Tianjing Normal University	1992	Washington State University	Literature	Associate Professor
Scholar 14	M	1986	Peking University	1993	Harvard University	Anthropology	Professor

3.2.3.2 Over one-third of scholars have no desire in returning to China

Figure 3.2 shows that over one-third of the respondents (36.8%) would not return to China, 26.5% might return, 16.2% would definitely return, and 20.6% were not sure yet. Regarding their schedule for returning to work in China, 19.1% would return within the next three years, 14.7% would return after three years, 27.9% would not return, and 38.2% did not have a specific timetable to return.

3.2.3.3 A majority obtained a bachelor's degree in China and most of them obtained a doctorate degree in the US

As shown in Table 3.9, the proportions of those who obtained a bachelor's degree, master's degree, and doctorate degree in China were 97.1%, 61.4%, and 30%, respectively. Most of these Chinese scholars would then stay in the US to obtain their American doctoral qualifications. Therefore, China has paid a high and long-term cost for the growth of Chinese scholars, while the US has retained China's intellectual talent through the last doctoral process and the green card residency. Undoubtedly, it seems that the developing countries have been robbed of talent by developed countries because the former is on the periphery of the knowledge research system. As long as there exists an unbalanced development and an unequal competition between countries, then the academic talent outflow from developing countries to developed countries will continue.

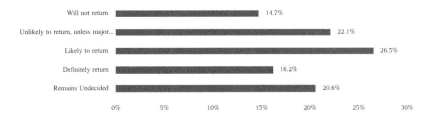

Figure 3.2 Intentions for returning to China ($n = 68$).

Table 3.9 Level of degree obtained by Chinese scholars staying in the US

Country	Bachelor's degree		Master's degree		Doctorate degree	
	Number of scholars	%	Number of scholars	%	Number of scholars	%
China	68	97.1	43	61.4	21	30
US	1	1.4	16	22.9	38	54.3
Other countries	0	0	1	1.4	5	7.1
No degree obtained	1	1.4	10	14.3	6	8.6

3.2.4 Why do Chinese academic talent choose to stay in the US?

By the beginning of the 21st century, although the pull from China is increasing and the US is gradually declining due to decreased academic career opportunities, a number of the most outstanding academic talent have chosen to remain in the US. It cannot be denied that the US is at the centre of world knowledge and research for many disciplines. This brings an obvious advantage for the US in terms of academic environment and academic career development platforms.

3.2.4.1 Career development determined their choice of whether to stay in the US

In the US, the academic platform is well-established and there are more opportunities for academic development. As for the 14 interviewees, regardless of whether they hold the position of Assistant Professor, Associate Professor, or Full Professor, they are all in a better professional development environment and status compared to if they were in China. Scholars in science and engineering have independent laboratories and scientific research teams, while those in humanities and social sciences have their research centres or academic fields, where they can independently supervise doctoral students. Only one anthropology scholar openly spoke about the possibility of returning to work in one of China's famous universities if the academic position he held in the US does not go well. On the other hand, the remaining 13 interviewees remarked that they would stay in the US to advance their academic career.

The interviewees believe that in the US, they had superior academic platforms and a more ideal peer-to-peer support culture. Having a standardized academic system and method of evaluation were conducive to their academic development. Comparatively speaking, the domestic academic community had an impetuous atmosphere and focused on utilitarian and quantitative evaluation. The existence of unpleasant phenomena, such as academic corruption, made the interviewees worried about the possible return to China.

Scholar 1 (who is a male Associate Professor in Psychology) illustrated his reasons for staying in the US:

> I do psychological measurements. First of all, there are too many internal affairs that involve too much energy in China. Second, there is a discrepancy between the development in China and the development here; and China is still in a state of following up the development abroad. Besides, on a personal matter, my wife is also in the US, and she has not yet graduated from her doctorate.

Some scholars believed that America was in the international centre of their disciplines. For example, Scholars 8 and 7 mentioned,

> As for the field of medicine I am engaged in, there is a huge gap between China and the US. It will take 20 years for China to catch up. The reason why I stay in the US is mainly because what I am currently doing is cutting-edge. I cannot do

it if I were to return to China. In the US, I can contribute to the whole disciplinary field. Additionally, there are age restrictions in the policies and talent programmes in China. There is no way I'd be able to contribute once I'm over 50.

(Scholar 8)

In China, the "academic oligarchs", such as a certain number of academicians, have too much control, which has suppressed the academic innovation and the growth of young scholars. The influence and power of those individuals should be reduced.

(Scholar 7)

The complicated interpersonal relationship in China discouraged Chinese scholars in the US from returning home. The survey shows that complicated interpersonal relationships in China have a negative effect on scholars' desire to return home. As shown in Table 3.10, 64.7% of the respondents believed that the presence of complicated interpersonal relationships at work made them reluctant to return to China. The main factors that impeded those scholars to return to full-time work in China were by-and-large the social relationship, overly complicated academic network, and the strong influence of academic authority on the allocation of financial resources.

The strong administrative power in the academic environment is not conducive to Chinese scholars' decision to return home. In China, the administration has a relatively strong power, which has hindered the decision making of certain

Table 3.10 Negative factors affecting US Chinese scholars' willingness of returning to China

Push factors from China	%	Pull factors from the US	%
Complicated interpersonal relationship	64.7	Ideal working conditions	20.6
Strong administrative influence from China	55.9	Political freedom	11.8
Limited career development	33.8	Direct and simple interpersonal relationship	11.8
A better future for children in the US than in China	25.0	Good working culture	11.8
Poor life quality in China	19.1	A better future for children	10.3
Lack of academic exchange with foreign scholars	17.6	Freedom of choice	10.3
Family members reluctant to return home	17.6	High living standards	7.4
Lack of personal freedom of choice	10.3	Other reasons	5.9
Lack of scientific research conditions and equipment	8.8	Reluctant to give up American citizenship	2.9
Degree majors studied abroad and not applicable back in home country	5.9	None	2.9

groups of Chinese scholars in the US to not want to return home. The respondents reported that the strong administrative power was an important factor (accounting for 55.9%) in preventing them from teaching in China. It can be concluded that the continuous reform of the administrative system and the de-administration of universities and scientific research institutions are some of the important measures that could be used in attracting overseas talent to return home.

3.2.4.2 Family elements have become increasingly important factors

The Chinese culture has always attached great importance to kinship and family responsibilities. Because of this, the decision to leave or stay in the US is not necessarily an individual's decision, but most likely a combined decision of an entire family after weighing its pros and cons. Family factors, such as the spouse's intention to stay or not, the children's education and career development opportunities, and the family responsibilities for their elders, have a direct impact on the scholars' decision to stay or to leave. Of the survey respondents, 17.6% said that the reason why they did not return to China was because their family members were unwilling to return.

Among all the family factors, education for the children was of extreme importance. Some interviewees held the belief that once their children reached elementary or middle school, and should they decide to return back home to China, the children would not adapt to China's highly competitive and test-oriented education environment. It would also be difficult for the youngsters to meet the requirements of their Chinese language competencies (views of Scholars 5 and 11). Among all the survey respondents, 58.8% and 86.8% reported that they hoped their children would receive basic education and higher education, respectively, in America. Of them, 25% thought their children would have a better future in the US than in China. The test-oriented education pattern and insufficient quality education resources in China have led the overseas talent to become concerned about their children's education if they were to go back home. The dominant position of the US in the world's higher education system attracted them to stay in the US.

It was observed that there existed a model of one family living in two countries among the Chinese scholars. If the whole family could not reach a consensus on whether to return, the alternative was for the family to live in two countries, that is, the spouse engaged in the academic profession (often the male) would return home alone first, and then the other partner, together with their school-aged children, would continue to reside in the US.

3.2.4.3 The economic factor was still the key reason for Chinese scholars staying in the US

Economic income is very important for any profession. The respondents had a very positive comment on the economic income and overall living conditions in the US. Those who believe that their economic income was either very high or high accounted for 39.7% and 23.5%, respectively. Those who believe that their lives were either very good or good accounted for 44.1% and 42.6%, respectively. In addition, 76.9% of the respondents agreed or strongly agreed that the economic income in American universities was higher than that of similar universities in China. With the improvement of research conditions in Chinese universities and the increase in the remuneration for high-end talent, the income gaps between those engaged in academic profession in the US and China have been marginal and the economic factor is no longer as important as it once was back in the 1980s and 1990s. However, the salary of Chinese university academics is still considerably low and lacks international competitiveness. In 2008, Qian Yingyi, Dean of the School of Economics and Management of Tsinghua University, sent job invitations to 20 high-level overseas talent. Only one accepted the invitation; the rest went to Singapore, Hong Kong, and other Anglo-European countries. It is said that low salary was one of the main reasons for them in giving up work opportunities in the domestic market. In recent years, Mainland Chinese universities have made a tremendous improvement in their hardware facilities and scientific conditions, but they still cannot compare with those universities based in Anglo-European countries and regions, Japan, Singapore, or Hong Kong (China). According to a survey conducted by Laura Rumbley, Ivan Pacheco, Philip Altabch in 2008 on the academic salaries in 15 countries globally, the academic salary in China was by-and-large towards the lower end in terms of starting salary, highest salary, and average salary, with the figures being $682, $1,845, and $1,182, respectively (Rumbley et al., 2008, p. 39).

3.2.4.4 Immigration motives induced academic talent to stay in the US

The vast majority of the respondents were academic immigrants and obtaining American green card or citizenship was one of their goals with staying in the US. In the survey, most of the respondents have obtained their green card or become an American citizen. The survey showed that at the time of going abroad, 38.6% held F-type student visas, 48.5% held visiting scholar or student visas (with 41.4% holding J1 visiting scholar visas and 7.1% holding visiting student visas), 5.7% held H-type work visas, and none of them were American permanent resident or citizen. At the time of the survey in 2011, 30% of them were American citizens, 42.9% were American permanent residents, and 12.9% held H-type work visas. It can be estimated that up to 72.9% have obtained their American green cards or citizenship. It was very unlikely that they would give up their American green cards or citizenship for full-time work in China.

3.2.4.5 Other pulling forces from the US

Some survey respondents thought staying in the US was helpful for their career development, in terms of having an ideal working condition (20.6%), good working culture (11.8%), simple and direct interpersonal relationships (11.8%), and the freedom of choice (10.3%). Aside from this, it was also conducive to their children's development and the living standard in the US was relatively high in comparison to China (see Table 3.10).

Some interviewees believed that the American academic environment encouraged innovation. For example, Scholar 5 talked about his academic development:

> The most important factors that have influenced my academic growth were: First and most important, having the opportunity to encounter great tutors and professors; second, the existence of a free and open academic environment in the US, which encourages me to continuously challenge one's boundaries and creating this new disciplinary concept.

Some interviewees believed that the academic system in the US was relatively mature and conducive for innovation. For instance, Scholar 13 said:

> The academic community in the US is relatively favourable. There are a few fuzzy and grey areas, but the rules are clear-cut and transparent. Whether it is promotion, publication of works or papers, programme application, they are all based on relatively standardized and clear performance guidelines. Moreover, the intellectual properties in the US are completely free from other stakeholder's constraints and non-academic influential factors. The researchers can concentrate purely on their research.

3.2.5 Factors triggering Chinese academic talent in the US to return to China

As mentioned above, there are not only forces from China and the US that make Chinese talent stay in the US, but also factors that make them return to China, namely the pulling forces from China and the pushing ones from the US. With its continuous social and economic development in the past 40 years, China has been moving away from the periphery to semi-centre of the world's academic system. The academic environment has been gradually improving. As there are a growing number of favourable factors in attracting overseas Chinese scholars to return to China for academic careers, more and more overseas talent have come back to work in China. The survey results show that career development, family members' intention to return home, children's education and growth, social status, and other unfavourable factors that used to hinder the return of these academic talent, are turning into favourable ones that attract them back (see Table 3.11).

3.2.5.1 Pulling forces from China

First, the search for opportunities and platforms for career development is the primary factor in determining overseas Chinese scholars in returning to China. With regard to the academic talent who have returned and those who have not yet returned, they are beginning to become aware of the many attractive factors for returning to China. Shi Yigong (2016) believed that the advantages were, first and foremost, the level of student quality in China, and with it, a highly qualified and skilled academic team could be forged, which is conducive to achieving valuable research outcomes. Second, the scientific equipment and hardware conditions were as good as, if not better than, those of universities and scientific institutions

Table 3.11 Favourable factors attracting Chinese scholars in the US to return home

Pull factors from China	%	Push factors from the US	%
Favourable career development in China	71.6	Inadequate sense of belonging	38.2
Attractive Chinese culture	37.3	High living pressures and quick living pace	14.7
Family members willing to return to China	37.3	Life is monotonous	10.3
Higher social status in China than abroad	34.3	Other reasons	10.3
Willing to participate in China's reform	31.3	Job instability	4.7
Higher living quality	25.4	Poor social security	1.7
A better future for children in China than in the US	13.4	None	20.6
Higher economic income in China than in the US	11.9		

in developed countries. The third was the development platforms and the opportunity to be innovative in their chosen disciplinary fields. There is a high probability that if a Chinese PhD graduate stayed in the US for their academic career, they will not be admitted into the research universities in the US. By contrast, if they were to return to China, they would have the chance to enter research universities in large cities such as Beijing and Shanghai, where there are more opportunities for career development and sophisticated platforms to play with. The fourth is the academic autonomy and sense of ownership of their intellectual property. They can be a participant and potentially even a leader, not a bystander, in China's development. A group of scientists and scholars such as Shi Yigong, Rao Yi, and Tian Guoqiang have flourished in their academic development after returning to China, which undoubtedly become an exemplar for attracting noteworthy talent in returning to China. A series of overseas talent programmes developed by the Chinese government and universities have gradually shown a positive effect in attracting a number of distinguished academic talent to work in Chinese research universities.

Second, Chinese culture and social identity lead overseas Chinese scholars to consider returning to China. A sense of identity with Chinese culture and the lack of belonging in the US are actually two sides of the same coin, which is one important cultural factor attracting Chinese scholars in the US to return to China. When there is a stable political environment in China and the economic income gap between the Chinese and US citizens shrinks, the role of social and cultural factors will be further highlighted. The sense of belonging in a Chinese culture and acceptance in the society will attract more Chinese scholars to return from the US.

Third, the family factors can not only cause Chinese scholars in the US to stay there, but also propel them to return to China. According to the survey, 37.3% reported that their close family members are hopeful for their return back home. Parents and family members based in China can act as an anchor in attracting them to return. The survey showed that the scholars who returned and the scholars who are still in the US emphasized that their parents and family play a major role in their decision of returning to China.

Fourth, social status is also a key factor for Chinese scholars in the US to consider returning to China. From the survey, 34.3% of the respondents believed that their social status was higher when they were working in China than in the US. Overseas academics require tremendous effort in order to achieve a certain level of professional development, but the social status remains below their expectations. As such, they feel that they have a higher social status once they return to China for work.

3.2.5.2 Pushing forces from the US

As shown in Table 3.11, the potential factors from the US that caused Chinese scholars in the US to return to China are as follows: Lack of belonging, high-pressure living conditions and monotonous lifestyle, job instability, and poor social security. Since the economic crisis in 2008, higher education funding in the US has been reduced, and with it, the expenditure in universities and research institutions has been cut. This resulted in a laborious effort to raise the salary of academics. Meanwhile, job opportunities are in short supply and competition has intensified. The changing macro environment and uncertain career prospects have made the US lose its advantages that originally attracted scholars to study in the US.

Some interviewees referred to this as a "glass ceiling" phenomenon for Chinese scholars who were navigating their career in the US. Scholar 7 described two examples in detail:

> There is a glass ceiling phenomenon in the US. I did not feel it much when I was a student but when I became a faculty, it has become much more obvious now. The more you climb up, the more obvious this phenomenon is. There are two examples: the first is this faculty recruitment done geographically. The originally shortlisted 4 candidates were all of Chinese heritage, and it was obvious that some of the other professors thought this was not good enough, so a fifth candidate was enlisted, not of Chinese origin. And surprisingly, or not so surprisingly, as a result, the finalist who got the position was in fact the fifth one. Of all four Chinese candidates, there certainly was some areas that they were lacking, but surely, one of them was much more qualified than the chosen one. The second example is of one of my former postdocs' experiences. He had very strong professional abilities and ranked first in the interview at Columbia University, but he still did not get the position. Later on, he ended up returning to China.

Scholar 2, a Chinese female who was based in the US, spoke of another "glass ceiling" phenomenon where the dual prejudice of gender and race hindered career development:

> The career development of Chinese scholars in the US is faced with a so-called glass ceiling phenomenon. As a non-Caucasian and female, the

authority and degree of respect are not as high as those of white male. Moreover, those who have returned for one year or longer are mostly men because men have higher desires and pursuits for leadership and be leaders than women. In the US, it is hard for them to get into leadership, while it is easier for them to be entrusted with important positions upon their arrival into China.

3.2.6 Views of overseas Chinese scholars on the academic career environment in China and the US

According to the abovementioned survey results, academic environment and career development are the primary factors that affect the scholars' choice of staying in the US. In the following section, a comparison will be made in terms of those scholars' perception about the academic careers in China and in the US. Previous studies have not looked into the influence of academic career development characteristics and environment on talent retention in China and the US. This study found that these differences were crucial in determining Chinese academic scholars' decision to stay in the US and not return to China.

3.2.6.1 Differences in academic environment and systems between China and the US

The academic environment and academic systems are composed of four dimensions. The first dimension is the social environment, which includes academic freedom and academic integrity. The second aspect is the environment at the organizational and institutional level, such as academic management, academic promotion, academic evaluation, and the global status of the academic system. The third one is the interpersonal and cultural environment, such as the professionalism of academic colleagues, interpersonal relationship, and culture in the academic community. The fourth dimension is the infrastructure for research, such as the research conditions, library resources, and research funding. Across these four dimensions, most of the survey respondents believed that, in general, the US was better than China.

As shown in Table 3.12, through the survey across 13 aspects, like academic environment, academic system, academic conditions, academic management, and interpersonal relationships, it was found that Chinese scholars in the US believed that the US was better than China in 11 of these aspects. More than 80% of the survey respondents believed that the US was better than China in the following six aspects: (a) The academic promotion in American universities is more standardized; (b) the work in the US can be at the academic centre of the field; (c) academic ethics and academic integrity are more valued in American academia; (d) the American academic evaluation system is more conducive to conducting valuable research; (e) the management style within American universities is better than that of Chinese ones; (f) American universities have much more abundant library resources compared to the Chinese universities.

Table 3.12 Scholars' comparison of the academic career between China and the US

State-ment	Aspects	Disagree (%)	Neutral (%)	Agree (%)	Strongly agree (%)	Agree and strongly agree (%)
1	Academic promotion in American universities is more standardized	0	10.8	40	49.2	89.2
1	Working in the US can be at the academic centre of the field	1.5	9.2	46.1	43.1	89.2
1	Academic ethics and academic integrity are more valued in American academia	0	10.8	32.3	56.9	89.2
2	The American academic evaluation system is more conducive to conducting valuable research	3.1	10.8	46.2	40	86.2
3	Management in American universities is better than that in Chinese ones	0	15.4	41.5	43.1	84.6
4	American universities have more library resources than Chinese ones	46	15.4	27.7	52.3	80
5	The scientific research conditions in American universities are better than those Chinese universities in similar tiers	7.7	13.8	35.4	43.1	78.5
6	Economic income in American universities is higher than that of similar Chinese universities	3.1	20	46.2	30.8	77
7	Interpersonal relationship in American academia is not as complicated as in China	7.7	15.4	32.3	44.6	76.9
8	American academic colleagues are more supportive in their professional development	0	27.7	43.1	29.2	72.3
9	Working at an American university is much more conducive to career development	3.1	29.2	38.5	29.2	67.7
10	The research funding in American universities is much higher than that of similar universities in China	15.4	43.1	32.3	9.2	41.5
11	Working in American universities is more rewarding	6.2	56.9	16.9	20	36.7

Note: The sample $n = 65$; strongly disagree = 1, disagree = 2, Neutral = 3, agree = 4, strongly agree = 5; the results for strongly disagree are 0, which has been omitted from this table.

3.2.6.2 The gap in the economic benefits of academic professions between China and the US narrowed down

Academic talent mainly pursue career development and work achievements, but economic returns and material conditions are the life necessities. In terms of work rewards, they are further divided into material rewards and achievement recognitions. Most of the survey respondents believed that the economic income in American universities was higher than that of similar universities in China. However, the gap between China and the US has been narrowed down in the past decade. Furthermore, as shown in Table 3.12, only 41.5% agreed that the scientific research funding obtained in the US was higher than that in China. Generally, the economic benefits of pursuing an academic career in China were lower than in the US. A higher housing and living expenditure in metropolitan cities, such as Shanghai and Beijing, have also made overseas academic talent feel the growing economic pressure.

3.2.7 Cooperation with academic counterparts in China

Chinese scholars in the US have their own academic expertise and academic and social network. They know their academic frontiers and have their own research teams and laboratories or research centres. They can cooperate with domestic institutions and counterparts through various ways to achieve the transfer and sharing of knowledge, technology, and resources. The following part will analyze the collaborative patterns between Chinese scholars in the US and their counterparts in Mainland China, the beneficiaries, existing problems, and their level of satisfaction.

Scholars in the US have advantages in transnational knowledge and technology transfer and cooperation. They are familiar with domestic and international communities. They are located at the centre of international knowledge and technology platforms and have the close-knit ties and willingness to make contributions to domestic scientific research and higher education. However, when dealing with transnational knowledge and technology transfer and cooperation, problems and challenges are still arising, including information asymmetry, difficulty in finding suitable scientific research partners, the inability to adapt to domestic scientific research, and management style.

3.2.7.1 The function of academic network and strong ties in forming a cooperative network and partnership

Sun Xiao'e and Bian Yianjie (2011) found that the mutual complementary relationship of strong and weak ties in social networks successfully promoted the transnational collaboration between Chinese American scholars and their counterparts in China. Strong ties provided connection, rapport, and constructive support for cooperation. The alma mater or former working organizations of US Chinese scholars become their important cooperating institutions. As alumni, their affection for their alma mater makes them willing to provide various kinds of services or even work part-time there. For example, Scholar 2, as a Changjiang Scholars Programs awardee, has now returned to work in the university of which he graduated.

3.2.7.2 American Chinese scholars have strong intentions for cooperation

In recent years, domestic talent introduction policies strongly advocate overseas scholars to return for short-term work. There are various policies and programmes in colleges and universities to attract overseas scholars to return to work for a short period of time. In essence, we may ask, how long can these overseas Chinese scholars return to work in China each year? The survey showed that 26.8% were willing to return to work for a period of two months every year, 18.3% for one month, and 11.3% for three months. Those who were not willing or unable to return for work accounted for 5.6%. It can be concluded that overseas Chinese scholars were more enthusiastic about returning to work for a short period, which is very helpful for improving overseas academic talent policies in terms of short-term service.

3.2.7.3 One-third did not cooperate with domestic counterparts

As shown in Table 3.13, the respondents' main collaborators were foreign counterparts abroad, Chinese counterparts abroad, and Chinese counterparts in Mainland China. Among them, 32.3% had no cooperation with Chinese counterparts in Mainland China. It showed that a majority of Chinese scholars prefer to work with cooperating colleagues in foreign countries, including foreigners and overseas Chinese scholars.

The frequency of communication between Chinese scholars in the US and their domestic counterparts were mainly on a single basis every 2 to 5 months (20.0%), once a month (18.5%), once every half year (12.3%), and once for longer than one year (13.8%). Those who never communicated with domestic colleagues accounted for 10.8%. The relatively modest number of collaborators and low communication frequency indicated that Chinese scholars in the US did not have strong academic exchange and cooperation with scholars in China. This implies that their substantial and extensive cooperation needs to be strengthened.

3.2.7.4 The main cooperative forms are academic visits, cooperative scientific research, and co-publication

Figure 3.3 shows that 41.5% respondents had no specific cooperation projects with their domestic counterparts. Among those who had collaboration projects, their cooperation forms largely involved writing academic papers in China, co-publication, and conducting collaborative research projects. Academic exchange visits, cooperative scientific research, and cooperative publication were common, and scholars could decide the cooperative forms from the individual aspect. However, more substantial cooperative forms, such as establishing joint research centres or laboratories, creating a domestic research base, or promoting disciplinary construction and talent cultivation in China were very rare, which called for organizational and institutional support.

3.2.7.5 It is difficult to find suitable domestic colleagues for cooperation

According to the survey, 16.9% of the respondents indicated that there were no problems in cooperating with Chinese academic colleagues. Others identified the following problems: Difficulty in finding suitable cooperative partners, difficulty

From brain drain to brain circulation 71

Table 3.13 Collaborative object of Chinese scholars in the US

Collaborators	Over 10 people		5–10 people		3–4 people		1–2 people		None	
	Number	%	Number	%	Number	%	Number	%	Number	%
Scholars from Mainland China	5	7.7	10	15.4	10	15.4	19	29.2	21	32.3
Chinese scholars abroad	5	7.7	19	29.2	13	20.0	15	23.1	13	20.0
Chinese scholars in Hong Kong, Macao, and Taiwan	0	0	3	4.5	5	7.7	14	21.5	43	66.2
Foreign scholars abroad	20	30.8	21	32.3	10	15.4	6	9.2	8	12.3

72 From brain drain to brain circulation

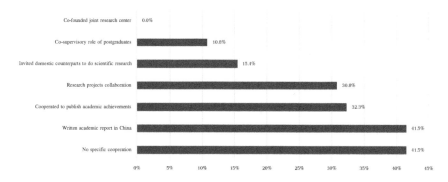

Figure 3.3 Forms of contribution Chinese scholars in the US made for China.

in cooperation because of difference in academic training at home and abroad, and lack of common research questions, among others (see Table 3.14).

3.2.7.6 Cooperation enhances the knowledge and technology transfer

Nearly half of the respondents stated that cooperation was mutually beneficial and a win-win for all parties involved, with the respondents themselves and their domestic collaborators being the main beneficiaries. Among the participants, 26.2% believed that the main beneficiaries were their domestic partners, 18.5% believed that the main beneficiaries were the two institutions involved in the project, 3.1% believed themselves as the main beneficiary, and 3.1% believed that the main beneficiaries were the Chinese institutions. It can be concluded that nearly all of them have benefited from the collaboration, but the knowledge and technology transfer mainly flowed from the US to the Chinese counterpart.

Scholar 7 (majored in Geography, male) shared his experience of cooperating with domestic scholars:

Table 3.14 Major problems in cooperation with Chinese academic colleagues ($n = 65$)

Problem	Percentage	Frequency
Difficult to find suitable cooperation partners	23.	15
Difficult to cooperate due to different academic training at home and abroad	2	13
Different research questions arising from different development stage at home and abroad	15.4	10
Lack of research fields for mutual interests	9.2	6
Other uncategorized issues	9.2	6
Different research methods	4.7	3
Different research writing styles	1.5	1
None	16.9	11

I have a long-term cooperation with a female professor in XX Institute of the Chinese Academy of Sciences who has studied in the US and returned to work in China very early on. Her research field was related to geography. I was satisfied with our cooperation, we worked complementary to one another. We collaborated to write our research paper and have published many high-quality articles. She is retired now. I'm currently working with her students, who are all very outstanding individuals. For a long time, I have trained dozens of students and post-doctorates for China, who have returned to work in different institutions in China. One works in the Meteorological Bureau. One is a chief scientist, with whom I have close working connection with. The collaboration with domestic colleagues is mainly to cultivate talent and a few of them are there to conduct collaborative research projects.

3.2.7.7 American Chinese scholars hold positive attitudes towards the cooperation effects with domestic counterparts

Figure 3.4 shows that Chinese scholars in the US hold a positive attitude towards their domestic collaboration counterparts, with 7.7% strongly satisfied, 27.7% very satisfied.

Chen Xuefei et al. (2003) found that the cooperation between overseas academic talent and returnees could contribute to the domestic academic community in various forms: Becoming high-level visiting scholars, leading and participating in the construction of disciplines, cooperating in scientific research and publication, building overseas and domestic scientific bases, promoting talent exchange, teaching courses, cultivating talent, introducing scientific projects, bringing in new technology and equipment, and reforming and improving management systems in China.

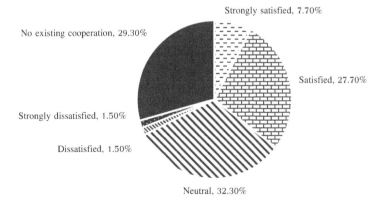

Figure 3.4 Satisfactory levels of collaborative partnership with Mainland Chinese counterparts ($n = 65$).

3.2.8 Summary

With respect to the nature of academic profession and the impact of globalization on the flow of talent, parallel development of brain drain, brain gain, and talent circulation are the inevitable trends of the global talent flow.

3.2.8.1 Push and pull factors leading Chinese academic talent to stay in the US

The international flow of academic talent is structural, dynamic, and competitive in the market, whose direction of flow, scale, and characteristics vary with the changes in the macro environment and academic professional environment of the source country and the receiving country. During different historical periods, the factors that have influenced academic talent's flow between China and the US can be divided into four levels. The first one is the macro-institutional environment. This includes the differences and development level of politics, economy, culture, education, and the research environment, combined with the macro-government systems and policy variables, such as visa application, immigration standards, overseas talent policies, and so forth. The second is the academic system and institutional organizational environment between China and the US. The third are the factors of disciplinary and academic community. The fourth are the individual factors, such as their personal characteristics, attributes, attitudes, and family circumstances. Family members' mobility and attitudes have a profound effect on scholars travelling internationally because it is not only an individual's decision, but also the collective decision made by the family as a whole.

3.2.8.2 The micro-level factors become prominent in influencing talent's choice of staying in the US

With the change in social and economic development trends, factors that influence Chinese overseas scholars' choice of staying in the US have also changed. As the differences in the economic and social development levels between China and the US diminish, the meso- and micro-level factors become much more prominent.

Before the 1980s, the main body of overseas students were publicly sponsored ones, whose mission was to return to China to serve the motherland. Since the 1990s, the overseas students have become more diversified. A majority of them were self-sponsored students who pursued personal development and individual well-being. Beginning in the 21st century, individual career growth, family, and cultural factors have begun to play a major role in overseas Chinese scholars' decision of international mobility. It is evident that when the macro political and economic environment and Sino-US relations are stable, micro-level factors become increasingly important to determine the transnational mobility. Among the career factors, the academic career environment and career growth are of great importance. Some Chinese scholars in the US encountered the glass ceiling phenomenon. Facing the bottleneck of career development, they paid more attention to domestic cooperation and even considered their return to China. Meanwhile, the choice of returning to China varied by academic field, gender, age, marital status, job title, and nationality situation.

3.2.8.3 The improvement of domestic academic environment enhances overseas Chinese scholars' intention to return to China

For those Chinese scholars in the US, career environment and development opportunities are often the primary factors affecting their choice to stay. As long as there is significant difference in academic career environment between China and the US, and the domestic academic environment is not improved fundamentally, it is difficult to attract a large number of overseas high-level talent to return. In order to attract the best and brightest overseas Chinese scholars to return to China, it is necessary to investigate the relationship between the academic career environment and talent flow at home and abroad.

3.3 Trends and reflection on the international flow of Chinese academic talent

3.3.1 Emerging trends on Chinese scholars' international mobility

Since the 1980s, the international flows of Chinese academic talent have demonstrated the following trends:

First, the positions of the source countries and receiving countries of academic talent's international flow have changed. China has moved from the peripheral to a semi-centre position in the global academic mobility market. From the perspective of government investment, and the scale and development speed of higher education and scientific research, China's position in the world's system has undergone gradual changes. China's rise as a major host and sending country of international students and scholars is very significant for China and the world academic community.

Second, the push-pull factors leading to China's academics' international mobility have changed when the macro environment stabilized, and the meso- and micro-level factors have played an increasingly important role. In the late 20th century, the main factors that determined the direction of talent flow were the economic and political ones. However, in the early 21st century, the societal and cultural factors and individual's career development elements have increased in importance. In terms of career factors, the academic career environment and career development space are of utmost importance. The migrants' characteristics and their transnational space and knowledge network have drawn in considerable attention. Some overseas Chinese scholars had encountered glass ceiling or career development bottlenecks in the host countries and began to consider returning to China. The policy factors of the source and recipient countries play a very important role in the trend of talent flow.

Third, the direction of the international flow of Chinese academic talent has shifted from one-way talent flow to the coexistence of talent drain, talent gain, and talent circulation. For a long period of time, China has faced the challenge of brain drain. However, the past decade has witnessed the returning tide of Chinese talent. Talent with overseas academic background, whether working at home or abroad, have established transnational academic networks, conducted various academic cooperation and communication, and jointly built academic communities at home and abroad.

Fourth, policy factors are of utmost importance for attracting Chinese overseas scholars to return to China. Policies in China and the host countries have been crucial in attracting Chinese scholars to return home. Overseas academics have high expectations on governments' talent policies. Since 2004, China has issued the green card policy, but with a relatively high threshold.

3.3.2 Reflection on the global mobility of Chinese academics

The global mobility of Chinese talent needs to be viewed from a dynamic and developmental perspective. It is useless to blindly emphasize its negative effects. Instead, active measures need to be adopted to attract outstanding overseas talent to return to China or to serve the motherland through various forms. The Chinese governments' publicly sponsored overseas education should focus not only on the dispatch of talent, but also on attracting talent to return to China. Favourable systems and policies to take advantage of the returnees need to be optimized.

In the 20th century, the mainstream flows of talent were from developing countries to developed countries. At present, the global mobility of scholars has become more complex and dynamic. Meanwhile, the most developed countries remain the major destination of high-level academic talent. The reasons why these countries can attract outstanding foreign students and academic talent are due to their advantages in research, and higher education system. These countries have a favourable research condition, access to advanced technology and equipment, and an open academic atmosphere with high-level peer groups, as well as generous quality of resources. With the increasing globalization and internationalization of higher education, the pace of China's integration into the world's knowledge and higher education system is expected to be enhanced and deepened. The flow of Chinese talent in the international market is bound to accelerate.

We need to fully realize the seriousness of the outflow of academic talent in China. As long as China is open for educational exchanges, there will always be the phenomenon of brain drain and brain gain. The proportion of returnees in China remains between one-third to two-thirds, with the return rate of publicly funded students much higher than that of self-financed ones. It is worth paying attention to the fact that the higher the individual's education degree is, the lower the possibility that the individual would return. For example, the return rate of Chinese PhDs in the fields of science and engineering in the US has remained between 10% and 20% during the past decades.

The phenomenon of staying abroad does not mean we have permanently lost these academics. Favourable policies and measures can completely enable knowledge diasporas to play the role of a network node of knowledge transfer in the global knowledge neural network. As Welch and Zhang (2008) proposed, the knowledge diasporas are bridging the domestic and international academic communities as the node of international knowledge neural network. The concept of diaspora describes the intermediate state of overseas talent, indicating the temporary and dynamic development of them staying abroad. These knowledge diasporas can bridge the gap between science and education in the north and the south. Knowledge and technological transfer of talent are key processes in attracting diaspora scholars, which can enhance the relationship between knowledge-intensive and less-intensive countries. Chinese scholars working in overseas higher education and scientific institutions can maintain close academic contacts with domestic colleagues and research institutions. They can also carry out various forms of scientific research and establish reliable programme cooperation. To compete for global talent in the globalized environment, it is necessary to examine the talent flow with a comprehensive viewpoint.

The academic profession is a highly mobile profession. Globalization has led to massive, market-oriented and diversified trends in academic talent mobility. Academic talent not only belong to a certain institution, region, and country, but also to the specific discipline and its academic community. As an invisible college, the academic community goes beyond national boundaries. In a sense, the institutional and national affiliation of academic talent are changeable. Therefore, in terms of the intrinsic characteristics of academic talent, the inherent nature of academic professions, and the basic principle of academic careers, international flow can meet the needs of academics. The academic disciplinary identity and pursuit of knowledge are void of national boundaries. Academics in the same discipline have a strong sense of cross-institutional and cross-national identity.

References

Altbach, P. G. (1998). *Comparative higher education: Knowledge, the university, and development*. Ablex Pub. Corp.

Altbach, P. G. (2004). Globalization and the universities: Myths and realities in an unequal world. *Tertiary Education and Management*, *10*(1), 3–25.

Cao, C. (2009). Zhongguo de "rencai liushi", "rencai huigui", "rencai xunhuan" [Brain drain, brain gain and brain circulation]. *Kexue Wenhua Pinglun [Science & Culture Review]*, *6*(1), 13–32.

Chen, X. F. et al. (2003). *Liuxue Jiaoyu de Chengben yu Shouyi: Woguo gaige kaifang yilai gongpai liuxue xiaoyi yanjiu [Costs and returns: A study on the efficiency of government-sponsored overseas education since 1978]*. Jiaoyu Kexue Chubanshe. Educational Science Publishing House.

Zhongguo Jiaoyu Zaixian(2017). Zhongguo Chuguo Liuxue Fazhan Qushi baogao 2017 [Development trends of study abroad in China in 2017]. Retrieved June 20, 2019, from https://www.eol.cn/html/lx/report2017/yi.shtml.

Chinese Governmental Website. (2019, March 28). 2018 Woguo chuguo liuxue renyuan qingkuang tongji [Statistics of Chinese overseas students in 2018]. Retrieved June 28, 2019, from http://www.gov.cn/xinwen/2019-03/28/content_5377626.htm

Finn, M. (2005). *Stay rates of foreign doctorate recipients from US universities*. Oak Ridge Institute for Science and Education.

Gürüz, K. (2011). *Higher education and international student mobility in the global knowledge economy*. State University of New York Press.

Institute of International Education (IIE). (2017). (n.d.). Project atlas. Retrieved June 29, 2019, from https://www.iie.org/ResearchandInsights/Project-Atlas/Explore-Data

Institute of International Education (IIE). (2018). (n.d.). America's open portal data. The top 20 universities in the US accepting international students in 2018. Retrieved June 21, 2019, from https://www.iie.org/Research-and-Insights/Open-Doors/Data^International-Students?7Leading-Host-Institutions

Institute of International Education (IIE). (n.d.). America's open portal data. Retrieved June 20, 2019, from https://www.iie.org/opendoors

Kim, D., Bankart, S., & Isdell, L. (2011). International doctorates: Trends and analysis on their decision to stay in US. *Higher Education, 62*(2), 141–161.

Li, M. (2008). *Gaodeng jiaoyu guoji shichang: zhongguo xuesheng de quanqiu liudong [International higher education market: Global mobility of Chinese students]*. Shanghai Jiaoyu Chubanshe. Shanghai Education Publishing House.

Ministry of Education (MOE) of China. (2018) (n.d.). 2017 Nian chuguo liuxue、huiguo fuwu guimo shuangzengzhang [Double growth in the scale of study abroad and return service in 2017]. Retrieved March 30, 2019, from http://www.moe.gov.cn/jyb_xwfb/gzdt_gzdt/s5987/201803/t20180329_331771.html

Ministry of Education (MOE) of China. (2019) (n.d.). 2018 Niandu woguo chuguo liuxue renyuan qingkuang tongji [Statistics of Chinese overseas students in 2018]. Retrieved March 27, 2019, from http://www.moe.gov.cn/jyb_xwfb/gzdt_gzdt/s5987/201903/t20190327_375704.html

Zhongguo Tongji Nianjian. (2018). Jiaoyu: Liuxuesheng he liuxue renyuan qingkuang [China statistical yearbook 2018: Education of postgraduate and overseas students]. Retrieved June 28, 2019, from http://www.stats.gov.aVtjsj/ndsj/2018/indexch.htm

Rumbley, L., Pacheco, I., & Altabch, P. (2008). *International comparison of academic salaries: An exploratory study*. Center for International Higher Education, Boston College.

Shi, Y. G. (2016). Qianren jihua de biyao he jinpo [The necessity and urgency of the Thousand Talents Plan]. Retrieved June 22, 2019, from http://www.1000plan.org/superblog/461/21

Sun, X. E., & Bian, Y. J. (2011). Liumei kexuejia de guonei canyu jiqi shehui wangluo qiangruo guanxi jiashe de zai tantao [Transnational participation and social networking: Interaction between strong and weak ties of Chinese American scientists]. *Shehui [Chinese Journal of Sociology], 31*(2), 194–215.

Wang, H. Y. (2009). *Zhongguo Liuxue Rencai Fazhan Baogao (2009) [Report of Chinese overseas personnel (2009)]*. Jixie Gongye Chubanshe. China Machine Press.

Welch, A. and Zhang, Z. (2008). Higher education and global talent flows: Brain drain, overseas Chinese intellectuals, and diasporic knowledge networks. *Higher Education Policy, 21*(4), 1–19.

Yang, Y., & Liu, X. L. (2014). Xiangzhi xiangshi xiangguan—Zhongmei liuxue 35nian huigu [Acquaintances, intimates and friends: China-US 35 years scholarly exchange]. *Shenzhou Xueren [China Scholars Abroad], 10*, 1215.

Ye, F. S. (2001). *Rencai Zhanzheng [Talent war]*. Zhongguo Wenlian Chubanshe. China Federation of Literary and Art Press.

Zweig, D., & Chen, C. G. (1995). *China's brain drain to the United States: Views of overseas Chinese students and scholars in the 1990s*. Institute of East Asian Studies, University of California.

4 From luring back to taking advantage of talent

Overseas academic talent policies and their implementation

Chapter 3 elaborated on the trend in mobility and the characteristics and significance of Chinese academic talent; the focus in this chapter is on the government's policies for attracting overseas talent, the effects of their implementation, and suggestions for policy improvement. Since overseas academic talent policies are closely related to Chinese students going abroad, the chapter considers this issue as well.

In the 40 years since China's reform and opening-up, the flow of Chinese talent studying abroad and returning home has grown from a trickle to a historic surge. Although there have been twists and turns in the relevant policies and systems, they are becoming increasingly detailed and improved as a whole. Overseas education has expanded from prioritizing training to take employment into account. At the same time, the recruitment of talent has shifted from an emphasis on individuals returning to work to include overseas students and Chinese scholars staying abroad to serve the home country in various dimensions.

4.1 Historical evolution of overseas academic talent policies

Following the developmental characteristics of China's overseas education and talent policies, this section divides the 40-year history of these policies into five periods. The first is the early stage of reform and opening-up (1978–1983), in which the focus was on the planning and administrative management involved with dispatching talent, especially publicly funded initiatives. The second period was characterized by intensive opening-up (1984–1991), when the focus was on the dispatch and return of talent. In the third period, characterized by market-oriented transformation (1992–2000), the focus was equally on returning to work and serving the country. In the fourth period, the focus was on the global competition for talent (2001–2007), especially improving the process of returning to work and serving the country. In the fifth period (2008–present), the focus has been on attracting key high-level innovative and entrepreneurial talent.

In the first two periods, overseas talent policies underwent a major shift to active dispatching and promoting the repatriation and development of overseas talent policy. In the third period, China transformed its management mode from a planned economy to a market economy, in the process establishing a special organization, the China Scholarship Council (CSC), to engage with both publicly funded and

DOI: 10.4324/9781003424611-4

self-financed individuals who study abroad and implemented the overseas talent policy of "freedom to come and go". Marked by China's accession to the World Trade Organization (WTO), the fourth period inaugurated a new era for studying abroad, with a transformation in the policies governing overseas talent.

The key national policies have thus shifted from dispatching and returning to encouraging overseas talent to serve the country, resulting in the establishment of a complete policy system of talent going abroad and either returning to work or staying abroad. During the fifth stage, which began in 2008, the overseas talent policies have shifted from a focus on attracting talent to highlighting key skills and attracting the right people, including high-level overseas talent, by improving the system for appealing to and using high-level overseas talent. During this time, it has become necessary to expand the implementation of policies for attracting such talent through initiatives such as Changjiang Scholars Program and the Thousand Talent Program that provide a solid system and talent base for China to enhance its higher education and scientific research outputs as part of the effort to build an innovative country and compete in the global arena.

4.1.1 The early stage of reform and opening-up (1978–1983)

The policies at the early stage of reform and opening-up focused on dispatching Chinese citizens for training, particularly with public funding and in the fields of planning and administrative management. During this stage, under the leadership of Deng Xiaoping, China gradually restored its relations with other countries around the world, and the policy of studying abroad began to shift. Government-sponsored overseas education opportunities facilitated relations between China and foreign countries and broadened the horizons of those studying abroad. The government's publicity and emphasis on overseas education created a desire in the public for the opportunity to study abroad. However, the beneficiaries of publicly sponsored study-abroad programmes remained limited to a small cohort of university students, graduates, and visiting scholars (State Council, 1986), a situation that was far from meeting the needs of Chinese industries for research talent and the next generation of students. As a result, studying abroad at one's own expense became an increasingly important pathway. In 1981, the State Council approved and forwarded the *Request for Instructions on Self-financed Studying Abroad* and *Interim Provisions on Self-financed Studying Abroad* (henceforth referred to as "Request" and "Interim Provisions", respectively). These guidelines were later issued by seven departments, including the Ministries of Education and Foreign Affairs, stipulating the scope of, and procedures associated with, the policies and other issues related to self-financed study abroad. The Request and Interim Provisions identified this form of study abroad as a way to cultivate talent and established that, regarding overseas education in China, self-financed and publicly sponsored students should be treated the same.

From 1978 to 1983, the central government increased the funding for academic talent to study abroad in an effort to strengthen its management system. In 1978, the selection criteria for publicly sponsored personnel to study abroad were excellent academic performance or extensive on-the-job experience, the aim being to cultivate elite students. The Request and Interim Provisions stipulated that self-financed study-abroad students who were in-service teachers should specialize in the fields of technology or business and be subject to the same selection criteria as publicly sponsored students, with approval from their work units and supervisory departments, before reporting to the Ministry of Education for inclusion in the national plan. They were then sent abroad according to the procedures followed by publicly sponsored students (General Office of the Beijing Municipal People's Government, 1981; Overseas Chinese Affairs Office of the State Council, 1984). In the *Report on the Management of Overseas Students Conference* issued in 1980, the focus of government policy began to shift from sending students to study abroad to luring high-level academic talent back to China (He, 1998).

For talented academics trained overseas who returned to China, the government adopted mandatory administrative management measures, allocating work uniformly after they returned to China. In 1983, the Ministry of Labor and Personnel, Ministry of Education, Ministry of Public Security, and Ministry of Finance issued the *Interim Measures of the Dispatch of International Graduates*, which stipulated that the relevant ministries and commissions, as well as provinces, municipalities, and autonomous regions, jointly formulate annual allocation plans for international graduates. In principle, upon graduation, those who belonged to a work unit before going abroad were to return to their original units. The government would allocate jobs to the students whom it sponsored and did not belong to work units, while those who studied abroad at their own expense would return to their hometowns, where they would be recruited by the local personnel departments.

Talent studying abroad, then, was not only forced to return to China but also assigned to work units, this being one of the main features of the planned economy era. The state invested a vast amount of resources in cultivating this high-level academic talent in the rising generation, and publicly sponsored overseas education was regarded as an investment by the state in reserving academic and scientific research talent. In order to ensure a good return on the investment, the state implemented centralized management and deployment to ensure that students would return to China after completing their studies.

4.1.2 The period of intensive opening-up (1984–1991)

The period from 1984–1991 was characterized by an equal emphasis on the dispatch and return of academics. The central government began to attach importance to the systematic cultivation of talent returning to work in China, for instance, by creating post-doctoral work opportunities at Li Zhengdao's suggestion and establishing the Chinese Service Centre for Scholarly Exchange (CSCSE), a research start-up fund for overseas students returning to China. In 1985, China began to finance and build post-doctoral scientific research stations and has thus far reached the second stage of its plan to convince overseas students to return by applying fresh approaches to difficulties associated with resettlement issues (Cheng, 2009, p. 298).

In 1988, what was then the State Education Commission held the 13th Enlarged Meeting of All Members and decided to implement the principle of "encouragement of talent flow, reasonable competition and two-way selection", thus allowing overseas students to choose their jobs freely and establishing a "service centre for scholarly exchange" (Cheng, 2009). In April 1989, the aforementioned CSCSE was officially established and formed cooperative relationships with relevant institutions at home and abroad. The CSCSE has been committed to helping returnees search for work units, handle dispatch and settlement procedures, transfer organizational relationships, deal with file storage, handle vocational applications for returning home, apply for business licences, make investments, evaluate and authenticate their foreign academic degrees and credentials, receive support through a "scientific research start-up fund for returnees from abroad", and deal with similar matters. This comprehensive and multifunctional service system for scholarly exchange has continued to operate until the present.

The state not only provided opportunities for high-level overseas returnees to make full use of their expertise by improving the relevant policies and systems but also established agencies to help them solve practical problems after returning home and obtain financial support for scientific research. In October 1989, Hou Yibin, who had studied in the Netherlands, proposed to the central government the establishment of a fund to support the development of returned students. President Jiang Zemin agreed to the suggestion and, on January 17, 1990, advised the State Education Commissioner to allocate 20% of the total annual funds for overseas students for their resettlement upon returning to China so as to address their scientific research funding and housing problems. Accordingly, in 1990, the then State Education Commission established the Research Subsidy for Returned Overseas Students, which was renamed the Ministry of Education Research Start-up Fund for Returned Overseas Students in 1997. The scheme was mainly utilized in the preparation for and implementation of returnees' scientific research activities. The criteria for beneficiaries were being younger than 45, having obtained a doctoral degree at home or abroad, having studied abroad for more than one year, and engaging in teaching and scientific research after returning to China.

The state used its news outlets to inform students studying abroad about this initiative. For example, in May 1987, the China Education News Agency began publishing its *China Scholars Abroad* magazine. In 1995, the then State Education Commission revamped the website for its Supply and Demand Information for Overseas Talent, Technology and Program, renaming it the China Study Abroad Network. This website has become a well-known brand and an important channel for overseas students to learn about China's Encouraging Overseas Students to Return to China policy as well as domestic job opportunities.

Since 1987, publicly sponsored personnel must sign the Study-Abroad Agreement with their dispatching unit before studying abroad and, during this time, have a sponsor. The agreement, once signed, imposes compulsory two-way constraints on publicly sponsored study-abroad personnel and organizations. In 1987, the number of self-funded Chinese international students exceeded 100,000, this form of studying abroad having become the pathway for as much as 90% of those receiving an overseas education.

4.1.3 The period of market-oriented transformation (1992–2000): Emphasis on returning to work for and to serve the country

4.1.3.1 Policies for luring overseas academic talent back to work in China

Since 1992, policies for high-level academic talent overseas to return to serve China have taken shape. Two kinds of policies related to attracting talent and employment by encouraging citizens to "return to work" and "serve the country" have been implemented. In August 1992, the National Natural Science Foundation of China (NSF) presented the *Trial Measures for the National Natural Science Foundation of China to Set up Special Fund for Overseas Students Returning to China for Short-term Work and Lectures*, which were officially implemented in 1994. The special fund targeted outstanding young and middle-aged scientific and technological experts (including those who had obtained long-term or permanent residency in foreign countries). Later that year, the NSF issued the *Administrative Measures for Overseas Young Scholars' Cooperative Research Fund*, which encouraged young scholars overseas to conduct cooperative research. Both of these NSF funds concerned high-level talent within and without the educational system.

In October 1992, the then State Education Commission began implementing the regulation *Certificate of Returned Personnel From Studying Abroad*, which has gradually evolved from a certificate for purchasing a domestic duty-free car to one of identity and experience allowing talent to enjoy several preferential policies or conveniences set up by central and local governments in terms of starting businesses, analyzing job prospects, transferring household registration, enrolling children in school, purchasing a place of residence, and authenticating academic degrees. The policy was welcomed by domestic management agencies on all levels and in all walks of life (Cheng, 2009). In 1992, Li Tieying, State Councillor and Director of the State Education Commission, put forward as a general policy for managing overseas education in China "supporting studying abroad, encouraging [graduates] to return, and enabling the freedom of choice to come and go". The Third Plenary Session of the 14th Chinese Communist Party's (CPCs) Central Committee in 1993 confirmed this policy in the *Resolution on Issues Concerning the Establishment of a Socialist Market Economic System*.

In September 1997, the report of the 15th National Congress of the CPC included language about "encouraging overseas students to return to work or serve the motherland in a suitable way", thus establishing the work principle of attracting overseas students to "return to work" and "serve the motherland". In May 1998, the Ministry of Education implemented the 985 Project as part of its effort to improve China's first-class universities. The central government invested billions of RMB, 20% of which served to hire overseas scholars. Later on, a number of ministries and commissions introduced further plans to support outstanding talent on their return to China.

The policies designed to encourage talent to return to China for long-term work included the aforementioned Hundred Talent Program established by the Chinese Academy of Sciences (CAS) in 1994, which was the first talent support plan launched in China. Its aim was to recruit outstanding talent with doctoral degrees from domestic and overseas institutions. In 1998, the party's Central Committee and the State Council made the major decision to build a national innovation system, in the context of which the CAS would launch a pilot project for knowledge innovation. The CAS added the Attraction of Foreign Outstanding Talent programme, a plan to recruit 100 distinguished scholars from abroad each year within three years and continue attracting academic leaders from abroad. The criteria for the programme were that the scholars be under 45 years of age, have at least two years of scientific research experience, and have independently led projects after obtaining their doctoral degrees (China Education and Research Network, 2001). Then, in 2000, the *Opinions on Encouraging Overseas High-level Talent to Return to Work in China* was issued for the purpose of encouraging high-level talent overseas to return in a systemic and organized manner. It is, then, clear that the national policy attached great importance to high-level overseas talent.

4.1.3.2 Policies to encourage overseas academic talent to serve China

In 1996, the former State Education Commission issued the *Measures for the Implementation of the Special Fund of the State Education Commission for Sponsoring the Short-term Return of Overseas Students to Work in China* and launched the Chunhui Plan to support the temporary return of outstanding overseas students. In November 2000, the Ministry of Education issued the *Ministry of Education Chunhui Plan Implementation Measures for Overseas Talent Returning to China on Academic Leave (in Trial)*. The academic retention programme is part of the Chunhui Plan, with the recruitment effort targeting Chinese overseas students who hold the position of assistant professor or higher at prestigious overseas universities. The scope of the funding includes inviting talent to participate in international academic conferences, seminars, cooperative scientific research and educational initiatives, and other short-term service activities. In 2004, the Ministry of Education issued its *Notice on Further Improving the Chunhui Plan*.

In August 1998, the Ministry joined forces with Hong Kong industrialist Li Ka-shing to establish the Changjiang Scholars Award Program, which created a system of specially appointed professorships and the Changjiang Scholars Achievement Award to encourage renowned Chinese scholars overseas to return temporarily to China and to undertake collaborative research projects. Since 1999, this system has undergone continuous improvement in terms of the implementation process and has achieved significant results. In 2004, the ministry issued new *Changjiang Scholars Recruitment Measures* that allowed scholars in the fields of the humanities and social sciences to apply for the Changjiang Scholars Award. The number of visiting professors was increased from 10 to 100 in that year, with an annual working period of no less than two months, and the annual working period for the distinguished professors was set at no less than nine months, with the corresponding employment contract being shortened from three to five years (Huang & Bian, 2006).

4.1.4 The period of global competition for talent (2001–2007): Improving the system for returning to work and serving China

4.1.4.1 Policies to encourage overseas academic talent to return to work in China

By this stage, the country had clearly defined the scope of overseas high-level talent, was making gradual improvements in its programmes for attracting talent, and had established merit-based funding and focused resources on attracting the overseas talent most urgently needed for its nation-building plans. In other words, the original talent-attraction programme had been continuously improved. Meanwhile, new talent-attraction programmes emerged, in which "returning to work" and "serving the country" were grouped in the same category. The same programme, however, may have had distinct policies for various groups of students.

In March 2005, the Ministry of Human Resources, the Ministry of Education, the Ministry of Science and Technology, and the Ministry of Finance jointly issued *A Guideline on Defining Overseas Educated Graduates in the Attraction of Overseas Talent* (hereafter "Guideline"). This document clearly defined "high-level graduates" as those who hold the title of at least associate professor, have a degree from a foreign higher education or scientific research institution, have favourable career development prospects, and work with an independent team or have mastered cutting-edge knowledge in their fields.

4.1.2.2 Improving the policy systems for overseas academic talent to serve the country

In May 2001, the Ministry of Education, Ministry of Science and Technology, Ministry of Personnel, Ministry of Public Security, and Ministry of Finance jointly issued the *Opinions on Encouraging Overseas Students to Serve China in Various Forms*, which stipulated seven ways to serve the country, five of which were specific to high-level academic talent: (1) Employment as a part-time professional, technician, or consultant in an honorary position in a domestic university, research institution, key (open) lab, engineering and technology research centre, one of various other enterprises and institutions, or, in the case of qualified overseas students, as a post-doctoral fellow at a domestic research station; (2) conducting cooperative research at domestic universities, research institutions, and enterprises involving advanced scientific technology and equipment and funds; (3) working on domestic scientific research projects or foreign scientific R&D relevant to research groups; (4) encouraging overseas students to help domestic employers cultivate talent by drawing on overseas scientific research, education, and training institutions in cooperation with domestic units; (5) travelling to western China to engage in technical recruitment, scientific and technological research, consulting services, or other academic and technical exchanges. This document represented a milestone for overseas high-level talent as the first time that policy-making in China recognized the need for overseas students to serve the country even without returning home.

In this period, some talent programmes developed into programmes that combined "returning to serve the country" and "serving the country", such as the Hundred Talent Program. This programme entered the second phase of its knowledge-innovation pilot project in 2001, when the Chinese Academy of Sciences issued the *CAS Management Measures for Attracting Outstanding Talent from Abroad*. This programme included recruiting outstanding talent to return to China to work for an extended period (hereafter "outstanding talent") and famous overseas scholars to return to do so for a short period of time (hereafter "famous scholars"). The outstanding talent were Chinese experts or scholars and those willing to give up their foreign nationality to settle in China; the criteria included holding a doctorate degree and at least the position of assistant professor or a corresponding position abroad. The criteria for the famous scholars were having obtained the position of at least associate professor or a corresponding position abroad. In 2006, the Hundred Talent Program entered its third phase. In order to align the cultivation of talent with the deployment of major projects and important directional projects, the programme was split into tracks according to the funding source and amount, including the Recruitment of Foreign Outstanding Talent, Domestic Hundred Talent Program, Project-oriented Hundred Talent Program, National Science Fund for Outstanding Young Scholars, and so forth.

In addition, the state began to pay attention to the concerns of overseas talent after returning to China and issued policies to create favourable conditions for high-level talent in terms of the work environment, salary allowances, scientific research funding, housing, insurance, family visits, employment of family members, and children's schooling. On February 5, 2006, the Ministry of Education issued the *Notice on Handling the ID Certificate of High-level Overseas Students*, which confirmed that this work was being undertaken by the China Study-Abroad Service Centre. The *Opinions on the Green Channel for Overseas High-level Talent Returning to Work in China* issued in 2007 regulated, in a comprehensive and systematic way, the provision of services and conveniences for returnees in terms of the entry and exit policies, residency, children's schooling, and spousal employment. With the approval of the relevant competent departments, returnees could be exempted from restrictions on the number of staff, position target, total amount of salary, and location of their household registration before going abroad, being directly appointed to the corresponding level of their professional and technical titles without the restriction of their years of service and receiving preferential treatment in terms of entry into, exit from, and residence within China.

The visa and permanent residency systems have become important for the long- and short-term return (or arrival) of talent to work in China. At this stage, high-level overseas talent who obtained foreign nationality were also prioritized. Specifically, on March 26, 2002, the Ministry of Public Security, Ministry of Foreign Affairs, Ministry of Education, Ministry of Science and Technology, Ministry of Personnel, Ministry of Labor and Social Security, Ministry of Foreign Trade and Economic Cooperation, Overseas Chinese Affairs Office of the State Council, and State

Administration of Foreign Experts Affairs jointly formulated the *Regulations on Facilitating the Entry and Residence of Foreign High-level Talent and Investors*, which enabled foreign academic talent to apply for the F (visit-type) visa for two to five years with multiple entries and a stay of no more than one year each time as well as a foreign residence permit valid for two to five years and a multiple-return Z visa (work-type) within the same period. In 2004, the Ministry of Foreign Affairs and Ministry of Public Security implemented the *Administrative Measures for the Approval of Permanent Residence of Foreigners in China*, which stipulated that, once their applications are approved, the Chinese government may grant foreigners permanent residency and that defined qualified applicants as those who had made significant and outstanding contributions to China and helped to fill a special need in the country.

4.1.5 The period of attracting high-level innovative and entrepreneurial talent (2008–present)

In December 2008, the General Office of the Central Committee of the CPC issued the *Opinions of the Central Talent Work Coordination Group on the Implementation of the Plan for the Attraction of Overseas High-level Talent* (hereafter the "Thousand Talent Program") and the *Interim Measures for the Attraction of Overseas High-level Talent*. In order to fulfil the strategic goals for national development, these two policies focused on attracting and supporting a select group of scientists and leading talent in the coming five to ten years to work in China on innovation and entrepreneurship. The hope was that they would make breakthroughs in key technologies, develop high-tech industries, and support emerging disciplines in key national innovation projects and laboratories, central enterprises and state-owned commercial financial institutions, and various industrial parks and zones focusing on high-tech development. The early phase of the Thousand Talent Program targeted experienced scientists and leading talent, and, in 2010, a new Thousand Youth Talent Program (TYTP) was added. In 2011, the Thousand Talent Program for Foreign Experts was also added according to the nationality of applicants. The *Notice on the Application of the Thousand Talent Program* in 2012 stipulated that, starting with the eighth round, the Thousand Talent Program would consist of five sub-programmes: The Long-term Program for Innovative Talent, Short-term Program for Innovative Talent, Program for Entrepreneurial Talent, Thousand Talent Program for Foreign Experts, and TYTP.

On March 11, 2011, an inter-ministerial joint conference on the service work for overseas students returning to China was held in Beijing that resulted in the issuance and implementation of the *Administrative Measures for the Approval of Foreigners' Permanent Residence in China*, which further lowered the threshold for overseas students with foreign nationalities returning to China to apply for permanent residency. In addition, the *Opinions on Further Improving the Usage of Chinese Permanent Residency (Green Card)* was issued to solve the problem of "permanent residency" holders enjoying the privileges of Chinese citizens (Dong, 2011).

China's national overseas talent policy system, then, initially had as its core the Thousand Talent Program, which was, in turn, supported by local talent policies. The talent policies have tended to be diversified in terms of the target audiences, with multiple levels of talent-attraction policies and a combination of policies for "returning to serve the country" and "serving the country while staying abroad". Over the past few years, this series of high-level Talent Programs has received significant investment and has exerted a nationwide impact, so its implementation merits examination. Taking permanent residency associated with the TYTP as an example, the following discussion explores the implementation effect as well as existing problems and concludes with some suggestions for policy improvements.

4.2 The implementation of the Overseas High-level Talent Program

Since the 1990s, in order to meet the needs associated with economic transformation and upgrading, the construction of first-class universities, the rapid development of high-tech industries, and the development of an innovative country and to support its increasingly prominent role in the international arena, China has been urgently cultivating and attracting high-level international talent. Such talent has become an important dimension of human capital for all industries in China since local training alone cannot meet the needs of the new era. Pursuing a strategy of developing the country through science and education and strengthening its innovative vigour, the central and local governments have formulated and organized numerous programmes to participate in the global competition for human capital. These programmes have fundamentally reversed China's high-level international talent shortage, laying a solid foundation for comprehensively nurturing higher education and research capabilities and realizing the transformation from a large human resource country to a strong human resource country, building a knowledge-based and innovative economy, and fostering a new environment in which to engage in the global competition for talent.

The impact of the implementation of overseas high-level talent recruitment more than 20 years ago has been exceptional and far-reaching, alleviating the serious shortage of high-level international innovative and entrepreneurial talent in China. The analysis here concerns mainly the effectiveness of, and problems with, the Thousand Talent Program for Young People.

4.2.1 Satisfying the needs of talent and establishing a multi-support policy system for the recruitment of talent

It is useful to distinguish among the policies relating to young talent those that restrict application conditions, provide support from the state, and pertain to the application procedures. The supportive policies can be further divided based on their guarantees, rewards, and development in relation to the benefits received by the talent, as Figure 4.1 shows.

The aim of the favourable guarantee policies is to meet the needs of the talent facing a new living and working environment and to allow for a smooth transition into it. It is assumed that those who benefit from the policies become invested

From luring back to taking advantage of talent 89

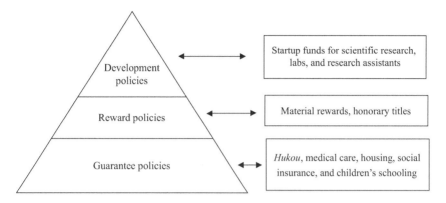

Figure 4.1 Classification of policies for Thousand Youth Talent Program awardees.

in undertaking scientific research when provided with comfortable and stable living conditions. The one-off material rewards and honourable recognition serve to attract outstanding talent. The development policies are, then, intended to establish the conditions in which talent can make further breakthroughs in their careers. Young talent with academic goals may opt to return to China not only to benefit economically but also for better academic prospects thanks to the supportive domestic policies. The new arrivals' needs include research start-up funds and laboratories in advanced facilities that are staffed with research assistants.

The central government offers TYTP awardees a living allowance of RMB 500,000 and a research grant of RMB 1–3 million for three years while basing other working conditions and living benefits on the existing policies of the plan. Local governments and employers have complementary policies regarding scientific research start-up funds, housing subsidies, and annual salary packages to ensure that young talent can concentrate on the work at hand. Institutions such as Tsinghua University and Zhejiang University also provide 1 to 1 matching of research funds of RMB 1–3 million for each TYTP awardee. The annual salary package offered by universities ranges from RMB 300,000 to 600,000; those of the University of Science and Technology of China, Beijing Normal University, and Xiamen University range from RMB 500,000 to 600,000.

4.2.2 Creating a concerted talent recruitment and utilization mechanism

The central government, local governments, and employers have created a concerted talent recruitment and utilization mechanism, but problems of utilitarianism and excessive competition persist. The leading and demonstration effects exerted by national Talent Programs have driven the talent programmes of various localities and institutions, thus shaping the organization and implementation of the programmes and policies at the national, local, and university (institutional) levels.

These organizations draw on each other's strengths to attract, deploy, and promote the recruitment and utilization of high-level talent as a whole through joint efforts.

At the strategic national level, the Central Organization Department and Ministry of Human Resources and Social Security in conjunction with the Ministry of Education, Ministry of Science and Technology, Chinese Academy of Sciences, Chinese Academy of Engineering, Ministry of Foreign Affairs, Development and Reform Commission, Ministry of Industry and Information Technology, Ministry of Public Security, Ministry of Finance, Overseas Chinese Affairs Office, Natural Science Foundation, Foreign Affairs Bureau, Chinese Association for Science and Technology, and other departments have formed a working group for attracting high-level overseas talent. The group has responsibility for the organizational leadership and coordination of the TYTP. This being a national-level talent-attraction programme, the central government has established clear requirements for recruitment, and a platform jointly set up by multiple departments will be tasked with evaluating the candidates, announcing the shortlist, and allocating the national off-time grant and research start-up funds. In this case, the state stipulates only the implementation criteria and not specific plans, thereby leaving room for local governments to compete for outstanding talent.

At the local level, local governments have issued policies and regulations based on the central Talent Program and made commitments regarding the entry and exit, settlement, social insurance, and remuneration of talent. The goal of the Shanghai Thousand Talent Program, for example, is to attract high-level overseas talent for which the need is urgent in the coming five to ten years based on the national major strategies and strategic goals for that city and to establish 20 to 30 municipal-level innovation and entrepreneurship bases for the talent in appropriate enterprises, universities, research institutes, and industrial parks. In addition, Shanghai is setting aside "a one-time" living subsidy of RMB 1 million for attracting and retaining talent by reducing the costs associated with resettlement and taxation and maximizing salary.

The implementation of various university policies also directly affects the recruitment and usefulness of young talent. After a letter of intent regarding employment has been signed by an employer and overseas talent, they apply to the platform according to the requirements of the declaration notice. High-level young scholars are crucial to efforts to improve the core competitiveness of universities and implement strategies for strengthening them. Universities and research institutions, as direct beneficiaries of the recruitment of talent, likewise provide matching material rewards and research start-up funds.

This concerted talent recruitment mechanism has, then, been government-led and employer-initiated. Looking to them as the main locus of talent recruitment and concentration, the partnership has helped universities and research institutions to consolidate and strengthen their talent cultivation and scientific research, promoted the construction of a number of key universities, supported research departments and key disciplines, and, thus, enhanced the international competitiveness of China's higher education system. As a result, China's scientific outputs have improved year by year, so that now, in terms of the number of published academic papers, the country is among the top-ranked globally in some disciplines. Likewise, China's capacity to provide postgraduate training has increased to the point that it now educates about as many PhD students as the US. However, there are many kinds of talent programmes at various levels, resulting in negative consequences of repeated awards reflected in various "talent hats" (titles), excessive competition for talent, and the prevalence of utilitarianism.

4.2.3 The crucial role of returning overseas talent in higher education and scientific innovation

Since the implementation of the Hundred Talent Program by the Chinese Academy of Sciences in 1994, then, China has implemented various high-level talent programmes that have attracted a large number of high-level academics and researchers to its universities, scientific institutions, and private enterprises and cultivated their development. These individuals have come to constitute a significant force in the higher education, scientific research, and management sectors. By 2018, the Thousand Talent Program had sponsored 5,549 people, the TYTP had awarded 3,535 young researchers, and the Changjiang Scholars Program had supported 3,931 scientists and academics. The high-level talent that received these awards included leading figures in their disciplines at universities and others engaged in improving the academic institutional environment and its management by serving as department heads, chairs, or deans, thus playing active roles in building academic institutions and enhancing the academic environment.

The remarkable results of the TYTP in attracting young scientists to Chinese universities and scientific research institutions can be seen in Table 4.1. Thus, the number of awardees increased, with some 600 people having been recruited every year since 2015. An analysis of the listed TYTP awardees from 2011 to 2016 reveals that a plurality were post-doctoral fellows, with 246 candidates, accounting for 33.4% of the total, followed by assistant professors/researchers, with 178

Table 4.1 Number of TYTP awardees (2011–2018)

Round	Year/Month	Number of individuals	Percentage (%)
No.1	2011/1	143	4.0
No.2	2012/2	218	6.2
No.3	2012/7	177	5.0
No.4	2013	183	5.2
No.5	2014/1	396	11.2
No.6	2015/4	661	18.7
No.7	2016/3	558	15.8
No.8	2017/5	590	16.7
No.9	2018/2	609	17.2
Total		3,535	100.0

Data source: The author combined from the shortlists of the Thousand Youth Talent Program awardees.

individuals, accounting for 24.2%, and professors/researchers, with 142, accounting for 19.3% of the total group. The TYTP mainly targets those who are in the early stages of their academic careers, for example, post-doctoral fellows transitioning to independent scientific research after doctoral training and assistant professors at the stage of academic accumulation before receiving tenure. Working on the frontiers of academia with vigorous energy, these awardees have been prepared to enjoy an early outpouring of research. At the same time, they are under great pressure and in the process of building academic networks in specialist fields and academic teams and laboratories. Therefore, they represent potential academic talent and academic leaders. The TYTP awardees in this critical period of academic growth, by receiving financial and policy support as well as access to a suitable academic environment, are ready to develop into academic elites.

4.2.4 The impacts of the TYTP

The Thousand Talent Programs classify and manage overseas talent according to such criteria as nationality, age, time of returning to work in China, and type of talent, thereby reflecting the gradual improvement and refinement of talent-attraction policies. The talent programmes have broken through the traditional personnel system and implemented innovations in selection, recruitment, evaluation, employment, and so on. The radiation effects have guided personnel system reforms at universities and scientific research institutions, which have improved the talent management system and raised awareness of the importance of the international competition for talent. Drawing on the management system for recruiting talent, universities have reformed the personnel system and talent-management measures in such contexts as domestic and foreign open recruitment, peer review, the role of the primary investigator (PI), annual salaries, periods of employment, and other personnel systems. However, the dual-track system of employment and preference for overseas returnees has also led to an imbalance of interests between the overseas returnees and domestic-trained talent.

4.2.5 "Double First-class" universities attracting most TYTP awardees

The implementation of these plans and programmes relies on key universities and the CAS to attract talent according to the needs of the nation and higher education system. Also, the status, advantageous disciplines, and geographic location of universities affect their power to attract talent in a manner that can be described as "the stronger the university, the stronger the talent". The result has been the uneven development of talent across universities.

As Table 4.2 shows, the so-called "double first-class" universities have been most successful in attracting TYTP awardees, accounting for 67% of the total TYTP awardees, while the CAS and its subordinate institutes have recruited 13.7%. Though other colleges and universities are in urgent need of talent, they cannot compete with the double first-class institutions. This situation reflects the market mechanism behind the deployment of academic talent that will doubtless increase the stratification of colleges and universities.

From luring back to taking advantage of talent 93

Table 4.2 Institutional distribution of TYTP awardees by cohort (2011–2018)

Cohort/institution type		"Double first-class" universities	First-class discipline universities	Regular universities	Chinese Academy of Sciences	Other scientific institutions	Enterprises	Others	Total
1	Number	98	14	3	23	5	0	0	143
	%	68.5	9.8	2.1	16.1	3.5	0.0	0.0	
2	Number	148	13	8	37	7	5	0	218
	%	67.9	6.0	3.7	17.0	3.2	2.3	0.0	
3	Number	112	13	11	38	1	2	0	177
	%	63.3	7.3	6.2	21.5	0.6	1.1	0.0	
4	Number	112	14	10	38	7	2	0	183
	%	61.2	7.7	5.5	20.8	3.8	1.1	0.0	
5	Number	249	32	19	75	20	1	0	396
	%	62.9	8.1	4.8	18.9	5.1	0.3	0.0	
6	Number	435	54	56	94	19	1	2	661
	%	65.8	8.2	8.5	14.2	2.9	0.2	0.3	
7	Number	379	57	46	58	16	0	2	558
	%	67.9	10.2	8.2	10.4	2.9	0.0	0.4	
8	Number	403	60	42	69	14	1	1	590
	%	68.3	10.2	7.1	11.7	2.4	0.2	0.2	
9	Number	434	65	38	51	17	4	0	609
	%	71.3	10.7	6.2	8.4	2.8	0.7	0.0	
Total	number	2,370	322	233	483	106	16	5	3,535
	%	67.0	9.1	6.6	13.7	3.0	0.5	0.1	

Data source: The author combined from the shortlists of the Thousand Youth Talent Program awardees.

94 *From luring back to taking advantage of talent*

As Table 4.3 shows, there is a high concentration of TYTP awardees in the distribution of universities, mainly in those with double first-class status. For instance, universities with the number of TYTP awardees ranking in the top 20, CAS Shanghai Institute of Biological Sciences jointly attracted 59.8% of the total number. Among the top 20 institutions, 17 are double first-class universities, 9 of which (Peking University, Tsinghua University, Fudan University, Zhejiang University, Shanghai Jiao Tong University, Nanjing University, University of Science and Technology of China, Huazhong University of Science and Technology, and Sun Yat-sen University) hold significant advantages. Soochow University is the only shortlisted "first-class discipline" university, and Southern University of Science and Technology is the only emerging research-intensive university that has attracted TYTP awardees. These two universities have made outstanding achievements in attracting awardees thanks to their talent-attraction policies and the location advantage of the cities in which they are located. Southern University of Science and Technology attaches great importance to TYTP awardees, attracting 2, 7, and 7 in the second, third, and fourth cohorts, respectively, demonstrating the effectiveness of its innovative system for talent.

Overall, then, the distribution pattern of TYTP awardees is closely related to the academic status, discipline types, key disciplines, and geographical locations of the various universities. Those on the southeast coast and in Beijing have rich resources, a high degree of internationalization, and the ability to make enormous efforts to attract talent from overseas. Universities specializing in science and engineering have more visible advantages than those focusing on humanities. Some traditional universities, such as Renmin University of China, Shandong University, Jilin University, and Nankai University, have attracted relatively small numbers of TYTP awardees. In addition to the geographical and policy factors, the number of overseas scholars attracted by institutions has a certain correlation with their popularity and discipline platforms because academic talent attaches great importance to the academic environment and career development platforms to play a professional role (Li et al., 2018).

4.2.6 *Implementation of an international open talent recruitment system*

In order to solve the problems of information asymmetry and the division of the domestic and international talent market, the TYTP launched a website that provides information for overseas high-level talent about returning to China to pursue opportunities for innovation and entrepreneurship, building a unified platform for display, inquiry, publicity, and communication for all regions and departments to engage in the recruitment of high-level overseas talent. In December 2012, the first online recruitment activity for high-level overseas talent began, and the results of the recruitment were gradually made public. The construction of the talent-attraction network platform has facilitated communication and the sharing of information between the supply and demand sides, improved the efficiency of talent attraction, and enhanced the fairness and transparency of recruitment. At the same time, the network faces challenges regarding talent security and the standardized

Table 4.3 Number of shortlisted Thousand Youth Talent Program awardees at top 20 institutions (2011–2018)

No.	Institution	Number of Thousand Youth Talent Program awardees	Percentage in the total number of Thousand Youth Talent Program awardees (%)	Institution type
1	Tsinghua University	221	6.3%	Double first-class university
2	Zhejiang University	199	5.6%	Double first-class university
3	Peking University	196	5.5%	Double first-class university
4	University of Science and Technology of China	183	5.2%	Double first-class university
5	Shanghai Jiao Tong University	157	4.4%	Double first-class university
6	Fudan University	136	3.8%	Double first-class university
7	Nanjing University	124	3.5%	Double first-class university
8	Huazhong University of Science and Technology	114	3.2%	Double first-class university
9	Sun Yat-sen University	113	3.2%	Double first-class university
10	Wuhan University	88	2.5%	Double first-class university
11	Tongji University	71	2%	Double first-class university
12	Shanghai Institute of Biological Sciences, CAS	66	1.9%	Chinese Academy of Science
13	Southern University of Science and Technology	65	1.8%	Regular university
14	University of Electronic Science and Technology of China	63	1.8%	Double first-class university
15	Sichuan University	61	1.7%	Double first-class university
16	Xi'an Jiao Tong University	59	1.7%	Double first-class university
17	Beihang University	54	1.5%	Double first-class university
18	Xiamen University	53	1.5%	Double first-class university
19	Tianjin University	51	1.4%	Double first-class university
20	Soochow University	39	1.1%	First-class discipline university
	Total	2,113	59.8%	

Data source: The author combined from the shortlists of the Thousand Youth Talent Program awardees.

management of talent information. In the era of the Internet and data storage, ways to manage and serve overseas talent will be an urgent concern for departments at all levels. Gao (2012) found information asymmetry in talent attraction and argued that, in the big data era, mastery of the relevant data will confer an advantage in attracting international talent.

4.3 Problems and countermeasures in overseas high-level talent-attraction policy

4.3.1 Existing problems

The 20 years since the implementation of the programmes for the recruitment of high-level overseas talent have witnessed substantial achievements, but many problems have arisen that need to be addressed. First, talent programmes tend to be project-based, unbalanced, and unconventional and, as a result, face sustainable development issues. Second, talent programmes have resulted in the stratification of scientists and academics and uneven development across institutions. Third, problems of connecting and matching the innovation in the personnel system and scientific research system have resulted in talent programmes which differ from the normal track for faculty promotion and development. Fourth, to address the problems of multiple leaders, repeated funding, and overlapping functions, it is necessary to rationalize the relationship among the government, employers, and third-party organizations and coordinate the project-based talent attraction and long-term market mechanisms. Fifth, competition in the complex international environment has complicated talent security and standardized management of talent information. As the situation worsens, it is imperative to evaluate the impact of the implementation of talent programmes. To solve the existing problems, work must be done to improve the policy measures and establish long-term mechanisms for attracting and utilizing overseas scientists and academics.

4.3.1.1 The sustainability of talent programmes and talent programme awardees

The design of talent programmes is based on cyclical goals. The retention of awardees after the implementation cycle requires systematic and sustainable policies. Deciding on the nature of a programme (i.e. whether it should be temporary, long-term, permanent, or cyclical), mapping out a long-term plan, and setting strategic goals at the policy-making stage are crucial to the sustainability and stability of talent programmes. Those with a long-term design must consider the sustainability of funding resources and continuity of policies.

In foreign countries, talent programmes clearly define the cycle and specify how often they can be renewed and for how long. For example, in 2000, Canada implemented the Canada Research Chair Program, investing $300 million per year towards the establishment of 2,000 research professorships in Canadian universities. The policy specified two categories of Canada Chairs, one being world-class scientists, with a period of seven years at C$200,000 per year and the possibility of renewal, and the others being rising academic stars at C$100,000 per year for five years with the possibility of renewal. By 2010, the programme had successfully recruited 1,845 chairs, including 546 scholars from abroad (334 from the US and a significant proportion from the UK) (Zha, 2014).

4.3.1.2 "Matthew effect" resulting from implementation of talent programmes

The implementation of talent programmes has, as mentioned, resulted in the agglomeration of high-level talent and unbalanced development across institutions. When there is a high degree of agglomeration in the free flow of talent, disciplinary leaders can often attract other talent to gather and join in. The double first-class universities enjoy dominant positions in the implementation of talent programmes. The significance of the implementation effect correlates with the length of the implementation time, bringing about unbalanced development across universities and certain disciplines.

Because both the Changjiang Scholars Program and Thousand Talent Program were designed to reward and fund the most promising talent, they were bound to strengthen strong institutions, regions, disciplines, and departments and weaken the weak ones over the long term. Promising young scientists and academics become concentrated in the double first-class universities, which then take advantage of the combined effect of the young talent programmes and the double first-class construction project to dominate talent recruitment, thereby further solidifying and strengthening their advantages. Meanwhile, the majority of ordinary universities face an unfavourable situation in terms of talent attraction and future development.

The talent programmes have achieved policy and system innovation through incremental reforms, providing experience relevant to the improvement of existing personnel and research systems, but they have also created a dual-track system of employment within institutions that is problematic for the academic environment. There is a wide gap in remuneration, resources, and development opportunities between awardees and other faculty members. Thus, the programmes have motivated a small number of the most talented people while also possibly discouraging the work of the majority of other talent. The improvement of higher education and scientific research depends not only on a small number of highly talented individuals but also on the commitment of the entire faculty in terms of attitude and working ability.

4.3.1.3 Need to optimize the leadership and organizational management system of talent programmes

Many central ministries and commissions have initiated their own talent programmes, and various talent programmes are overseen by various departments. The Thousand Talent Program is coordinated by several departments, an arrangement that inevitably causes problems when handling policies from multiple government departments and leaders. Talent programmes can easily become the performance projects of central ministries and commissions, leading to competition and departmentalization of overall interests. In addition, talent programmes need to strengthen effective coordination and achieve functional convergence with their organizational management systems and technical supervision platforms.

The implementation of talent programmes shows signs of strengthening the administrative tendency. The programmes have been developed and implemented to fulfil national development needs. The long-term implementation of this top-down, projects-based development mode will strengthen the administrative tendency of universities and scientific research institutions, highlight their developmental autonomy, and affect the formation of independent development mechanisms by institutions and disciplines.

4.3.1.4 Challenges associated with the international competition for talent

As the environment in which the competition for international talent takes place becomes increasingly complex and uncertain, it is necessary to dynamically adjust talent programme policies and heighten awareness of talent security. Recently, the recruitment of overseas talent has had to take into account changes in the strategy and immigration policies of the US pertaining to China. The US is highly alert to the rise of China, and the international environment is generally unfavourable to the recruitment of high-level overseas talent in China. The US containment policy towards China and changes in visa and immigration policies have created new uncertainties. The central government needs to adapt to the situation by assessing the talent security issues and optimizing talent programmes.

4.3.2 Suggestions and countermeasures

In 2018, *The Guidance Opinions on Classifying and Promoting the Reform of Talent Evaluation Mechanism*, and *Opinions on Deepening the Reform of Project Evaluation, Talent Evaluation and Institutional Assessment* released by the Central Committee of the Communist Party of China and the State Council provided guidance and a basis for improving the policies relating the recruitment of high-level overseas talent. The selection and use of talent in the implementation of overseas talent programmes should take into account the real contributions and intrinsic value of talent rather than academic background and identity characteristics so as to avoid the halo effect of the talent hats.

4.3.2.1 Integrating talent programmes so as to avoid overlap

The various talent programmes should be clearly positioned and identified as either temporary and periodic talent or long-term. Based on this classification, adjustments should be made to the overall system, and management and implementation measures should be improved. The Changjiang Scholars Program and Thousand Talent Program, for instance, having been implemented effectively and proven to be widely influential, can be transformed into long-term programmes with goals over more than ten years. Initiatives such as the Outstanding Youth Program and Hundred Talent Program can be treated as periodic and temporary non-conventional programmes. The programmes should also be differentiated based on their functions and targets so as to prevent "repeated crowning" and "multiple funding" and talent programmes from becoming projects for rewarding academic officials. Meanwhile, the overall salary level of academics should be increased and their working conditions improved.

4.3.2.2 Preventing vicious competition and the "Matthew effect" caused by the implementation of talent programmes

Practical measures should be taken to prevent the talent programmes from creating the Matthew effect, a winner-takes-all environment, and excessive concentration of talent. Policies should be made to guide the flow of high-level talent to universities in less-developed regions and provincial universities to achieve a more balanced distribution of talent and improve the overall level of higher education faculty.

4.3.2.3 Improving the organization and management of talent programmes

A further suggestion concerns improving top-level management and establishing a unified management committee to coordinate the various programmes. The creation of a talent management office or committee on the basis of the central talent programme can help to manage all talent programmes comprehensively. In the process of the top-level design and implementation of talent programmes, it is necessary to clarify further the responsibilities and roles of central government departments, the government as a whole, and talent programme implementation agencies such as universities, research institutes, and enterprises so as to ensure the openness, transparency, dynamic trackability, and adjustability of the programmes as they are implemented.

Also, optimization of screening and evaluation in talent programmes as well as the system for assessing and managing selected talent can enhance the transparency and credibility of the process. It is also necessary to strengthen the role of international peers in talent assessment, develop respective reasonable evaluation criteria for various disciplines and fields, combine objective indicators and peer judgements, and implement a principle of interest avoidance.

Other needs include the establishment or improvement of measures for talent information security and management of norms and the creation of a web-based, open, and transparent talent programme service system and platform. Additionally, the enhancement of the overseas talent information collection network of domestic and foreign institutions, private and government organizations, and professional and associated organization alliances can improve China's overseas talent information system and network service platform for configuring the supply and demand of talent. A key part of these efforts is data storage technology with improved institutional measures for talent security and information management.

4.3.2.4 Tracking various talent programmes and selected candidates through professional evaluation

There is a need to establish a database of select candidates from various talent programmes and conduct dynamic tracking for each of them. Meanwhile, a database of overseas high-level Chinese talent should also be established, and professional organizations or expert committees that are well-respected at home and abroad should track and regularly evaluate the implementation and effectiveness of the talent programmes. These systematic evaluations can inform adjustments of the talent programme system to refine its effects. Additionally, it is necessary to provide guidelines for the various kinds of talent programmes for provinces, cities, and universities so that they can be appropriately combined, streamlined, and refined (Li and Xu, 2018).

4.3.2.5 Balancing efforts to attract overseas talent and train domestic talent

Attention should be paid to balancing the development of unconventional talent programmes and regular talent and generally improving the remuneration for university faculty members. The personnel management system and distribution system that have proved successful in the implementation of the talent programmes can be applied, with modest adjustments, to the management of university faculty. Li Mei (2017), who studied the intentions of Chinese talent studying in the US to return to China and found that the career development platform and academic institutional environment were impediments to returning to China, argued that it is crucial to take advantage of both domestic-trained talent and overseas returnees.

References

Cheng, X. (2009). Tizhiwai de zengzhang yu tizhinei de daoxiang: gaige kaifang 30nian zhongguo liuxuesheng huiguo zhengce pingshu [The improvement outside the system and the instruction inside the system: Review of the 30-year policies for returned overseas students since the reform and opening-up in China]. In H. Y. Wang (Ed.), *Zhongguo Liuxue Rencai Fazhan Baogao [Report of Chinese overseas personnel]* (pp. 295–316). Jixie Gongye Chubanshe [China Machine Press].

China Education and Research Network. (2001) (n.d.). Zhongguo kexueyuan guanyu yinjin guowai jiechu rencai de guanli banfa [Management measures for introducing outstanding talents by the Chinese academy of sciences]. Retrieved June 22, 2019, from http://www.edu.cn/edu/jiao_yu_yan_jiu/ren_cai_pei_yang/zhong_ke_yuan/200603/t20060323_13412.shtml

Dong, G. Y. (2011). Waiguoji haigui rencai na zhongguo "Lvka" menkan jiangdi [The threshold of applying for Chinese "green card" has been lowered for overseas returnees with foreign nationalities]. *Zhognguo Gaoxiao Shizi Yanjiu [International Talent]*, 5, 6.

Gao, Z. P. (2012). Haiwai keji rencai huiliu yu xinxi buduicheng wenti yanjiu [On information asymmetry in the course of returning of oversea science and technology talents]. *Dangdai Qingnian Yanjiu [Contemporary Youth Research]*, 10, 25–31.

General Office of the Beijing Municipal People's Government. (1981) (n.d.). Bejingshi renminzhengfu zhuanfa guowuyuan pizhun jiaoyubu deng qige bumen《Guanyu zifei chuguo liuxue de qingshi》 de tongzhi [The Beijing municipal people's government forwarded the notice of the state council approving and forwarding the "request for instructions on self-financed studying abroad" by seven departments including the ministry of education]. Retrieved June 22, 2019, from http://www.beijing.gov.cn/zfxxgk/110001/szfwj/1981-02/18/content_8fd225ac62f745ed9afe65bc14f8e501.shtml

He, D. C. (1998). *Zhonghua remin gongheguo zhongyao jiaoyu wenxian 1976–1990 [Important educational documents of PRC, 1976–1990]*. Hainan Chubanshe Hainan Publishing House.

Huang, T. Y., & Bian, J. H. (2006). Changjiang xuezhe jiangli jihua [The significance and enlightment of the implementation of "changjiang scholars award program"]. *Zhognguo Gaoxiao Shizi Yanjiu [Research on University Teachers in China], 1*, 33–39.

Li, M. (2017). Zhongguo liumei xueshu rencai huiguo yixiang ji yingxiang yinsu fenxi [The willingness of returning to China and the push-pull factors leading to Chines academics' studying in the USA]. *Fudan Jiaoyu Liuntan [Fudan Education Forum], 15*(2), 79–86.

Li, M., Yang, R., & Wu, J. (2018). Translating transnational capital into professional development: A study of China's thousand youth talents scheme scholars. *Asia Pacific Education Review, 19*(2), 229–239.

Li, X. X., & Xu, F. (2018). Yanxu rencai jihua moshi yihuo huigui changtaihua shichang jizhi: guanyu shidai keji rencai zhengce de sikao [Continue talent-planning model or return to normalized talent-market mechanism: Study on S&T talent policy in new era]. *Zhongguo kexueyuan yuankan [Bulletin of Chinese Academy of Sciences], 33*(4), 442–446.

Overseas Chinese Affairs Office of the State Council. (1984) (n.d.). Guanyu Zifei chuguo liuxue de zanxing guding [Interim provisions on self-financed studying abroad]. Retrieved June 22, 2019, from http://www.gqb.gov.cn/node2/node3/node5/node9/node106/userobject7ai1352.html

State Council of China. (1986). Guowuyuan pizhuan guojia jiaoyu weiyuanhui 《Guanyu chuguo liuxue renyuan gongzuo de ruogan zanxing guiding》 de tongzhi [Some provisional regulations on the work of students studying abroad]. Retrieved June 22, 2019, from http://www.gov.cn/zhengce/content/2012-09/21/content_6092.htm

Zha, Q. (2014). What factors influence the direction of global brain circulation: The case of Chinese Canada research chairholders. *Compare: A Journal of Comparative and International Education, 46*(2), 214–234.

5 From returning to taking root

Institutional environment and patterns of professional development of overseas academic returnees

Driven by China's economic, technological, academic, and higher education development, higher education institutions (HEIs) in China have been thirsty to attract high-level returning talent since the reform and opening-up. Preferential treatment and high-status were offered to those returnees in order to fast-track their career development. However, as the number of returnees continues to rise, such advantage seems less significant. Only those who have been selected into talent programmes or honoured with the titles of talent and special treatment can have access to the special career promotion fast-track and development space. Such special treatment is a kind of symbol and mark of status, which exerts an important influence on producing the cultural capital and academic status that the Thousand Youth Talent Program (TYTP) awardees need. Based on the literature review and field research on the academic career development of overseas returnees, this chapter in particular conducts an in-depth qualitative investigation and provides a summary on the institutional environment and career development characteristics and patterns of the returned faculty in general, and the TYTP awardees in particular. The chapter aims to present their real state of academic life and career development milieu and examines the current academic working environment and organizational culture from the perspective of overseas returnees.

5.1 Literature review on the academic career development of returned faculty

In recent years, the research on academic returnees or the returnees as faculty members of HEIs has increasingly become a heated topic in investigating talent policy and the internationalization of higher education. The talent's structure and policy changes at the macro level, and the individuals' adaptation to the domestic environment, survival strategies, job satisfaction, and career development at the micro-economic level have been explored, from the perspectives of sociology, management, education, and psychology. This section briefly reviews the existing studies from the following aspects.

5.1.1 The changing trends of overseas returnees and related policy and management

In the field of international talent policy, the Center for China and Globalization (CCG) founded by Wang Huiyao has published a series of research outcomes and policy reports. The *Talent War* (Wang, 2009), *A Collection of Articles on Global*

Talent Strategies (Wang, 2015), the *Blue Book of Global Talent* series edited by his team, for example, *The 2013 Annual Report on the Development of Chinese Returnees* (Wang & Miao, 2013), focused on the statistical data and policy analysis and informed the returnees' characteristics, developmental trends, as well as the strategies and policies regarding Chinese returnees.

In the past decade, with the implementation of various national talent programmes, the national talent policy and its implementation have also become a heated topic of research (Sun, 2016). This kind of research focuses on the "Thousand Talent Program" (Chao, 2014), the "Thousand Youth Talent Program" (Sun & Zhang, 2017), the "Outstanding Talent" scientists (Cao & Suttmeier, 2001), the "Changjiang Scholars Program" (Li & Wu, 2016), and other talent projects. These studies examine the characteristics, distribution, influence, and academic productivity of the academics listed into various talent programmes through statistical data, résumé analysis, and quantitative analysis.

5.1.2 Reasons for the outflow and return of talent

The reasons for the outflow and return of Chinese talent in the international talent market has attracted a lot of attention of researchers. In the 1990s, Chen Changgui (Chen, 1994; Chen, 1995) conducted a research series on Chinese students in the US and Canada in terms of their intentions of returning to China, with the discussion of the two questions of "why have they outflowed?" and "why have they returned home?" The investigation revealed that the status of the participants and the length of time abroad, whether their spouses were also abroad and their attitude towards returning home, and how their evaluation of their interpersonal relationships at their affiliated domestic organizations affected their willingness for returning home. The comprehensive effect of the individual development prospects, economic factors, political factors, family factors, and adaptation towards social culture influenced their decision of returning home. Through the questionnaire surveys and interviews, Li Mei (2017) found that the scholars who studied in the US and had achieved success were unwilling to return home due to the influence of various factors, mainly including career development, the academic career environment, interpersonal relationships, family factors, and emigration intentions.

In exploring the motivation of the returned faculty included into the "Thousand Talent Programs", Ma at el. (2013) found that the influence of social and academic relationships, traditional cultural concepts, and national identities affected the returnees' decisions of returning home. Tian Haisong's (2012) research on the "Thousand Talent Program" in Tianjin showed that the personal development factor was the most important aspect affecting one's intention of return, which is followed by environmental factors, family factors, and policy factors.

5.1.3 Adaptation of the returned faculty

There are many studies on the adaptation of returned faculty. Most of the studies show that the returned faculty adapt well to domestic conditions and enjoy favourable working conditions and career development in China. Liu Rongjie (2010) studied the status of returned scholars from four "double first-class" universities in Shanghai and found that the returned faculty did not necessarily feel unaccustomed to the working environment, and they could quickly adapt to it. But there are also studies that find that the returned scholars face many challenges in adapting to their new jobs, the culture and interpersonal relations after they returned to China, and the level of adaptation is so low, that it is difficult for them to exert their subjective initiative (Li, 2013). Some young returnees in humanities are confronted with an "academic hard landing" (Zhu, 2017). Consequently, some researchers have investigated the adaptation model and factors influencing the returnees. Wang Rongrong (2012) argued that there were three main modes of social adaptation for returned talent: The first is assimilation by the domestic environment, the second is active and selective reconstruction of their lifestyles and modes of interpersonal communication, and the third is to return abroad because of the failure to adapt to the domestic environment. Zhang Donghai and Yuan Fengfeng (2014) summarized four types of strategies for adaptation to the academic system adopted by young returnees, namely, adapting, using systems, sticking to the post, and evading. Scholars have different opinions about the factors that affect the adaptation of returned scholars. Zhao Qing (2010) showed that adaptation to the working environment has the most significant effect on the adaptation to domestic circumstances, which is followed by adaptation to the organization and adaptation to interpersonal relationships. Zhang Donghai and Yuan Fengfeng (2014) argued that the excessively quantitative-oriented evaluation underlying the professional promotion mechanism and polarization in academic resource allocation, among other factors, affect adaptation.

5.1.4 Job satisfaction of the returned faculty

Analysis of the working status of the returned faculty from the angle of job satisfaction has also received considerable attention. Scholars believe that the factors affecting job satisfaction of returnees could be divided into external factors and individual factors. The former concerns the growth and development enabled by the university and society, academic support, management and culture, the work itself, material and mental returns as well as the working environment. Individual factors involve the returnees' accumulated working time, the length of stay abroad, gender, and so on (Xu, 2009). Yu Xiaofei (2009) found that the returnees had the highest level of satisfaction with the job itself but the lowest satisfaction regarding academic support. Growth and development, academic support, material and mental returns were the key factors affecting their job satisfaction. The questionnaire survey conducted by Li Yiying and Zhu Junwen (2018) on young overseas faculty (engaging in their first job upon return) found that returnees in different cities showed different degrees of satisfaction. Those in new first-tier cities had the lowest level of satisfaction while those in first- and second-tier cities showed a relatively higher level of satisfaction. The young returnees were least satisfied with the salary. In order to enhance the job satisfaction of returned faculty, it is necessary to take effective measures, including improving the system of remuneration, promotion, and evaluation; adopting scientific, friendly, standardized, and democratic management systems to reduce pressure on returnees; improving the remuneration incentive mechanism to improve their quality of life; and focusing on the construction of the "soft environment". It is especially essential to create a free academic environment, a fair institutional environment, an open cultural atmosphere, and an inclusive interpersonal atmosphere for returnees (Xu, 2009).

5.1.5 Academic career development of the returned faculty

As for the comparison between returnees and domestically trained scholars in terms of professional development and academic contributions, studies presented divided views. One view reveals that there is no significant difference in terms of research output between returnees and domestic scholars (Zhao, 2010). Another point of view argues that there is a difference in terms of academic performance between returnees and domestic scholars while the returnees have more advantages regarding their academic performance in many aspects (Rosen & Zweig, 2005). At the same time, the career development of returnees selected into talent programmes has received a growing amount of attention from researchers. Li Mei and her research team have conducted in-depth qualitative research on the academic development of the TYTP awardees and found that they enjoyed a favourable professional development career (Li et al., 2018).

In recent years, more research has focused on the relationship between transnational capital, career development, and the academic productivity of returned scholars. Relevant studies, mainly from the perspective of social capital, reveal the relationship between the returnees' transnational capital transfer and their career development on the basis of quantitative statistics of academic publications and social network analysis. The international cooperation network is one of the main factors that distinguish returned scholars from locals, and it has had a significant impact on the research output of returned scientists, which is notably conducive to the growth of their academic output in both quality and quantity (Lu, 2014; Chen et al., 2015). Moreover, international and domestic binary academic networks are conducive to their professional promotion. Zweig and other researchers (2004) argued that returnees can get higher returns on human capital than domestic scientists, returned scientists benefit more from preferential policies and a higher proportion of them hold academic leadership and administrative positions.

5.1.6 The role and influence of the academic returnees

Chen Xuefei and his colleagues (2003) argued that studying abroad brought great benefits to individuals and society. Individual benefits are related to the internal, institutional, and material forms of benefits, and institutional benefits are manifested in teaching, scientific research, international exchanges, and management. Chen Changgui et al. (2000) found that academic returnees played an important role as core faculty in teaching and scientific research. They raised the threshold of academic research, advanced disciplinary development, created a new generation of leaders for the discipline, improved their scientific research competence, and enriched international academic exchanges, radiating their influence and serving as network nodes connecting Chinese and foreign academic systems. Xu Rong et al. (2014) have proved, through a case study of overseas talent employed by Shanghai Jiao Tong University, that the employment of high-level overseas talent has promoted the rapid development of universities and disciplines.

5.1.7 The accumulation and transfer of transnational capital of the academic returnees

The academic community defines the capital that has been formed and accumulated during their study and work abroad as transnational capital, which is the knowledge, skills, experience, and social networks that academic talent accumulate in the process of transnational mobility and working in different countries and environments, including human capital, social capital, and cultural capital. Zweig et al. (2004) argued that returnees possess transnational human capital which is different from traditional human capital. The former is accumulated based on overseas learning experience and international education, which is difficult to be obtained in the home country (Lu et al., 2014). The second type of transnational capital owned by returnees is social and academic relations accumulated overseas and the resources that are contained in the relationship network. Cultural capital, in the form of educational qualifications and diplomas, is the third type of transnational capital of returnees. Transnational human and social capitals are embedded in academic talent, flowing with them among different countries, systems, and organizations. The knowledge, skills, and experience of returnees are unfolded and used in their work and career development in their transnational mobility and will be further appreciated and transferred. Transnational capital distinguishes academic talent with overseas educational and work experience from those who have been trained locally, in that the social networks, knowledge, and professional experience of the former are beyond the reach of the latter. Transnational capital has become a comparative advantage for returned scholars to pursue their academic careers.

By comparing returned scientists and researchers with their domestically trained counterparts, Lu et al. (2014) found that returned scholars have advantages in academic creativity and academic contributions. Chen et al. (2015) argued that the network of professional relations among the Thousand Youth Talent Program scholars (TYTPSs) has dual characteristics concerning both international and domestic circles, which has a significant impact on the professional promotion and academic productivity of returnees. The academic returnees possess a transnational network of cooperation on research publishing. The key co-authors of their papers are their doctoral and/or post-doctoral supervisors before and after their return to China.

To sum up, the range of research topics on the returned faculty in China has been constantly expanding, from macroscopic to mesoscopic, and then to microscopic levels. The research methods adopted involve questionnaire surveys, interviews, bibliometric statistics, and case studies. However, the existing research has some drawbacks as follows: First, it focuses on macroscopic and microcosmic research, and thus ignores the study of institutions and disciplines at the mesoscopic level. It regards the returned faculty as a whole entity. Few in-depth comparative studies have been conducted on academic returnees of different types, institutions, and regions. Second, there is a lack of studies on characteristics and influencing factors on the academic career development of academic returnees. Third, it emphasizes the external perspective of the government and institutions, but hardly examines the principal role and developmental characteristics of academic returnees from their own perception and perspectives.

5.2 The institutional environment and situation on the professional development of academic returnees

5.2.1 Research questions and research methods

5.2.1.1 Research questions

The "academic returnees" and "returned faculty" were once a group with a certain aura. They were once believed to enjoy relatively satisfactory academic work and academic career development after their return to China. In fact, academic returnees also need to adapt to the environment. This is a non-homogenous group. On the one hand, there are similarities in the developmental characteristics of this group; on the other hand, there are differences in their career development and personal milieu. Through in-depth qualitative research, this section reveals the milieu and characteristics of academic career development of academic returnees and their perceptions of, and views on, the academic system at home and abroad.

In the process of return or transnational flow, academic returnees usually face tasks and challenges relating to academic development and the construction of their academic platforms. Based on their accumulated overseas experience, returnees come to their home countries to develop their academic careers, which not only means a geographical change in their working environment, but also a transformation of the work-field and the institutional environment. After returning to Chinese universities, how do the returnees think about the impact of their foreign experience upon themselves? How do they perceive and look upon the institutional environment of career development? How do they build their academic career? What are the characteristics of their career development?

5.2.1.2 Research methods

This section mainly adopts the qualitative research method, and describes the main characteristics of the academic work of 15 returned faculty, based on interviews. The author and Chen Qiongqiong interviewed 15 returned faculty from double first-class universities in Shanghai and Xi'an, who were mainly returnees from the US, including eight in the fields of science and engineering (coded as NS) and seven in humanities and social sciences (coded as SS). Twelve of them were male. The interviewees had studied and worked in the US for 5–23 years and had been working in China for 3–11 years. The interviewees were selected through purposeful sampling. In the universities of Shanghai and Xi'an, invitation letters were sent to the returned faculty who were selected by gender, discipline, and professional title. Face-to-face semi-structured interviews were conducted, with each interview lasting for one to two hours. All of the interview data were transcribed. After a thorough analysis of the interview data, the authors classified the results of field investigation under three topics: First, the impact of overseas study and work on individuals; second, the perception and opinion of returned faculty on the institutional environment for academic career development; third, the milieu of professional development and academic characteristics of academic returnees.

5.2.2 Findings

5.2.2.1 The impact of studying and working abroad on individuals

Chinese academic returnees accumulate their human and social capital while studying and working abroad, and their overseas experience exerts a profound impact upon their professional competence and concepts. First of all, overseas experience has contributed to the training of professional competence, learning attitudes, and research methods of the returnees. In terms of professional competence, their overseas experience contributes to the improvement of their professional knowledge, enables them to learn about the frontier of the discipline, establishes their research field, and builds academic relationships. In terms of attitude and spirit, the overseas experience gives rise to their professional beliefs and enthusiasm, stimulates their passion for professional and scientific research, helps them to develop good working habits, fosters a sense of professional responsibility and mission, and makes them devoted to research with little concern for earthly gains. In terms of methodology, the overseas experience cultivates them to adopt a more rigorous methodology and academic writing standards. Second, studying and working abroad has changed the way of thinking of the returnees, influencing their values and their outlooks on life and on the world, which include respecting others, valuing the individuality of students, and recognizing the values of equality, freedom, tolerance, and pluralism. Third, it enables them to work and cooperate in an international environment, to broaden their international horizons, and to learn about the international code of conduct and norms. Foreign language competence and international social network advantages accumulated during their stay abroad are helpful for the returnees to publish English articles, to cooperate with their foreign counterparts, and to enhance their international influences. Table 5.1 lists the returnees' narratives about these influences.

5.2.2.2 Returned faculty's perception of the institutional environment of academic career development

Based on their personal experience and observation, returned faculty have their own views and thoughts on the positive and negative aspects of the domestic academic system and academic environment. Their perceived academic system environment may

Table 5.1 The impact of overseas study and work on individuals

Interviewees	Interview data	Concept
SS10	What influences me most, I think, is the way of thinking, and the way of problem-solving.	Ways of thinking
NS8	What I learned most from my stay in the US is that I learned how to respect others. Of course, we should also respect ourselves, learn to respect ourselves, and then respect others. And I also learned about how to do things conscientiously, how to do things in a down-to-earth manner, as well as adopting a pragmatic attitude and inclusive spirit towards colleagues and students.	Values and view of life
NS5	There is greater flexibility in academic research, that is, we can do any research that we are interested in, without worrying about doing something we are interested in but not meeting the needs of the country. During my five years' stay in the US, I learned how to do research. My teacher taught me to generate research questions hand-in-hand, and then taught me how to find solutions, as well as how to apply them to the information field. It is very difficult to explore this process all by myself without guidance. So, it was a very precious opportunity to learn under the guidance of such a good teacher. This is the biggest benefit of my study in the US, which helped me learn how to do scientific research.	Research ability and the transformation of research attitude and methods
NS5	The comparative advantage of overseas returnees is that their academic ability is relatively strong. However, for some domestically trained scholars, although their publication ability is not as strong as returnees, they have more advantages and are more likely to succeed in applying for research projects.	Comparison of advantages between overseas returnees and domestically trained scholars
NS6	Because you have the chance to connect with people from completely different educational backgrounds, your vision is broader, and you can better understand what different groups of people are thinking about, or what their purposes are. What impacted me the most is that I became more rigorous and more organized while doing things.	Open mindedness
NS8	I got the chance to know many American colleagues and friends, and I learned many things from them, including my mentor. I feel that their mentalities, and their minds, really had a great impact [on me].	Social circles and spiritual values attribution

Notes: Coding of interviewees; NS stands for Natural science; SS stands for Social science.

be coloured with personal emotions and subjective judgements, but it is precisely the perceived academic system and organizational environment that constitutes the field of their professional practice, which is constantly shaping working mentalities and the emotional experience of the returnees. The academic system environment experienced and considered by the returnees includes not only the macro environment, like the position of China's academic system in the world, but also the institutions, management, and working conditions at the institutional and disciplinary levels, such as administrative management, employment system, assessment system, student quality, team building, scientific research facilities and conditions, peer cooperation culture, and interpersonal relationships, etc. These circumstances and conditions have a potential impact on the career development and academic work of returnees, who, as self-motivated scholars, are also actively transforming and improving the local microenvironment in the process of adapting to that environment.

1. Does returning from the US but to work in China mean moving from the academic centre to the periphery?

The educational researchers represented by Altbach (2004) has adopted the "centre–periphery" world system theory to explain the position of different academic systems in relation to the world academic system. The returned scholars have a clear understanding of the changes brought about by their return to work in China from American academic centres. The returnees believe that American academic standards have had a profound impact on China. There is a gap between the Chinese academic community and the international first-class counterparts in terms of scientific research, and the academic exchanges between China and foreign countries are unequal. But there are also returnees who are optimistic about China's integration into the global academic community and believe that China is slowly heading towards the world academic centre. A number of interviewees reflected on China's position in the world academic system, and some of their comments are as follows:

> We are on the edge of the (global) academic circle. We all follow Western standards in publishing articles, and we are all following the Western Way, so we are on the edge. However, we are slowly making it to the center of the knowledge system, and our understanding of scientific research as well as our understanding of knowledge has also changed.
>
> (NS1 in Science and Engineering)

> So, I think there is a gap between the Chinese academic community and the world academic community. There's a lot of internationalization and a lot of communication, but in most cases, it is not an equal academic exchange. That is to say, the exchange between Chinese scientists and top-level foreign scientists is not reciprocal. Nevertheless, China has its own strength, namely, it has abundant human resources and more students.
>
> (NS8 in Science and Engineering)

From returning to taking root 111

> It may sound extreme, but I think by choosing to stay away from the United States, I am moving away from the core academic circle. Of course, we will still have exchanges, but slowly, that academic circle will not recognize you as much as it used to when you were active there.
>
> (NS7 in Science and Engineering)

The interviewees criticized the academic hollowing-out caused by the blind pursuit of American academic standards and the limitations of the academic authorities of their discipline who, restrained by their past experience, were unable to bring Chinese academic research to the international frontier. Whereas one returnee (SS3) believes that if he stays in the US, he can only go to a second- or third-tier university, but back in China, he can go to a leading academic centre, like one of the top research universities in Beijing or Shanghai. Thus, although Chinese academia is not the centre of the world's academic system, he has made it to the centre of the Chinese academic system.

2. The government has invested heavily in scientific research, providing favourable scientific research conditions, sufficient resources, and better hardware and facilities.

In recent decades, the Chinese government has had a positive impact on the investment in research resources, funding, and projects of universities and research institutes through the construction of "Project 211", "Project 985", and double first-class programmes. The returnees have found that domestic scientific research conditions and investments are even better than those in the US. For example, NS6 expressed,

> I think China offers considerable financial support for academic research, especially over the past two years. For example, the Ministry of Education and the Ministry of Science and Technology have increased their funding by almost 50% annually, which has resulted in generous financial support for researchers. In terms of hardware, China has gradually reached the international leading level.

Returnee NS2, who is in the field of science and engineering, is very satisfied with the scientific research conditions and research atmosphere of his unit. He said,

> When I just came back, I found the hardware here is far more advanced than that of Johns Hopkins University. Here, we share a lot of things in the same building. It is very convenient to access all the equipment under the charge of the project manager and you can use it as if you owned it. The hardware equipment is good, and there is not much interference in the orientation or the project selection. Researchers can basically do whatever they want, and I think it's a pretty accommodating environment.

3. Top-notch universities adopt the "up-or-out" employment system and follow international standards for scientific research assessment.

Influenced by the "new public management" wave, the Chinese universities have been carrying out the reform of their personnel employment systems and performance management since the beginning of the 21st century. The life-time job system has given way to the contract system. Representing the top of the pyramid, double first-class universities started their employment system reform even earlier and have been implementing it strictly. Some Science and Engineering departments follow international standards in terms of faculty assessment.

According to a returnee (NS5) in the field of science and engineering in a double first-class university in Shanghai, his school has 55 faculty members, among whom returnees account for 80%. His school follows the standards for foreign academic systems and adopts the "either promotion or leave" employment system. It also refers to international standards for the assessment of scientific research. The interviewee NS5 said,

> First of all, the tenure track was introduced from the United States. The returnees mostly get the professional title of associate professor in two or three years. Our assessment is actually more demanding than that of the United States. Our tenure track requires that we must win the national title of outstanding young scholar within six years. If you get it, you pass; Otherwise, you will be dismissed. Now, the policy has loosened. Well-known overseas scholars are invited to evaluate a teacher's performance over the past six years to see if he or she meets the standards. If he or she meets the standards, he or she will stay. If not, the person will be dismissed. Second, international standards are also referred to for the evaluation of scientific research. Our department has produced a list of top international journals and prestigious conferences. Every professor, associate professor, and lecturer is required to complete a certain number of articles published on the list of journals. Generally speaking, a professor should publish three to four articles, and an associate professor at least two. If they fail to meet the requirements, they will be hired with a lower salary package.

4. The interpersonal relationship in China has both positive and negative effects.

Social relations and interpersonal relationships have different connotations and meanings in different cultures. The close interpersonal relationships and the close contact and cooperation among colleagues in Chinese workplaces, where colleagues interact and cooperate closely, may bring positive emotional and professional support and prevent individuals from feeling alienated. SS3 in anthropology is very sensitive to the aloofness among Americans:

> Individuals in American society, even in their own words, are quite aloof to each other. I myself have experienced that feeling, for I am a foreigner, and American society shows a notable trend of atomization. Comparatively speaking, the United States has a limited culture and resources while China has so many interesting things for me to explore, to experience, and to feel.

However, if the interpersonal and human factors weigh too much in academic activities, it will cause negative effects such as the "banding together" culture. Some returnees think that the "banding together" and "circle" (*quanzi*) culture is not conducive to the formation of a high-performing academic team. For example, some interviewees illustrated,

> So many of our domestic academic teams are not the academic teams in the real sense of the term, as they are maintained through some other mechanism. What is the mechanism? Sometimes we just avoid the topic. When you are abroad, you often see two or three scholars working together for their entire lives, and they draw on each other's expertise to make up for their own weaknesses. It is hardly seen at home, at least in the short term, because of such a mechanism.
> (SS10 in Humanities and Social Science)

> The phenomenon of banding together is widely seen. New recruits from overseas academic institutions may not have unique backgrounds, or they just stand for themselves, but at home you may find there are groups with distinct boundaries among them. I think it is very difficult to pursue development back home in China if you have no support. For example, if a new recruit has the same status and conditions as I do, and if he is a student of a very prestigious professor in China or has a special relationship, it will be a lot easier for him to grow.
> (NS6 in Science and Engineering)

5. Academic work is affected by the quasi-government institution atmosphere and the system of the units (*danweizhi*).

The interviewees majoring in science and engineering as well as those in humanities and social sciences all mentioned the impact of the quasi-government institutional atmosphere, the planned system, and the system of units (*danweizhi*) that impact upon university management, culture, and interpersonal relationships. For example, some interviewees illustrated,

> I think in terms of work, a lot of people hold bureaucracy-oriented thoughts. For example, in the United States you will be respected for yourself. But in China the respect people have for you has something to do with your position and the power that is behind you.
> (NS6 in Science and Engineering)

> So, China's universities are not ivory towers in nature because they are not independent institutions for knowledge production. They are still under the control of the system of units which not only imposes many administrative constraints on academic operations, but also creates a cultural atmosphere that affects communication among individuals.
> (SS3 in Humanities and Social Science)

6. Domestic research mentality is impetuous and the academic community tends to be utilitarian.

In recent years, various ranking and evaluation systems have disturbed academic research activities in China. The reform of the personnel system of universities attaches too much importance to research performance and the quantitative evaluation of the faculty's performance. In terms of the academic and faculty evaluation, the "five only" phenomenon of "only papers, only talent labels, only professional titles, only academic degrees, and only awards" prevails, which affects the ecological environment of academic circles, and fuels the trend to seek quick gains. It has been criticized by the returned faculty:

> People are anxious. Everyone wants to get a project in a hurry and then rushes to finish it, hardly thinking if he can go further in the project. I think it's a matter of mindset [...] It's not the case that one learns more advanced things in the United States than in China, but when I was in the United States, I could afford to be devoted to what I was doing.
> (NS7 in Science and Engineering)

> I feel we are more like businessmen. We are not just a team of knowledge producers and knowledge creators, as we have become businessmen tasked with knowledge dissemination and circulation. It is pathetic.
> (SS10 in Humanities and Social Science)

7. The academic evaluation system is not conducive to academic innovation and cooperation.

The over-quantified performance management and unreasonable academic evaluation systems in China are not conducive to academic innovation and cooperation. At present, several colleges and universities have strict regulations on the recognition of academic achievements, generally only the publications under the first authorship of work units and the first individual authorship can be recognized. Only the project leader is recognized in the project evaluation, while the contribution of the research team fails to receive due attention. SS10 compares the differences in academic evaluation between China and other countries:

> The academic evaluation system causes a lot of problems for cooperation. For example, what are the institutional guarantees for academic cooperation abroad? For example, when we publish an article abroad, the first author aside, the second, third and fourth authors are all given due consideration. But at home, for example, in the XX University, only the first author is considered, which not only stifles cooperation and creativity, but also makes people eager for quick results, such that it is even possible for researchers to ignore long-term academic development prospects in order to publish SSCI articles.

NS6 thinks that the reward system in China results in seeking quick gains,

> I think the current reward system is for utilitarian purposes. There are clear criteria specifying which journals you should publish your work in and what kind of rewards you will get if you are the author. [...] Especially when it comes to paper publishing, you are required to be the first author, or belong to the leading unit, which makes it very hard for you to cooperate with others, especially those facing the same requirements.

8. Chinese students in similar universities show great competence, but they need to cultivate their mindset getting down to what they are doing.

As all the interviewees were faculty of double first-class universities, they believed that the students in double first-class universities were excellent enough, but some students have been affected by the impetuous culture of society and it is difficult for them to get down to their scientific research. NS6 said,

> The students in Chinese universities are more capable, both in terms of development at the intellectual level and also possessing a solid foundation of education, more so than their international peers at corresponding universities. But it is not so easy to cultivate them since some Chinese students are affected by bad social practices and can hardly be devoted to their work, which is quite different from the case in foreign countries.

5.2.2.3 The milieu of professional development and academic work characteristics of the returned faculty

1. The academic work of the returned faculty is characterized by internationalization.

Returnees' overseas experience has had a profound impact on the internationalization of their academic work since their academic work shows more prominent international characteristics and orientation, than that of their local colleagues. The internationalization orientation is reflected in their teaching, scientific research, management, and service. In regard to the language of instruction, teaching method, and educational ideas, they try to keep in line with international best practices. Returnees attach importance to classroom discussions, bring in international teaching materials, conduct bilingual or pure-English teaching, and offer new courses. They respect the individuality of students and treat them equally, with the focus laid on fostering their academic interests. In scientific research, they are more inclined to engage in international emerging fields and inter-disciplines. In terms of academic visions, they have international foresight; they know about the research trends of their peers in international academic circles. They have advantages in publishing in international academic journals, and they find it easy to get along with their international peers. When it comes to academic work, NS7 in the field of science and engineering is very proud of his international publishing ability:

> I can be focused on what I am doing, and my articles are surely much better than those by local colleagues. First, I am better in research and writing. And I also boast a good reputation in the academic community abroad. With all the factors combined, I am totally different from them. It is hard for others to publish one SCI article, but for me, even five or six articles can be done within two years.

2. The returned faculty take the initiative to create a local "mini environment" that is conducive to academic innovation.

The returned faculty do not passively adapt to the academic organization and working environment in China, but actively improve the institutional environment and create a "small environment" conducive to their career development and academic innovation when conditions permit.

For example, the research institute where the science and engineering scholar NS2 works has created an excellent development space with unique features, because the researchers at the Research Institute B of University A where he is working, are mostly returnees from the US. As more and more people come back, they are slowly changing the academic environment and creating an academic culture that, although is not very wide-ranging, has means to achieve a cultural change and a kind of academic freedom in this rising institution. Such a microcosmic environment is the enclave for the academic system and environmental innovation created by the returned research team. Such "micro-spaces" have a good disciplinary culture and an organizational atmosphere, that also has an institutional space detached from the original system and culture. Each PI (Principal Investigator) enjoys the right of independence and autonomy, including the recognition of priorities, free choice of scientific research topics, sharing of research equipment and resources, etc. It is like creating an island in the vast ocean of existing academic institutions, an "enclave" that is conducive to academic innovation.

3. The returned faculty, based on what they have learned abroad, make efforts to enhance the students' character and academic capabilities.

Some returned faculty members who have studied under the supervision of well-known scholars in Western countries have been deeply influenced by their mentors in terms of pursuing academic study, learning to be, dedication, and academic spirit. After they return to China, they have incorporated such spirit into their own research and talent training practices, paying great attention to the cultivation of students' personality and academic ability. They said,

> The training for students is intended to improve them rather than to meet the needs of the project. I probably spend a lot more energy in training the

students than other teachers because when I was abroad, my tutor spent a lot of time and energy on me.

(NS1 in Science and Engineering)

So, I think that I influence them more, in terms of what the attitude towards learning should be, and learning what to do, since I am duty-bound to teach and educate them. As for academic training, what I stress is the right way of doing academic work, and I have high requirements upon their visions, the depth of their knowledge, their inter-disciplinary knowledge, and their reading of relevant literature. At the same time, some of the work they do is up to a high theoretical level, it's quite original and challenging.

(NS8 in Science and Engineering)

4. Some returned faculty have high academic aspirations and work long hours every day.

Some of the returned faculty show strong career and academic ambitions. Those in science and engineering often work at the office or laboratory from morning to night. For example, NS7 is a typical case.

I should say that I like to read my things in the office by myself from 20:00 to 24:00 PM every night. It is a habit that I formed in the United States. Others find it is hard to stay up until 12 o'clock every night, but I think it is nothing. I spend every night this way.

But extra-long working hours are bad for physical health and sustainable development. In recent years, many tragedies of young talent dying at an early age have occurred, and the pressure and health problems of young and middle-aged faculty need urgent attention from all relevant parties. The administrative and management departments should take into account the psychological load and the pressure faced by teachers when carrying out reforms regarding faculty management.

5. The adaptation of returned faculty to the domestic academic environment varies from person to person.

Most of the returned faculty are well adapted to their current environment after returning to China, but some of the interviewees plan to go abroad again due to their work dissatisfaction. For example, NS8, a scholar in the field of science and engineering, who has studied and worked in the US for 20 years, is in this situation. After working for nearly four years at a double first-class university in Shanghai, he plans to return to the US. He does not want to fit into the small circle of China, but he is devoted to offering classes, guiding students, and doing research. On this point, the field survey found that the interviewees from the universities in the western part of China face even greater challenges to adapt to the domestic environment, as their universities lack good scientific research conditions and management systems.

After returning back, you have to start over and redefine your academic interests; you have to go through a process to get the funding for your research so that there is a period of adaptation. It may be a short period for some people, but it may be longer for others, depending on the institution you work with and what you do. If it is short, it may be one or two years; but if it is long, it may last for four or five years or even longer. After I came back, it wasn't until this year that I actually resumed my research. When I came back, I had the worst-case scenario in mind; but when it did happen, I went through a long process of suffering setbacks and disappointments.

(SS10 in Humanities and Social Science)

6. Some returned faculty face academic and economic difficulties.

Some young returnees face various challenges, such as difficulties in establishing a disciplinary team, applying for a research project, publishing a paper in Chinese, building an interpersonal network, and integrating into the domestic academic circles, as well as the difficulties in resting on their laurels due to low income and financial pressure, so it is hard for them to devote themselves to academic work. For example, NS8 considers himself an "outsider" of the domestic academic circle.

The biggest difficulty, I think, is that if you're in China, you have to be part of the Chinese community. Because if you're not in the community, good things will not come your way, and you will be marginalized. I'm an outsider roughly, but I'm doing things like an insider, like training students and offering classes. I teach students very well, and they enjoy my class. I've trained a lot of students.

Many interviewees felt quite dissatisfied with the low income, thinking that the young faculty's income was so low that it was difficult for them to be devoted to academic research in terms of having their own peace of mind.

Low salaries for academics leave young faculty unable to work devotedly, with no sense of dignity.

(SS3 in Humanities and Social Science)

In view of the general pay level in China, my salary is quite high. But for me, it is actually much lower than the pay I earned when I was teaching in an American university, it's only about one fifth or one fourth of what I got at that time.

(NS6 in Science and Engineering)

In terms of the system, there is still some disparities between China and Western countries. For example, at home we get an annual pay of about RMB 200,000 or $30,000. But as a faculty member in the US, the pay is much higher, reaching more than $80,000.

(NS5 in Science and Engineering)

7. There are differences in the career development among the returned faculty.

Compared with their domestic counterparts, the returned faculty show their own characteristics in advancing their academic career. The returnees differ in their experiences relating to academic work and professional development due to their differences in career development stage, the geographic location of work, the type of institution, and discipline. First of all, whether or not there is a label, the title and the talent programme support exert a crucial impact upon the development course and promotion speed of returnees. Second, the economic incomes and career development circumstances for the returnees, who are in different stages of career development, also differ. Senior scholars upon returning to China receive high salaries and enjoy a good package whereas everything is difficult for post-doctoral fellows and the lecturers who have just started their careers. It will be difficult to get things started. Third, factors at the institutional level and the academic platform also affect the career development of returnees. Fourth, returnees from different regions and cities also face very different environments and circumstances for development. Although Beijing and Shanghai are the centres of Chinese academia, home to many top-notch universities, high housing prices, high living costs, and high work pressure also affect the development of returnees. The universities in western China are thirsty for talent, but their academic platforms and management systems on the whole need to be improved.

In a word, through field investigation, this study found that returnee scholars believe that the academic system and environment in China have a positive side, and the academic system and environment on the whole, is being improved. The positive factors include the hefty investment of resources, advanced hardware and infrastructure, the overall competency of students who are in research-oriented universities, and local micro-spaces that allow for much freedom and independence from the disciplinary platform where returnees concentrate. But there are still many problems, such as the university's bureaucratic management, interpersonal factors and banding-together culture, over-emphasis on performance and performance evaluation, low salaries for academics, and insufficient academic support, which restrict the professional development and academic innovation of returnees. The academic career development of the returned teachers is international, individualistic, and is achieved through using their own initiative. The returnees benefit from translating their transnational capital into their strengths at home.

The returned faculty interact with the external academic system and the institutional environment, which influences the pattern and characteristics of their academic career development. The returnees' successful development and work embodies an excellent academic system and organizational environment, involving governmental policy support, the inclusiveness and openness of the city, policy support from the university, and a reasonable personnel management system. Only by creating a sound external environment, can the returnees embrace an ideal development space and platform. It has been found that returnees use their initiative for innovation. They construct a local microenvironment, participate in discipline management, and promote the continuous improvement of China's academic system and university governance, through interactions with the environment while exerting agency.

5.3 The academic career development and transnational capital transfer of the Thousand Youth Talent Program scholars

5.3.1 Research questions and research methods

5.3.1.1 Research background

The attraction and use of overseas high-level talent is not only a competitive strategy for universities, but also a necessary prerequisite for universities to gain superior status and social prestige. The promulgation and implementation of various national talent programmes has provided an opportunity for research-oriented universities to attract overseas high-level talent. Among the high-level talent projects, the TYTP is one of the most effectively implemented talent programmes. As of August 2018, a total of 3,535 overseas young scientists have been awarded as TYTPSs. Most of the TYTP scholars work within double first-class universities, and the high concentration of top-notch talent further affects progress in universities and disciplines in the new round of development. The market mechanism plays a fundamental role in the allocation of talent and institutions.

The government and universities provide the TYTPSs with strong policy support and favourable working conditions, so that they can have a higher starting point for their academic career, better working treatment and conditions, and a better career development platform when they come back to China. At the same time, the government and universities hold high expectations and requirements for scientific research contributions and achievements of the TYTPSs. However, what are the working conditions like for these young scientists who have been selected into the Thousand Youth Talent Program? What are the characteristics of their academic career development? These issues are directly related to the effectiveness of the implementation of the Thousand Youth Talent Program, the sustainable development of these TYTP awardees, and their value representation and hence need in-depth field investigation. The existing studies have examined the policy, structure, characteristics, academic productivity, and the impact of the TYTPSs as a whole based on the quantitative description, but few qualitative studies have examined their academic career development and the process of their transnational capital accumulation and transfer. Based on semi-structured interviews, this section depicts and analyzes the characteristics of academic career development of the TYTP awardees from double first-class and "first-class discipline" universities in Shanghai and Jiangsu, in order to shed light on how to improve talent policies and the academic career development environment for the talent.

5.3.1.2 Research questions

The young academic returnees who return to China often face the challenge of academic development and academic platform construction. Can the young scholars who are accumulating strengths or climbing up in their academic careers achieve sustainable development and maintain their strengths in scientific research to play a leading role in scientific research and talent training after they return to China? In this section, 22 returned TYTP scholars from four double first-class universities in

Shanghai and one university with first-class disciplines in Jiangsu were involved in the survey. An in-depth interview with the youth talent and an analysis of their CVs show the patterns of their career development and the role of their transnational capital after they return to China. The research questions are as follows:

(1) What kind of transnational capital have the TYTPSs accumulated during their academic growth and overseas study/work?
(2) What is the situation of the TYTPSs in terms of laboratory building, team building, and research project application?
(3) What are the characteristics of the academic career development of the TYTP awardees?
(4) What is the role of identity and transnational capital in the career development of the TYTP awardees?

5.3.1.3 Research methods

This section is mainly based on in-depth interviews with, and analysis of, CVs of the 22 young talent. From August to December 2016, the research team conducted semi-structured interviews with 15 TYTP scholars from four double first-class universities in Shanghai. To cover different types of institutions, from July to November 2018, the research team further conducted in-depth interviews with seven TYTP scholars from a "first-class discipline" university in Jiangsu Province.

The basic information about the interviewees is shown in Table 5.2. The interviewees are selected from different universities, disciplines, rounds, and academic backgrounds. They returned to China between 2011 and 2017, mostly from the US, Canada, Japan, and European countries, and include 20 male and 2 female scholars. Each interview lasted for one to two hours. With the consent of the interviewees, the researcher recorded the interviews and then transcribed the recording into text. In this section, the author constructed an analytical framework based on concepts and theoretical instruments in the related literature as well as the results of the field study. The academic career development of interviewees can be summarized into four themes: Growth trajectory and capital accumulation, construction of career development spaces, patterns of professional development, and the characteristics of academic work.

5.3.2 The theoretical perspective of the TYTP scholars

5.3.2.1 Transnational capital accumulation and transfer of the Thousand Youth Talent Program awardees

Eligibility for the TYTP is attributable to their accumulated transnational capital, including their academic experience, their qualification was obtained from prestigious universities, academic relationship network, knowledge creation, and academic productivity. The cultural and social capital of the TYTPSs is accumulated and transferred during the process of their international flow and professional

Table 5.2 Basic information of the interviewees

No.	Gender	Round	Year of return	Title	Overseas study/work country	Discipline	Type of university
TYTPS1	M	6	2014	Researcher	Switzerland	Life sciences	Double first-class university
TYTPS 2	M	6	2015	Researcher	Netherlands	Environment and earth sciences	Double first-class university
TYTPS 3	M	5	2014	Prof.	Japan	Electronic information science	Double first-class university
TYTPS 4	M	6	2015	Prof.	America	Ecology	Double first-class university
TYTPS 5	M	2	2011	Prof.	America	Ecology	Double first-class university
TYTPS 6	M	1	2011	Prof.	America & Japan	Chemistry	Double first-class university
TYTPS 7	M	2	2012	Prof.	America	Life sciences	Double first-class university
TYTPS 8	M	1	2011	Prof.	America	Material science and engineering	Double first-class university
TYTPS 9	M	6	2016	Prof.	Canada & Denmark	Eco-geography	Double first-class university
TYTPS 10	M	5	2014	Prof.	America & Japan	Ocean and earth sciences	Double first-class university
TYTPS 11	M	3	2012	Researcher	America & Singapore	Materials science and engineering	Double first-class university
TYTPS 12	M	3	2012	Researcher	America	Physics	Double first-class university
TYTPS 13	M	3	2012	Researcher	America	Astronomy and astrophysics	Double first-class university
TYTPS 14	M	3	2012	Prof.	America	Mathematics	Double first-class university
TYTPS 15	F	4	2012	Researcher	America	Life medicine	Double first-class university
TYTPS 16	M	1	2011	Researcher	Canada & America	Analytical chemistry	First-class discipline university
TYTPS 17	M	6	2015	Researcher	America	Energy science	First-class discipline university
TYTPS 18	M	3	2012	Researcher	Singapore & England	Optoelectronic information science	First-class discipline university
TYTPS 19	M	7	2016	Researcher	Singapore & America	Radiation medicine	First-class discipline university
TYTPS 20	M	5	2013	Researcher	America	Radiation medicine	First-class discipline university
TYTPS 21	M	8	2017	Researcher	England	Energy & materials	First-class discipline university
TYTPS 22	F	5	2013	Researcher	America	Energy science	First-class discipline university

Note: TYTPS refers to Thousand Youth Talent Program scholar.

practice. Zweig et al. (2004) not only put forward the concept of transnational capital of returned scholars, but also, through empirical research, illustrated that returned scholars have an advantage over the local talent in several aspects. The returnees choose to come back to China in order to translate their transnational capital accumulated abroad into career development capital in China. Transnational capital cannot function independently since it will only function in a certain space-time and institutional environment. Part of the reason for their return is that they believe that the knowledge, technology, and experience they have accumulated abroad can be put into greater use when they return home than if they stay abroad.

When the TYTPSs return home, they need to re-accumulate and transfer their transnational capital. Lu Xiao (2014) found that the impact of returnee status decreases with the passage of time. For their own development, the returnees need to re-establish a network of academic relations in China. The TYTP scholars, based on their academic status and disciplinary platform of their universities, as well as their honour of being awarded the title of Thousand Youth Talent, shall reinforce their transnational capital and endeavour to localize the capital.

5.3.2.2 The analytical framework for the academic career development of the TYTP awardees

The TYTPSs have achieved a promotion in their academic title after they return, directly changing from a post-doctoral fellow or assistant professor abroad, to an associate or full professor. This leap has saved them years of time that their domestic counterparts spend climbing the ladder for professional promotion. At the beginning of their career back in China, they lead the research team to carry out research and graduate student training in the capacity as a full professor or a post-doctoral supervisor. Of course, this kind of leap-frog development also brings challenges. First of all, in pushing forward the frontiers of scientific research, most of the academic research abroad is done in cooperation with the supervisor or the research team. After they return, they may not be able to continue with the research in the same direction or field. Second, they lack the accumulation and working experience in the domestic academic circle and have to explore various academic resources. Li et al. (2018) described the professional life of the TYTPSs through qualitative research. They found that, on the one hand, the TYTPSs have made irreplaceable contributions to the development of their disciplines, expanded disciplinary development, enhanced academic productivity, readily contributed to the development of the academic community, and advanced the internationalization of the disciplines. On the other hand, their academic development is also confronted with multiple dilemmas: The construction of the laboratory entails sustained research funding; the construction of the research platform consumes considerable energy and financial resources; they can only rely on graduate students to set up small teams since it is difficult to recruit the ideal competent core personnel for the discipline, which results in greater pressure that they must face.

In order to analyze the process, patterns, and influencing factors of the academic career development of the TYTP scholars, an analytical framework is constructed based on literature review, logical thinking, and field investigation (see Figure 5.1).

124 *From returning to taking root*

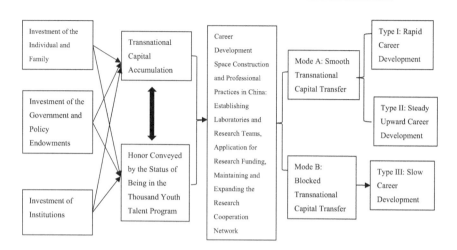

Figure 5.1 An analytical framework for the career development of the Thousand Youth Talent Program Scholars.

As shown in Figure 5.1, the career path for the TYTPSs is as follows: The investment in education of the individual, family, institution, and government and policy endowments – transnational capital accumulation and the honour conveyed by the status of being in the TYTP – career development space construction and professional practice in China – transnational capital transfer – career development. The cultural and human capital (educational qualifications, knowledge, experience, capabilities) accumulated before returning to China will not only manifest its value through academic practice, but will also have increased in value through the acquisition of the "Thousand Youth Talent" status. The title of the TYTPSs is not only the symbolic capital endowed by the policy, but also an academic position and role constructed through the interaction between an individual and the academic community in the relevant field. Such a status is capable of propelling and encouraging the academic career development of the TYTP awardees, which is reflected not only in the privilege and promotion paths granted by the policy, but also in the difference between them and other returnees as well as domestic scholars in accessing resources. Through the operation and transformation of human capital and social capital in both domestic and international academic spaces, the TYTP scholars gain a continuous accumulation, transfer, and appreciation of capital. Their knowledge production process is also based on communication and grafting between domestic and international academic spaces.

The academic practice of the TYTP scholars after they return to China includes the construction of their career development space, the establishment of laboratories and research platforms, the establishment of research teams, applications for research funding, the maintenance and expansion of the cooperative research network, knowledge production, and talent development in national and international academic networks. In the course of translating all kinds of capital into their academic career practice after they return home, due to internal and external factors, their transnational capital transfer shows two modes: Mode A, which has a smooth transfer and mode B which has a blocked transfer. Mode A enables rapid career development of individuals (Type I) and steady upward development (Type II). Model B shows slow and difficult career development (Type III). Obviously, this section focuses on the early stage of career development for the TYTP awardees, i.e. within seven years after they began to work. Follow-up research is needed to study their development at later stages.

5.3.3 Research findings

5.3.3.1 The growth trajectory and capital accumulation of the TYTP awardees

5.3.3.1.1 THE ACADEMIC GROWTH TRACK AT HOME AND ABROAD

The capital accumulation of the TYTP scholars is comparatively more than the whole higher education stage and post-doctoral stage. After returning to China, they continue to accumulate their human and social capital. The TYTP scholars go through a long process of growth through obtaining their bachelor's degree, their master's degree, and their doctor's degree, and pursuing post-doctoral study. Their pre-employment growth period is also a period of human and social capital accumulation. As indicated by the interviewees' CVs, 22 of the TYTP scholars have studied and worked abroad for an average of 8.5 years; among them, the shortest time abroad was 4 years and 15 years for the longest. All the TYTP scholars have received excellent higher education and have the experience of studying and working in famous universities or research institutions abroad. Table 5.3 summarizes three main modes of educational background of the TYTP awardees. Type I is the domestic-educated mode; the TYTP scholar 4, TYTPS 6, and TYTPS 10 belong to this type. They have received undergraduate and postgraduate education in the Chinese mainland, went abroad for post-doctoral studies for one to two terms, and then returned to China for work. Type II is a mixed training type A. The young researchers get their bachelor's degree and master's degree in China, and then go abroad for further study. TYTPS 1, TYTPS 2, TYTPS 3, TYTPS 5, TYTPS 8, TYTPS 9, and TYTPS 14 belong to this type. This type can be further divided into A1 and A2. A1 refers to those who engage in post-doctoral research after obtaining the doctoral degree abroad; A2 refers to those who return to China after obtaining the master's and the doctor's degrees and foreign post-doctoral experience. Type III is the mixed training type B. This group of young scholars (TYTPS 7, TYTPS 11, TYTPS 13, TYTPS 15) obtain their bachelor's degree in China and the master's degree abroad, do post-doctoral study abroad, and then return to China for work.

The higher education and post-doctoral study experience of the TYTP scholars belong to the human capital and social capital accumulation process during their apprenticeship, which can be summarized as follows: First, the three types of training patterns show that China's higher education has laid a solid foundation for the growth of young academic talent. In particular, Type I, the TYTP scholars who

Table 5.3 TYTPS' higher education and training background

Type	Bachelor education	Master education	Doctoral education	Post-doctoral training
Type I domestic education background: Bachelor & Master & Doctoral degrees in China + post-doctoral training abroad	domestic	domestic	domestic	overseas
Type II mixed education background – A1 type: Bachelor & Master degrees in China + Doctoral degree & post-doctoral training abroad	domestic	domestic	overseas	overseas
Type II mixed education background – A2 type: Bachelor & Master degrees in China + Master & Doctoral degrees & post-doctoral training abroad	domestic	domestic & overseas	overseas	overseas
Type III mixed education background B: Bachelor degree in China + Master & Doctoral degrees & post-doctoral training abroad	domestic	overseas	overseas	overseas

receive a Chinese domestic education and academic training for their bachelor's, master's, and doctor's degrees, and then they do post-doctoral study or short-term work abroad, which fully shows that with the in-depth implementation of the double first-class in China, Chinese universities have all the necessary capabilities to cultivate young scholars. Second, having a mixed international and domestic higher education and post-doctoral study experience is conducive to the cultivation of young academics and to their capital accumulation in the academic space at home and abroad. Third, the post-doctoral study experience at foreign prestigious universities has become a stepping stone for young scholars to be selected into the TYTP. All of the participants have, for a period of time, done post-doctoral study in prestigious universities or research institutions abroad and entered into international leading academic centres, where they have accumulated academic research capabilities and academic relationships and thus laid the foundation for their own academic development and the manifestation of their strengths in the future. As domestic research universities implicitly emphasize the conditions of having international experience when recruiting faculty, those who have received undergraduate and postgraduate training in China tend to do post-doctoral research in developed countries for a period of time, in order to enhance their competitiveness in the academic labour market after returning to China. Among the interviewees, those who have obtained all the bachelor's, master's, and doctor's degrees and done post-doctoral study abroad are very rare, and maybe such talent tend to stay abroad.

5.3.3.1.2 IDENTITY CONSTRUCTION AND TRANSNATIONAL SOCIAL CAPITAL ACCUMULATION

Studying at well-known universities abroad is not only a process of transnational human capital and the accumulation of social relations, but also a process of identity construction. As young scientists, the TYTP scholars have been enrolled in prestigious universities abroad, so they are members of the academic network of prestigious universities, boasting resources, qualifications, identities, and labels related to the prestigious universities, which hold a far-reaching impact on their future academic career development. As illustrated by TYTP scholar 3,

> For many students in Japan, they have the special title "students from Tokyo University", which indicates they are very intelligent (so this is an honour). Yes. That was one of the factors motivating me to enter the University of Tokyo, and the platform in itself provided a good opportunity for me because during my stay at the University of Tokyo, I was in contact with all of the top scientists in Japan. The people in my own circle and those I get along with are all the best in Japan.

5.3.3.2 The construction of career development space for the TYTP awardees

The construction of career development space for the TYTP scholars not only involves the physical environment and laboratory space, but also research teams, research funding, projects, scientific research partnerships, and interpersonal networks.

5.3.3.2.1 LABORATORY AND DISCIPLINARY PLATFORM CONSTRUCTION

The laboratory and scientific research conditions are essential to meet the needs of experimental science. Most of the interviewees have set up independent laboratories, but some of the TYTP scholars worry that the funding for the operation of the laboratory platform may not be sustainable after the TYTP term expires, and they have to apply for projects from the government, the non-public sector, and corporate enterprises. In addition to setting up laboratories, the TYTP scholars rely on the overall scientific research platform of the discipline to build academic teams. For example, the "Master (Academician[1] – a member of a body of elected elite scientists) + Team Development Mode" initiated by University B in the 1990s has exerted notable influence upon the improvement of the overall discipline. TYTPS 17 strongly agrees with this mode, which in his view, provides the young scientist with a good development platform:

> University B has been seeking to develop and improve the master + team development mode since the 1990s. If a master is followed by a group of young and middle-aged scientists, a research direction will be established in a timely manner. For young people to go for innovation, my experience shows that you still need a platform to rely on; to be independent too soon may not be such a good thing. It's better to work on a platform.

5.3.3.2.2 BUILDING SMALL AND MEDIUM-SIZED SCIENTIFIC RESEARCH TEAMS

There are two modes for the TYTP scholars to build a research team for the discipline: One is to join a research team which is led by a senior professor, and the other is to build an independent disciplinary team. Some TYTP awardees rely solely on their own independent research teams; while some make use of both models.

The research teams of the TYTP scholars are usually small in size and mainly made up of postgraduates, with the number and competence of the team members subject to restrictions. As shown in Table 5.4, the research teams of the TYTP scholars are mostly small and mid-sized teams, with less than ten members who are mostly working towards a master's degree or a doctor's degree in each of the teams. Among the interviewees, six of them have no more than five members in their teams; a small number of the people in the TYTP who returned to China relatively early have big research teams. Due to the preference for foreign academic degrees and educational backgrounds in the domestic academic community, outstanding undergraduates and postgraduates prioritize going abroad for further study; PhDs choose to go abroad to do post-doctoral work in order to accumulate transnational capital and realize the appreciation of their human capital. The interviewees reported that the recruitment

Table 5.4 TYTP scholars' research teams

Interviewees	Year of return	Professor, Associate Professor, Assistant Professor	Research assistant	Postdoc	Doctoral student	Master student	Total number
TYTPS 1	2014	0	0	0	2	3	5
TYTPS 2	2015	0	0	1	2	2	5
TYTPS 3	2014	0	2	0	2	2	6
TYTPS 4	2015	0	0	1	4	2	7
TYTPS 5	2011	0	1	0	5	3	9
TYTPS 6	2011	0	1	1	6	9	17
TYTPS 7	2012	2	1	0	7	2	12
TYTPS 8	2011	0	1	0	3	3	7
TYTPS 9	2016	0	1	1	1	1	4
TYTPS 10	2014	0	0	0	1	2	3
TYTPS 11	2012	0	0	0	4	3	7
TYTPS 12	2012	0	0	1	1	2	4
TYTPS 13	2012	0	0	0	4	1	5
TYTPS 14	2012	6	0	8	4	1	19
TYTPS 15	2012	0	1	1	5	4	11
TYTPS 16	2012	0	0	1	2	7	10
TYTPS 17	2017	0	0	0	2	6	8
TYTPS 18	2012	2	1	4	2	8	17
TYTPS 19	2016	0	0	0	2	8	10
TYTPS 20	2013	7	3	3	6	18	37
TYTPS 21	2017	0	0	2	3	9	14
TYTPS 22	2016	0	0	1	3	8	12

of postgraduates and post-doctoral students was constrained by research funds and universities' status, and it was difficult to arrange staff according to research needs.

Two TYTP scientists working in a double first-class university shared the dilemmas encountered by them in building research teams:

> I think the gap between China and foreign countries does not lie in hardware or funding. In fact, what we lack most is the talent. We cannot recruit competent personnel, and our postgraduates aren't good enough to do the work. We have good ideas, while others still have good ideas. Although my ideas are comparable to those of our foreign counterparts, like those from MIT and Harvard, it may take a good three years to materialize my ideas because I have no good helpers since many talented students have gone to the US. That is the crux of the problem. It's hard to recruit excellent and really insightful people since competent and ambitious people have gone abroad. This is the point. Moreover, national policy guidance plays a role here. One must have overseas experience to be accepted. Even if you have done great at home, you still need to go abroad, which is dictated by the national policy. So, everyone goes abroad for as long as they can.
> (TYTPS 1)

> My academic team consists of four PhDs and one master. To be honest, there is one thing that is different from what I expected. When I was abroad, I thought it might be hard to get funding and there should be many students back in China. But when I am back, things are opposite to what I thought. After I came to XX University, I found there was no problem to get research funding through this platform. However, it is hard to recruit competent students. It is hard to recruit excellent postgraduates since many of the undergraduates are going abroad. Most of the postgraduate students are recruited from outside this university, and to be frank, I'm very dissatisfied with some of the postgraduates' academic performance.
> (TYTPS 13)

5.3.3.2.3 ACCESS TO RESEARCH PROJECTS AND FUNDING

The TYTP scholars are more successful in applying for research projects and obtaining research funding than domestic scholars. Most of them engage in independent scientific research projects, and some of them also conduct a number of scientific research projects in cooperation with teams of their own and other universities. On the whole, they enjoy abundant research funding, which indicates that the increase of national investment in scientific research is conducive to promoting the development of scientific research and the growth of young scientists. For instance, TYTPS 13 illustrated,

> I thought it would be easy for us to recruit good students, but harder to access funds. However, when I came back, I found that the funding is not a problem. I have research funding from the TYTP, and I get the funding support from the

National Science Foundation. Moreover, some senior researchers have invited me to join their big projects. I have also joined in the "project 973", and the key project of the Ministry of Science and Technology, in other words, I have joined quite a few important projects and the funding was never a problem.

5.3.3.2.4 CONDUCTING COOPERATIVE SCIENTIFIC RESEARCH AND BUILDING INTERPERSONAL NETWORKS

For the returnees who are selected into the TYTP, the research cooperation and interpersonal network construction is sometimes smooth and at other times is tough. A major factor for the smooth development of the TYTP scholars is that they have already joined the key discipline platform. In terms of disciplinary development in research-oriented universities, the development of some key disciplines adopts the "master (academician) + scientific research team" approach, which is very conducive to the growth of the TYTP scholars and the development of disciplines. TYTPS 20 describes the development of his research team:

> Our research teams are like this: our college is under the leadership of Academician XX, and our team is under my charge. I have won the support of the National Science Fund for Distinguished Young Scholars this year or the title of "Outstanding Youth" (QY); and I am also a TYTPS and EY (short for "Excellent Youth", meaning those selected into the Science Fund Program for Distinguished Young Scholars). I lead some young people, and we are a very young team. Our members are mostly born after 1985 or in the 1990s, including laboratory assistants, lecturers, associate professors, and research assistants, all of whom add up to about ten.

However, the tendency of overemphasizing the quantified academic performance in domestic academic evaluation system and the rule of recognizing only the contribution of the first author and the first person in charge are not conducive to promoting cooperation among scholars. As TYTPS 13 elaborated,

> [In scientific research] I think maybe 60% of work is done by myself and 40% is done through cooperation with other people, mainly with returnees. All the young people here are returnees. Why is it difficult for domestic scholars and researchers to have substantial cooperation? One reason is related to the cultural factor. Everyone wants to be in charge of the project. The other reason is related to the scientific research recognition and evaluation system, which only recognizes the first author and the first person in charge, and thus actually discourages cooperation.

5.3.3.3 The patterns of the academic career development of the TYTP awardees

How can young scientists who are well educated abroad transfer their research paradigms, academic networks, knowledge, and technology to China? Will they be

From returning to taking root 131

able to continue their innovation and academic productivity after leaving the relative academic centres? What are the milieu and development status of the TYTP scholars during the process of their returning to work in China?

The academic career development of the TYTP scholars is positively correlated with their contribution to, and role in, the disciplinary construction, and there are internal differences in the academic career development among the TYTP scholars after they returned home. The TYTP awardees who enjoy smooth academic career development make more prominent contributions to disciplinary development while those who are struggling with academic career development make limited contributions to the disciplinary development, or even fail to conduct original research, and experience a mediocre academic performance and have a declining sense of fulfilment, as well as a poor sense of belonging to the discipline and organization. According to empirical observation, it is true that some returnees can hardly acclimatize or find it difficult to innovate after their return to China.

In the process of the TYTP awardees returning to work in China, supporting measures and policies for them at different levels show certain differences, which have a great impact on the TYTP awardees in the early stage of their career development. As for the institutional support, there is mainly policy support from the university and the discipline (college).

The college provides a microenvironment for academic career development; the discipline community, the funds, and facilities provided by the college exert a significant impact on the TYTP awardees. Due to factors related to individuals, organizations, disciplines, and policies, the academic career development of the TYTP scholars show different development patterns, which can be classified into fast-developing, steadily rising, and slow-developing patterns. The characteristics of, and factors behind, these patterns will be explained through the analysis upon the interview data below.

Table 5.5 shows the three types of career development of the TYTP scholars from the five aspects which consist of interpersonal relationships and organizational support, financial resources and funding, scientific research projects, laboratory and team building, research direction, and academic publication.

5.3.3.3.1 TYPE I: RAPID CAREER DEVELOPMENT

Most of the TYTP awardees enjoy rapid career development, and 10 out of the 22 interviewees belong to this type. With their academic accumulation, favourable policy conditions, and good academic platform, they boast rapid academic career development. They have successfully established research teams, built scientific research laboratories, entered the core circle of the domestic discipline community, applied for scientific research projects, and published high-quality research papers.

The TYTP scholars in rapid career development follow a straight upward path in professional development. After they returned to China, in the early stage of their career development they have been recognized and have been appointed as heads of the research teams or entrusted with important missions. TYTPS 7 has won the honour of EY; TYTPS 20 has won the honour as Excellent Youth (EY)

Table 5.5 Analysis of three types of career development of the TYTP scholars

Type	Interpersonal relationship and organizational support	Research funding and research projects	Lab and team building	Research interests	Publications	Interviewees
Type I: Rapid career development	Good	Sufficient funding and research projects	Sufficient physical space and laboratory facilities; good quantity and quality of research team members	Continue + extend	Both high quality and quantity	TYTPS 1, 3, 4, 5, 7, 14, 15, 17, 20, 21
Type II: Steadily upward career development	Good	Sufficient funding and research projects	Physical space, laboratory facilities, and the quality of the team members are relatively good	Continue + extend	Small quantity and high quality or high quantity and relatively high quality	TYTPS 2, 6, 8, 11, 12, 16, 18, 22
Type III: Slow career development/ start-up career development	Insufficient interpersonal cooperation and limited organizational support	Not enough funding, and a few research projects	Laboratory space and facilities still need to be built, and the number of team members is few and their quality is relatively poor	Break + explore new research areas	Low quantity but high quality	TYTPS 9, 10, 13, 19

and Outstanding Youth (OY); and TYTPS 3 and 21 are also typical cases in terms of achieving rapid development in young scientists.

The experience of TYTPS 3 can illustrate the career development of Type I. TYTPS 3 graduated from the double first-class University A in Shanghai. During his postgraduate stage, he studied under the guidance of a returnee from Japan. In 2005 he was honoured as an excellent graduate in Shanghai. He worked towards his doctor's degree, did post-doctoral work, and worked as a research fellow for nine years from 2005 to 2014 in Japan. After returning to China, he has been teaching at University A, his alma mater, and has published a series of high-level research papers and has won awards. After working for four years in China, he was appointed as the head of his department and the leader in his discipline.

TYTPS 3's success in academic growth testifies to the importance of one's educational background in relation to his/her academic growth. When he was working towards his master's degree, his supervisor recommended him to study in Japan. The three universities that have had the greatest academic influence on him (the double first-class university in China and well-known universities in Japan) have always been representative of the most important relationship network and social capital in his academic career. His outstanding educational background and rapport with his supervisor played very important roles in his academic growth. The Japanese university he studied at remains as an international platform that sustains his academic innovation and development after he returned to China. Each summer he goes to Japan to do research, to recruit his younger alumni and other returnees to become core members of his research team.

TYTPS 21 is another good example of a successful young scientist. He graduated from a double first-class university with a bachelor's degree; then graduated from a top university in the UK with a doctor's degree, and also did post-doctoral research in top universities in both China and the UK. After returning to China in 2017, he entered at University B, where he joined his post-doctoral supervisor's team. His former supervisor is an academician (*yuanshi*), who was also in charge of a laboratory there. As the academician supervisor cannot be in University B full time, he helped his supervisor lead the scientific research team.

TYTPS 21 is a lucky fellow because of his academician supervisor. Though he has been engaging in his discipline for a short period of time, his research develops smoothly. His research team consists of 14 members, including masters, PhDs, and post-doctoral fellows. From the selection of his employer to his being appointed as an independent PI (Principal Investigator), his academician supervisor always plays the role of the "significant other". The academician supervisor hopes that TYTPS 21 will help him play a big role at University B.

5.3.3.3.2 TYPE II: STEADILY UPWARD CAREER DEVELOPMENT

Among the interviewees, eight TYTP scholars indicated that their career is on a steady upward trajectory. These young scholars have set up their own independent laboratories and research teams to preside over, and participate in, many research projects. They have published a series of publications in core international journals, and accumulated

134 *From returning to taking root*

certain academic strengths; they are leading the scientific research team to explore frontier domains and building a team culture; they are satisfied with the work status of individuals and the team; and they are very optimistic about their future prospects. However, these young scholars do not have as strong academic connections and academic platforms as the Type I; but they stand firm and keep going upward.

5.3.3.3.3 TYPE III: SLOW CAREER DEVELOPMENT/START-UP CAREER DEVELOPMENT

There are very few TYTP scholars who have slow career development/start-up development. Their dissatisfaction with their own career development may be temporary, and after a period of time some may enjoy stable career development. The Type III includes the fellows selected into the TYTP who develop slowly in their careers (like TYTPS 10 and TYTPS 13) and those who have returned home for no more than two years (like TYTPS 9 and TYTPS 19). Some scholars refer to the phenomenon that the young returnees feel hindered in academic development as they experience an "academic hard landing" (Zhu, 2017). In fact, both TYTP scholars and other young returnee scholars face many challenges and changes when their identity shifts from an international student to an independent returnee scholar or even a disciplinary leader. If they do not have the support of the academic system, resource input, and interpersonal relationships at the level required for universities and disciplines, the so-called "academic hard landing" will occur during the period of transition. They may encounter many difficulties and setbacks regarding academic career promotion, unsatisfactory academic performance, lack of sustainable motivation for development, which are mainly attributable to the following factors: Failure to continue cooperation with overseas institutions, failure to go further in the direction of the research that was started abroad, a break in academic study and temporary academic depression, and the need to start over for academic accumulation and to explore new research directions; a less notable performance in getting academic papers published, the laboratory construction yet to be done, lack of core members in the academic team, the research direction is being explored, unsustainable research funding, and strenuous and time-consuming application for projects.

The TYTP scholars in their start-up career have to adapt to different circumstances. First, they change from a post-doctoral fellow to an independent research fellow and leader of the laboratory; second, they move from a foreign academic circle to the domestic one; third, they go from an overseas university research platform to the domestic university research platform. The period of adaptation differs from person to person. For some TYTP awardees, it takes just one or two years to get adapted to the new environment while for some others it takes three to five years or even longer. However, there are still a few of them that find it hard to get fully adapted to the new environment, so that they are finally content to be ordinary teachers and fail to fulfil the preset goals set for the TYTP.

Taking TYTPS 13 as an example. He is not satisfied with his career development after his return to China, and believes that the main reasons for the limited development are as follows:

> My academic publications are declining after my return to China because I fail to continue my cooperation with the academic community abroad (foreign supervisors). Instead, I explored new fields and directions at home. The students are not as good as I expected. The research conditions are less than satisfactory. Our department had promised me a machine room before my return, but even today I still haven't got that room yet.

Likewise, TYTPS 19 is not satisfied with the follow-up support of the university and his own career development. He was employed by University B as one of the TYTP scholars in 2016. He pointed out in the interview that the university generally failed to provide follow-up support for the TYTP awardees employed in recent years. He said,

> The young returnees over recent years generally indicate that after they were recruited, they were ignored to develop by themselves. You were given the salary according to the standard and recognized as a distinguished professor, but other supporting facilities were not sufficient.

TYTPS 19 further stated that when they were recruited, the capabilities of the TYTP awardee were almost at the same level, but their development differed sharply afterwards. The reason is that while a small number of the TYTP awardees enjoy support from certain academicians and develop rapidly, most of those who have little or no relationship with the academicians fail to gain policy support in the key period of growth and fail to play their expected role, which leads to a great waste of human resources (Xu, 2019).

5.3.3.4 Characteristics of the academic work of the TYTP awardee

5.3.3.4.1 TRANSNATIONAL: TRANSNATIONAL KNOWLEDGE GENERATION AND TRANSNATIONAL CAPITAL TRANSFORMATION

The transnational academic career development of the TYTP scholars is reflected in the transnational space for academic knowledge production, the transnational production process, and their international academic productivity. Through the transnational space construction for knowledge production, they have achieved their transnational academic and social capital transformation, knowledge production, and academic publishing.

For example, TYTPS 3 shares his story of transnational knowledge production and scientific research cooperation among three research-oriented universities in the US, Japan, and China as follows:

> The case with University P (of the United States) is like this: Professor L from University P is the top authority in our field. He is at an old age now, and his wife died the year before last year. Living alone, he finds that scientific research is too much for him, so he has transferred some of this basic stuff to my post-doctoral supervisor at University D in Japan so that we can carry on what he has done. This way, Professor L of University P is basically a back-up support for us.

TYTPS 3 has participated in transnational knowledge production for scientific research laboratories of three famous universities in the US, Japan, and China, and has directly entered the very frontier of the discipline. He has developed a very strong capacity for transnational cooperative scientific research. Most of the academic work in the traditional sense is done through cooperation, and knowledge production is attained within the same country. However, with the continuous development of transnational knowledge networks of migrant talent and the construction of transnational knowledge production spaces, knowledge production has transcended the boundaries between countries and institutions, giving rise to transnational knowledge production chains and academic chains. The academic relevance proposed by Gao Ziping (2014) refers to the pre-correlation, vertical correlation (the teaching inheritance), horizontal correlation (relevance to the academic team and academic communication network), and post-correlation (relevance to the academic orientation of the academic institutions and academic platforms which the returnees work with) between current research topics of returned scholars and the direction of their previous academic study.

5.3.3.4.2 INNOVATION: INNOVATIVE AND INTERDISCIPLINARY RESEARCH

The TYTP scholars are at the cutting edge of disciplinary development, who have the awareness and ability to explore new directions in interdisciplinary frontiers. Meanwhile, the TYTP awardee working on key disciplinary platforms often rely on the overall disciplinary platforms to carry out cooperative research and innovation. Many TYTP awardees admit that they are at the frontier of their research in China. For example, TYTPS 17 said,

> Because our own platforms at the Energy Institute and at the Institute for Energy Materials and Innovation are also very large, and they support research on nanotechnology, characterization, testing, batteries, or computational simulations. Here we have very close research cooperation because our leader (Academician X) holds that among the teams and the research groups of the same college and research institute, there should be horizontal cooperation. Thus, in recruiting new members, we have clear targets in mind.

5.3.3.4.3 SELF-MOTIVATION: THE INTERNAL DRIVE FOR WORK

Although the role of the external policies and incentives for the academic career development of the TYTP scholars cannot be underestimated, their academic achievement is mainly attributable to the completion of their work which is self-motivated. Their ambition for academic pursuits and having a strong passion for scientific research and an academic profession are the key to their career success. They choose their academic career out of interest. Their interest in conducting scientific research outweighs their interest in administration, so most of them tend to avoid administrative work.

5.3.3.4.4 THE TRANSCENDENCE IN THE FORMATION OF ACADEMIC DEVELOPMENT PATHS ENDOWED BY THE STATUS OF TYTP SCHOLARS

Due to the effect of the policy on the TYTP awardee, the academic career development path of the TYTP scholar differs from that of ordinary teachers and returnees. Instead of achieving step-by-step promotion and development, they seem to have leap-frogs in professional promotion and undergo a quick identity transformation. Upon their return, they soon change from a post-doctoral fellow to a professor, and then the leader of the laboratory or the discipline. There is tension between their quick academic promotion and the accumulation of their academic reputation and academic status. The "label" has the implicit function of enhancing the reputation and prestige of the young fellow, generating a halo effect such that the young fellow is more valued by his leaders, colleagues, and students at the institution. Explicitly, the young fellow gets the job title promotion, greater economic and material benefits, leadership positions, and greater responsibilities. The label also brings invisible high expectations and more responsibilities; the TYTP scholars need to change from a super post-doctoral fellow to a professor within a short period of transition after they begin to work. In this process, they face all kinds of pressures and challenges.

5.3.3.4.5 OPPORTUNITIES AND CHALLENGES THAT COEXIST FOR ACADEMIC CAREER DEVELOPMENT

The TYTP scholars are provided with various degrees of policy support and favourable conditions for rapid academic development, but meanwhile they still face many difficulties and challenges. First of all, after the employment period of the TYTP is over, they face challenges related to resources and sustainable development in the construction of academic platforms and laboratories. Second, they face the contradiction between the long cycle of knowledge production and the short cycle of assessment. The recruitment and assessment for the TYTP at universities are both subject to a short cycle of less than five years, and the assessment is dominated by the examination that tends to quantify the research results. Third, there are challenges of talent recruitment and team structure in building research teams, and it is difficult to recruit high-quality researchers. Fourth, the young scientists face more substantial academic responsibilities, workloads, and psychological pressure. These young people work under great pressure for long hours and face heavy workloads every day. Sometimes they are worn out in trying to strike a balance between their personal life and work. In the process of interviewing the TYTP awardees, they generally indicated that they face extreme work and psychological pressures. On the one hand, this pressure is brought about by the evaluation and examination from the external institutional environment. For example, some colleges and universities require the TYTP awardee to compete for projects funded by the NSFC, to publish high-level papers in prestigious international journals, and to compete to win the title of "Outstanding Youth" (another talent programme in China). For the interviewees, it is normal to work overtime, and quite a number of them won't go home until 10 p.m. Besides, various laboratory and scientific research management work also makes them feel pressed for time. On the other hand, they feel anxiety because of the pursuit of their academic careers and ambitions. Some young scholars feel that after returning to China, their efficiency and scientific research performance are not as good as expected, and the halo and expectation conveyed by the status as one of the TYTP scholars has caused them to experience associated pressure.

This section outlines the academic growth trajectory and the process of transnational capital accumulation of the TYTP scholars through the completion of an in-depth field investigation, and describes how different forms of transnational capital impact the academic development of the TYTP scholars after their return as well as the mechanism therein. The study found that the majority of the TYTP scholars have smoothly set up laboratories and discipline platforms, established research teams, obtained research funding, and built interpersonal networks thanks to external support that has been provided and their own strengths, while constructing their own career development space. The human capital, cultural capital, and social capital of the TYTP scholars are the main transnational capital owned by them. Based on that, their status as returnees and their special "status" after being selected into the TYTP also translates into a kind of capital equivalent to a cultural symbol which affects their academic development, resource access, and status acquisition. The process of transformation and spread of transnational capital is integrated into their professional practices. Through teaching, talent training, and knowledge production, transnational capital exerts influence upon individuals and makes contributions to disciplines and organizations. In terms of the academic promotion and research practice of the TYTP awardee, the transnational social network and academic background have a direct influence on their transnational cooperative scientific research and academic publication. In the process of transnational capital transfer, there are three types of academic career development, depending on how smooth the degree of transition is, i.e. the fast-developing type, steadily rising type, and slow-developing type. The academic work of the TYTP scholar presents distinctive features among its members, i.e. transnational, innovative, self-motivated, and the transcendence in academic promotion. In the meantime, the talent also face heavy pressure, multiple difficulties, and challenges in terms of their work.

5.4 Reflections on the professional development of Chinese academic returnees

5.4.1 *The circulation of talent in the global academic labour market and the transnational academic network*

There is a growing trend of transnational academic mobility due to globalization and world economic integration, which also accelerate and intensify the integration of the transnational academic labour market. The transnational flow of academic talent, especially top scientists and scholars, is more important than ever before. The flow of academic returnees in the international academic labour market has eventuated against the background of the rising global academic capitalism. In the context of liberalism, academic capitalism shows that the academic activities of HEIs in the US and other developed countries follow the principles of the market, with the law of market value and that of exchange value permeating the teaching and research activities of HEIs.

The outflow, return, and circulation of academics have resulted in the continuous construction and development of transnational academic networks. Therefore, the transnational flow of talent which has been investigated with one-way and static concepts needs to be reconsidered with the concepts of dynamic and multi-directional flow and incorporated social networks. Dynamic and multi-directional mobility indicate that scholars are always in a constant state of movement in different academic organizations and nodes, and the mobility direction is also multi-dimensional and uncertain. The academic relationship and academic communication network established through the flow play a more important role in the accumulation and transfer of the transnational capital. The movement of academic talent space leads to the spread of innovative knowledge and the construction of transnational knowledge production networks. The mechanism of such mobility is a market-dominated allocation mechanism, in which academic personnel, as the carrier of capital, decide whether they flow and how to flow according to the academic environment and development platform provided by different academic institutions.

However, the effect of talent policy on the academic growth of different returnees is hidden behind the successful implementation of the talent plan. From the angle of space and location, returnees from different institutions and regions are in different positions, which affects their access to resources and career development. The consequence of mobility is to change the institutional environment and career development space of the subject by changing the physical location. Mobility offers the subject transnational capital and access to new social networks, enhancing their ability to cross institutional spaces and boundaries. This chapter investigates the transfer and transformation of transnational academic capital and social capital owned by the returnees and the TYTP awardees from the individual and micro perspective.

5.4.2 Returnees realize the transfer and spread of transnational capital through academic work

The returnees impart the transfer and spread of transnational capital through transnational flow and the adoption of professional practices. Their movement from international to domestic academic fields and transfer from one organization to another enables the transfer of all kinds of transnational capital that is possessed and carried by them in the international and domestic dual academic spaces. At the same time, the accumulation of human capital and social resources is sustainable. After their return to China, they could further accumulate transnational human and social capital.

The transfer and spread of returnees' transnational capital is embodied in their professional practices. At the same time, the transnational capital transfer and the

140 *From returning to taking root*

conversion of returnees produce a spillover effect, i.e. the academic practice after their return to China has promoted the development of academic disciplines and institutions, trained academic talent, produced academic knowledge, and built networks and connections between domestic and international academic circles. The returnees act as a bridge between domestic and foreign academic communities, promoting international academic cooperation and exchanges among local colleagues and peers. They are committed to setting cutting-edge research fields and research directions, expanding the development platform of all disciplines, and cultivating new areas for disciplinary development.

5.4.3 The meaning and value of the identity of the TYTP awardee

The TYTP scholars are returnees who have been granted a special status, and have the cultural symbol and identity endowed by the dual status of returnees and TYTP. Identity is a kind of membership which is endowed by nature or constructed by a social system determining the qualifications, treatment, rights, and responsibilities of the individual with a certain identity in the group to which he or she belongs. In relation to the talent programme, the identity of the TYTP scholar is a title, a label, and a position.

Through the selection mechanism, the TYTPS are given a special status, which holds symbolic significance and serves the important function of institutionalization. In other words, it is advantageous for them to obtain academic status, get a promotion, and have access to academic resources. They have access to a range of materials, financial, and policy benefits from central and local governments. At the same time, the units and departments where the TYTPS work offer corresponding treatment to them, like directly granting them senior professional titles and the arranging of research assistants for them.

5.4.4 The phased and diversified characteristics of returnees' academic career development

The development of returnees' academic career shows phased characteristics, particularities, and diversity. During the transition period of shifting from a foreign to a domestic form of career development, the returnees and the TYTP scholars exemplify phased characteristics. The TYTP scholars and other returnees all have to undergo changes in terms of their workplaces and identities. From working in foreign countries to arriving in China, the geographical change in the returnees' workplace make them face a different space for academic activities. Their career development and academic growth necessitate not only their adaptation to the change from the overseas academic system environment to the domestic academic environment and disciplinary development space, but also their rapid change of identities and roles, i.e. their change from a post-doctoral fellow/researcher as a semi-independent scholar or as a member of a disciplinary team abroad, to an independent scientist and teacher at home. If the first change is to adapt to the new working environment and field (the institution, academic community, and academic work system), the second change is more about the change in the career development stages as well as the identities and roles of the returnees. These two changes are intertwined, which are reflected in their career development afterwards.

The TYTPS share similarities in terms of their academic career development with other academic returnees. In the meantime, there are still aspects that distinguish them from ordinary academic returnees. The similarities are as follows: First of all, the TYTPS and returnees who have no title put a premium on building their own academic status and achievements in domestic and international academic platforms and space through the transformation of transnational academic capital. Second, their own academic development is subject to the influence of the relationship between the individual and the organization, the disciplinary system, and the structural environment. The talent and their environment are in a mutually reshaping relationship.

The career development of the TYTPS typifies relatively special characteristics in that they enjoy obvious advantages in academic development. This particularity is mainly reflected in the special policy support that comes with their status and the special requirements and expectations of the government, institutions, and disciplines. At the same time, as an excellent group of young scientists, the TYTPS have higher expectations upon themselves and are more motivated to make achievements. Despite facing various similar tasks and backgrounds, the returned faculty members are not a homogeneous group, as evidenced by the internal variability among them. Their career development in a variety of states as revealed in this chapter fully demonstrates such disparities and the particularities of personal milieu.

Note

1 Academician refers to a member of a body of elected elite scientists of the Chinese Academy of Sciences and the Chinese Academy of Engineering.

References

Altbach, P. G. (2004). Globalization and the universities: Myths and realities in an unequal world. *Tertiary Education and Management*, *10*(1), 3–25.

Cao, C., & Suttmeier, R. P. (2001). China's new scientific elite: Distinguished young scientists, the research environment and hopes for Chinese science. *The China Quarterly*, *168*, 960–984.

Chao, L. Q. (2014). Gaoxiao gaocengci haiguirencai xianzhuang jiqi zuoyong yanjiu [Study on the status and role of high-level returned talents in Chinese universities–Focus on the recruitment program of global experts]. *Dongnanya Yanjiu [Southeast Asian Studies]*, *4*, 57–63.

Chen, C. G. (1994). Woguo liumei xuezhe huigui yixiang de diaocha yu fenxi (I) [Investigation and analysis of the intention of Chinese scholars studying in the United States to return to China (I)]. *Gaodeng Jiaoyu Yanjiu [Journal of Higher Education]*, *4*, 23–37.

Chen, C. G. (1995). Woguo liumei xuezhe huigui yixiang de diaocha yu Fenxi (II) [Investigation and analysis of the intention of Chinese scholars studying in the United

States to return to China (II)]. *Gaodeng Jiaoyu Yanjiu [Journal of Higher Education]*, *1*, 51–65.

Chen, C. G., Gao, L. Y., & Lou, X. L. (2000). Weishenme huiguo yu huiguohou zenmeyang: Dui 471wei huiguo renyuan de diaocha yanjiu [Why and what happens after returning: A survey of 471 returnees]. *Zhongguo Gaodeng Jiaoyu [China Higher Education]*, *Z1*, 46–49.

Chen, D. H., Duan, Y. B., & Pan, Z. J. (2015). Eryuan guanxi wangluo dui haigui kexuejia chanchu de yingxiang: Yi Zhongguo "Qianren Jihua" weili [The impacts of ambidextrous network on returnee scientists productivity: Evidence from the 1000-youth elite program in China]. *Zhongguo Keji Luntan [Forum on Science and Technology in China]*, *9*, 143–147.

Chen, X. F. et al. (2003). *Liuxue Jiaoyu de Chengben yu Shouyi: Woguo gaigekaifang yilai gongpai liuxue xiaoyi yanjiu [The cost and benefit of studying abroad: The efficiency of studying abroad was studied since the reform and opening era]*. Jiaoyu Kexue Chubanshe [Educational Science Press].

Gao, Z. P. (2014). Xueshu xiangguanxing weidu de haiwai ligongke liuxue rencai huiliu Yiyuan yanjiu [Analysis on wishes of inverse flow of science and engineering rencai studying aboard in the dimension of academic correlation]. *Ziran Bianzhengfa Yanjiu [Studies in Dialectics of Nature]*, *6*, 74–81.

Li, F., & Wu, D. (2016). Gaodeng jiaoyu beijing ruhe yingxiang butong xueke keji rencai chengzhang: Yi jiaoyubu changjiang xuezhe tepin jiaoshou weili [How higher education background influence the growth of scientific and technical talents in different disciplines: Taking changjiang scholars as an example]. *Gaodeng Jiaoyu Yanjiu [Journal of Higher Education]*, *10*, 42–48.

Li, G. X. (2013). *Gaoxiao haigui jiaoshi zhiye bushiying wenti de yanjiu [A study on un-adaptation of overseas returnees in Chinese universities]* [Unpublished master's dissertation]. East China Normal University.

Li, M. (2017). Zhongguo liumei xueshu rencai huiguo yixiang jiqi yingxiang yinsu fenxi [The willingness of returning to China and the push-pull factors leading to Chinese academics' staying in the United States]. *Fudan Jiaoyu Luntan [Fudan Education Forum]*, *2*, 79–86.

Li, M., Yang, R., & Wu, J. (2018). Translating transnational capital into professional development: A study of China's thousand youth talents scheme scholars. *Asia Pacific Education Review*, *19*(2), 229–239.

Li, Y. Y., & Zhu, J. W. (2018). Gaoxiao haigui qingnian jiaoshi shoupinqi gongzuo manyidu de diyu chayi yanjiu: Jiyu 2008–2017 nian 20 suo chengshi diaocha shuju de fenxi [A comparative analysis on young returnee faculty job satisfaction during early career in different cities-based on the data of 20 cites from 2008 to 2017]. *Gaodeng Jiaoyu Yanjiu [Journal of Higher Education]*, *11*, 56–63.

Liu, R. J. (2010). *Gaoxiao "Haigui" jiaoshi shengcun huanjing yu shengcun zhuangtai yanjiu [The study about living environment and state of overseas returnees in Chinese universities]* [Unpublished master's dissertation]. Shanghai Jiao Tong University.

Lu, X. (2014). Haigui kexuejia de shehui ziben dui zhiye jinsheng yingxiang de shizheng yanjiu [Social network and career advancement: An empirical study on Chinese academic labor market]. *Kexue yu Shehui [Science and Society]*, *2*, 49–62.

Lu, X., Hong, W., & He, G. X. (2014). Haigui kexuejia de xueshu yu chuangxin: Quanguo keji gongzuozhe diaocha shuju yu fenxi [Academic performance and innovation of overseas returning scientists: A national survey of science and technology personnel].

Fudan Gonggong Xingzheng Pinglun [Fudan Public Administrative Review], *12*(2), 7–25.
Ma, W. H., Ma, X. N., & Geng, Y. (2013). "Qianren Jihua" xuezhe huigui de dongyin xueshuv youshi yu tiaozhan [The return of "thousand talent plan" scholars: Motivations, academic advantages and disadvantages]. *Qinghua Daxue Jiaoyu Yanjiu [Tsinghua Journal of Education]*, *1*, 94–97+103.
Rosen, S., & Zweig, D. (2005). Transnational capital: Valuing academic returnees in a globalizing China. In C. Li (Ed.), *Bridging mind across the Pacific: US-China educational exchanges 1978–2003* (pp. 111–132). Lexington Books.
Sun, Y. L. (2016). Woguo gaocengci rencai xiangmu xuanba wenti yanjiu [Research on problems of high-level talent programs' selection in China]. *Zhongguo Renli Ziyuan Kaifa [Human Resources Development of China]*, *9*, 82–87+92.
Sun, Y. T., & Zhang, S. (2017). Haiwai qingnian xueshu rencai yinjin zhengce xiaoying fenxi: Yi "Qingnian Qianren Jihua" xiangmu weili [An empirical study on the policy effect of young academic brain gain: An example of the TYTP candidates]. *Kexuexue Yanjiu [Studies in Science of Science]*, *4*, 511–519.
Tian, H. S. (2012). *Gaocengci liuxue renyuan huigui dongji ji fazhan yingxiang yinsu yanjiu [The research on the influencing factors of the motivation and development for the high-level graduates returned from abroad]* [Unpublished doctoral dissertation]. Tianjin University.
Wang, H. Y. (2009). *Rencai Zhanzheng [The war for talent]*. CITIC Press.
Wang, H. Y. (2015). *Guoji Rencai Zhanlue Wenji [International talent strategy collection]*. Party Building Reading Press.
Wang, H. Y., & Miao, L. (2013). *Zhongguo Haigui Fazhan Baogao 2013 [Report on the development of Chinese returnees (2013)]*. Social Sciences Academic Press.
Wang, R. R. (2012). *Haiwai rencai huigui yu shehui shiying yanjiu [A study on the return of oversea talents and their social adaptation after flowing back to China]* [Unpublished doctoral dissertation]. East China Normal University.
Xu, J. H. (2019). *Gaoxiao gaocengci rencai yinjin jiqi dui xueke fazhan de zuoyong yanjiu [The recruitment of high-level talents and their role in the disciplinary development at public research universities in China]* [Unpublished master's dissertation]. East China Normal University.
Xu, R., Li, W. & Liu, X. X. (2014). Haigui jiaoshi dui gaoxiao guojihua jianshe de zuoyong tantao: Yi Shanghai Jiaotong Daxue weili [A case study of overseas returnees' role in university globalization]. *Ningbo Daxue Xuebao (Jiaoyu Kexue Ban) [Journal of Ningbo University (Educational Science Edition)]*, *1*, 54–56.
Xu, X. J. (2009). Haigui jiaoshi gongzuo manyidu diaocha fenxi [Survey and analysis of job satisfaction of "overseas returnees" teachers]. *Renli Ziyuan [Human Resources]*, *21*, 35–37.
Yu, X. F. (2009). *Jiyu gongzuo manyidu shijiao de gaoxiao haigui jiaoshi renli ziyuan guanli zhengce yanjiu [Research on human resource management policies of oversea teachers in universities based on the perspective of job satisfaction]* [Unpublished master's dissertation]. Fudan University.
Zhang, D. H., & Yuan, F. F. (2014). Gaoxiao qingnian haigui jiaoshi dui woguo xueshu tizhi de shiying [A study on the adaptation of junior returnee faculties to China's academic]. *Jiaoshi Jiaoyu Yanjiu [Teacher Education Research]*, *5*, 62–67.
Zhao, Q. (2010). *Guiguo shiying de goucheng weidu yingxiang yinsu jiqi yu gongzuo manyidu de guanxi yanjiu [The research on dimensions, antecedents and job satisfaction*

effect of repatriate adjustment] [Unpublished master's dissertation]. East China Normal University.

Zhao, W. H. (2010). Haigui boshi yu bentu boshi zhiye chengjiu bijiao: Jiyu quanguo boshi zhiliang diaocha de tongji fenxi [Comparison of career achievements between overseas and local doctorates: A statistical analysis based on national doctoral quality survey]. *Zhongguo Gaojiao Yanjiu [China Higher Education Research], 11,* 47–50.

Zhu, J. N. (2017). Xueshu Yingzhuolu. Gaoxiao wenke qingnian haigui jiaoshi de gongzuo shiying yanjiu ["Academic hard landing": The working adjustment of returning young faculty in humanities and social sciences at Chinese universities]. *Fudan Jiaoyu Luntan [Fudan Education Forum], 3,* 87–92.

Zweig, D., Changgui, C., & Rosen, S. (2004). Globalization and transnational human capital: Overseas and returnee scholars to China. *The China Quarterly, 179,* 735–757.

6 From a peripheral player to a major hosting country

Policies and practices on international students in China

Since the reform and opening-up, in particular after China advanced into the 21st century, the prominence of inbound international student mobility in China has seen rapid development. This was reflected in the increasing number of international students, the optimized proportion of the international student body, the pursuit of a higher level of education by international students, an increasing number of institutions actively recruiting international students, and an improved capability in terms of cultivating international students. Recruiting international students is a major component of the opening-up of China's higher education. In the international student market, China used to be mainly exporting rather than being the recipient country of international students. However, nowadays, it has become one of the major countries which is attracting and recruiting international students. In 2016, China has become the third largest recipient county in the world for international students after the US and the UK, and is occupying 10% of the international student market (Institute of International Education, 2016). However, it should be noted that there are still many problems and deficiencies in providing educational services for international students in China, which are mainly manifested in accordance with the unitary principle for the education of international students, the unreasonable proportion of the international student body, the lower educational level of international students, and the sources of international students originating mainly from neighbouring and developing countries. Additionally, there are a few aspects that need to be improved, including the macro-management system in higher education, the higher education management models that could not meet the needs of training international students, the ability in offering quality graduate education to international students, and the pedagogical model and curriculum system.

Based on the above circumstances, Section 6.1 and Section 6.2 of this chapter describe and analyze the features of the policy and practice surrounding international students in China since the reform and opening-up, with a focus on Shanghai. Section 6.3 reveals the reasons why international students choose to study in China and examines the adaptation of international students in China through a survey of international students conducted at three research universities in Shanghai. Section 6.4 summarizes the current problems that exist in education for international students in China and puts forward suggestions to improve the quality of education for international students.

DOI: 10.4324/9781003424611-6

6.1 The features of the policy and practice on educational services for international students in China

6.1.1 Policies on the education of international students in China

Since the reform and opening-up, the government has been continuously promoting inbound international student mobility and improving related policies and institutions for administration.

Educational services were initially offered to international students during the period between 1978 and 1992. The Ministry of Education (MoE) approved Beijing's Language and Culture Institute (now Beijing Language and Culture University) to receive students from a French university to come to China at their own expense to study Chinese for a short period of time. This was the starting point of education development for self-financed international students in China. In 1979, the State Council approved the *Request for Standards for Hosting Self-financed Foreign Students*, which provided a charging basis for self-financed foreign education in China. In 1985, the then State Education Commission and other ministries formulated the *Measures for the Administration of Foreign Students*. During this period, the central government was in charge of education for international students in China, while colleges and universities had not yet obtained full autonomy regarding this matter. Thereafter, inbound international student mobility into China showed a positive and rising trend and an increasingly diversified student body between 1985 and 1992.

A continuous improvement can be observed in terms of the administrative policies for education services relating to international students in China since 1993. For instance, in 2000, the MoE issued the *Administrative Regulations for Higher Education Institutions to Accept Foreign Students*, the *Notice on the Implementation of the Annual Evaluation System of Chinese Government Scholarships*, and the *Measures for the Annual Evaluation of the Chinese Government Scholarships*. The MoE also issued the *Notice on Reforming the Measures for the Management of Academic Credentials for Foreign Students* in 2001.

In February 2004, the MoE issued the *2003–2007 Action Plan for Revitalizing Education*, in which it identifies "expanding the scale, improving the level, ensuring the quality and normalizing the administration" (MoE, 2004) as general guidelines for work surrounding international students in China. According to the guidelines, the government adjusted and formulated relevant policies and regulations to optimize the learning environment in China in a timely manner, established an education evaluation system for international students, reformed the scholarship system, and increased funds for studying. This was done to make the Chinese government scholarships play a key role in facilitating inbound international student mobility to China, to enhance the competitiveness of Chinese government scholarships in the international student market, and to attract more high-quality international students to study in China. Moreover, the government also actively expanded the cooperation with foreign governments and enterprises to establish scholarship programmes for international students. On September 1, 2004, the Department of International Cooperation and Exchange for the MoE began working on the information management system for foreign students in China, which was promoted and has been available nationwide since 2006. This was followed by the *Trial Measures for the*

Electronic Diploma and Certificate Registration of Foreign Students in Higher Education Institutions issued in 2007, the *Notice on Adjusting the Standard of Living Expenses of Foreign Students Financed by Scholarships*, issued by the MoE and the Ministry of Finance in 2008, and the *Notice on Carrying Out Preparatory Education for International Undergraduate Students Sponsored by the Chinese Government Scholarship* issued by the MoE in 2009.

In 2010, the *Studying in China Program* was promulgated and implemented to promote the rapid expansion of foreign education in China. It proposed the goal of hosting 500,000 international students at all levels in China by 2020, which included 150,000 students receiving higher education at that time, making China the largest destination in Asia for international students. Moreover, it put forward the "principles" for foreign education, i.e. "expanding the scale, optimizing the structure, standardizing the administration and ensuring quality".

Since September 2014, the MoE and the Ministry of Finance (MoF) have revised the government scholarship standards for excellent international students studying in China. The scholarship values ranged from RMB 59,200 to RMB 66,200 for undergraduate students, from RMB 70,200 to RMB 79,200 for master students, and from RMB 87,800 to RMB 99,800 for doctoral students (People Daily Online, 2012).

As a guiding policy document, *Several Suggestions on the Opening-up of Education in the New Era* (promulgated and implemented in May 2016) proposed to facilitate the "Belt and Road Initiative",[1] expanded the financial support scope of the Chinese Government Scholarship Fund, and offered the "Silk Road" (equivalent to the "Belt and Road") Chinese Government Scholarship, financing 10,000 students from countries along the "Belt and Road" to study or research in China. In 2016, the MoE issued the "Belt and Road" *Educational Action Plan*, which has formulated a new route map for the opening-up of higher education. Studying in China has become a strategy for achieving common aspirations for China and the countries along the "Belt and Road". It is conducive to cultivating a number of people who "know China", "become friends of China", and "become intimate with China". In particular, it is helpful for attracting a number of international students to study in China, pursuing PhDs., master's, and undergraduate degrees, as well as national elites and industry leaders to further their education (Ma & Zhou, 2018).

In the meantime, the central government attaches great importance to foreign education and the effective management of international students. The MoE issued *Regulations for the Quality of Higher Education for International Students in China (Trial)* in October 2015, in which the training goals, recruitment and admission, teaching and learning, administration and services, and support have all been clearly standardized.

6.1.2 The characteristics of international students in China

In the past 20 years, the scale of inbound international student mobility has gradually expanded, the level of education for international students has been improved, and the number of higher education institutions (HEIs) that accept international students has also increased. Hence, international students in China have demonstrated

148 *From a peripheral player to a major hosting country*

certain developmental characteristics in terms of the scale, countries of origin, types of education, and disciplinary distribution.

6.1.2.1 The increase of international students in China

The numbers of inbound international students between 1996 and 2018 are shown in Figure 6.1, the number of international students in China has increased from 41,200 in 1996 to 492,200 in 2018, indicating an increase of nearly 12 times in 20 years. After China's admission into the World Trade Organization (WTO) in December 2001, the number of international students in China between 2002 and 2008 showed a more noticeable rising trend relative to the period between 1996 and 2000. The average annual growth rate of international students in China was about 13% between 1996 and 2002, about 17% between 2002 and 2008, and 8% after 2008.

6.1.2.2 International students in China mainly from Asia, with a fast growth trend from the region along the "Belt and Road" countries

In the past decade, international students in China mainly come from Asian countries. Moreover, the number of international students from the region along the "Belt and Road" countries have increased dramatically. Between 2007 and 2016, international students in China mainly came from Asia, but the proportion of Asian students showed a downward trend, from 72.5% in 2007 to 59.8% in 2016. The largest growth

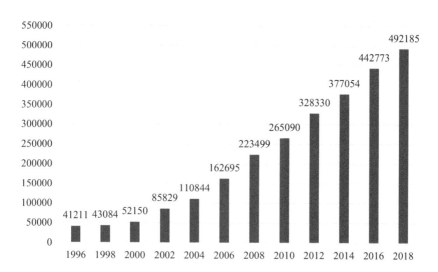

Figure 6.1 The number of international students in China between 1996 and 2018.

Source: The MoE (2018) *Department of International Cooperation and Exchange, Concise Statistics of International Students in China: 1996-2016*. Beijing: Department of International Cooperation and Exchanges, Ministry of Education; Ministry of Education (2019, 12 April), 2018 Statistics on International Students in China. Retrieved July 26, 2019, from http://www.moe.gov.cn/jyb_xwfb /gzdt_gzdt s5987/ 201904 /t20190412_377692.html.

rate is attributed to African students, increasing from 5,915 (3%) in 2007 to 61,594 (14%) in 2016, with an annual growth rate of 20% (Li & Fang, 2018).

Countries along the "Belt and Road" regions have emerged as a new source of international students' growth in China. China's education has different attractions for students from different countries. Asian students prefer to study in China. As shown in Table 6.1, the top five countries of origin of international students in China in most years are mainly Asian countries, such as South Korea, Japan, Indonesia, Vietnam, and Thailand, while only the US and Germany are shortlisted among Western countries. After China's accession to the WTO in 2001, the number of international students from different countries coming to China has been growing rapidly. Although the proportion of South Korean students in China had decreased yearly between 2003 and 2010, South Korea has almost always ranked first in terms of the number of international students for the past 20 years. The proportion of Japanese students had also decreased during the same period. After 2015, Japan has no longer been among the top five in terms of the number of international students in China. However, the number of international students from the

Table 6.1 Top 5 countries of origin of international students in China, 1998–2018

Year/country	Top 1	Top 2	Top 3	Top 4	Top 5
1998	Japan 14,524	South Korea 10,008	The US 3,832	Indonesia 1,770	Germany 89
2000	South Korea 16,787	Japan 13,806	The US 4,280	Indonesia 1,947	Germany 1,270
2002	South Korea 36,100	Japan 16,000	The US 7,400	Indonesia 2,900	Vietnam 2,300
2004	South Korea 43,617	Japan 19,059	The US 8,480	Vietnam 4,382	Indonesia 3,750
2006	South Korea 57,504	Japan 18,363	The US 11,784	Vietnam 7,310	Indonesia 5,652
2008	South Korea 66,806	The US 19,914	Japan 16,733	Vietnam 10,396	Russia 8,939
2010	South Korea 62,957	The US 19,668	Japan 16,808	Indonesia 13,177	Vietnam 13,018
2012	South Korea 63,488	The US 24,583	Japan 21,126	Indonesia 16,675	Russia 14,971
2014	South Korea 62,923	The US 24,203	Indonesia 21,296	Russia 17,202	Japan 15,057
2016	South Korea 70,540	The US 23,838	Indonesia 23,044	Pakistan 18,626	India 18,717
2018	South Korea 50,600	Indonesia 28,608	Pakistan 28,023	India 23,198	The US 20,996

Sources:
1. The MoE (2018). Department of International Cooperation and Exchange, *Concise Statistics of International Students in China: 1996–2016*. Beijing: Department of International Cooperation and Exchanges, Ministry of Education.
2. Ministry of Education (April 12, 2019). 2018 Statistics on International Students in China. Retrieved July 20, 2019, from http://www.moe.gov.cn/jyb_xwfb/gzdt_gzdts5987/ 201904 /t20190412_377692.html.

150 *From a peripheral player to a major hosting country*

US had increased yearly between 1998 and 2018. It even ranked among the top five in terms of the number of international students in China. This shows that the structure of the international student body in China has gradually changed, with a trend of source countries of international students in China diversified.

As shown in Table 6.2, the proportions and numbers for South Korean, Japanese, and American students in China have been decreasing yearly since 2004. The proportion of South Korean students had decreased from 39.4% in 2004 to 10.3% in 2018, and that of American students had decreased from 7.7% to 4.3%, while the proportion of Japanese students has decreased more severely, from 17.2% to 2.9%. In contrast, the students from countries along the "Belt and Road" regions have become a new source of growth. The top 15 countries of origin of international students in China in 2016 included 10 "Belt and Road" countries (Ma & Zhou, 2018). According to the 2018 statistics on international students in China, the statistics on the top ten countries of origin were: 50,600 from South Korean, 28,608 from Thailand, 28,023 from Pakistan, 23,198 from India, 20,996 from the US, 19,239 from Russia, 15,050 from Indonesia, 14,645 from Laos, 14,230 from Japan, and 11,784 from Kazakhstan (MoE, 2019). Among them, Pakistan, India, Russia, Indonesia, Laos, Kazakhstan, Vietnam, Bangladesh, Mongolia and Malaysia were all countries along the "Belt and Road" regions.

The structure of international students in China has been gradually optimized, but the proportion of students who hold academic degrees still needs to be improved. As far as the academic degree types of foreign students in China are concerned, Table 6.3 shows that non–degree-seeking students once reached more than 70% of the total number of foreign students before 2004, but this showed a gradual downward trend after 2005. While the degree-seeking students have taken on an upward trend, the proportion of these kinds of students had increased from 26.37% in 1998

Table 6.2 Proportions of Korean, American, and Japanese students to international students in China, 2004–2018

Year	Total number of international students in China	Korean students (%)	Japanese students (%)	American students (%)
2004	110,844	39.4	17.2	7.7
2006	162,695	35.3	11.3	7.2
2008	238,184	27.1	6.5	7.8
2010	265,090	25.2	6.3	7.5
2012	328,330	19.3	6.4	7.5
2014	377,054	16.7	4.0	6.4
2016	442,773	15.9	3.1	5.4
2018	492,185	10.3	2.9	4.3

Sources:
1. Ministry of Education (2018). *Concise Statistics of International Students in China: 2004–2016.* Beijing: Department of International Cooperation and Exchanges, Ministry of Education.
2. Ministry of Education (April 12, 2019). 2018 Statistics on International Students in China. Retrieved July 20, 2019, from http://www.moe.gov.cn/jyb_xwfb /gzdt_gzdt s5987/ 201904 /t20190412_377692 .html.

Table 6.3 Types of international students in China, 1998–2018

Year	Degree-seeking students Number	Percentage (%)	Non–degree-seeking students Number	Percentage (%)
1998	11,362	26.37	31,722	73.63
1999	11,479	25.67	33,232	74.33
2000	13,703	26.28	38,447	73.72
2001	16,650	40.39	45,219	59.61
2002	21,055	24.54	64,745	75.46
2003	24,616	31.67	53,099	68.33
2004	31,616	28.52	79,228	71.48
2005	44,851	31.79	96,236	68.21
2006	54,859	33.72	107,836	66.28
2007	68,213	34.89	127,290	65.11
2008	80,005	35.80	143,494	64.20
2009	93,450	39.23	144,734	60.77
2010	107,432	40.53	157,658	59.47
2011	118,837	40.61	173,774	59.39
2012	133,509	40.66	194,821	59.34
2013	147,890	41.48	208,609	58.52
2014	164,394	43.60	212,660	56.40
2015	184,799	46.47	212,836	53.53
2016	209,966	47.42	232,807	52.58
2017	241,543	49.40	247,629	50.60
2018	258,122	52.44	234,063	47.56

Sources:
1. Ministry of Education (2018). *Concise Statistics of International Students in China: 1998–2016.* Beijing: Department of International Cooperation and Exchanges, Ministry of Education.
2. Ministry of Education (April 12, 2019). 2018 Statistics on International Students in China. Retrieved July 20, 2019, from http://www.moe.gov.cn/jyb_xwfb/gzdt_gzdt s5987/201904/t20190412_377692.html.

to 52.44% in 2018. In 2018, the proportion of degree-seeking students exceeded the proportion of non–degree-seeking students for the first time.

Figure 6.2 shows that the number of undergraduate, master's, and doctoral students among degree-seeking students had increased year by year between 2000 and 2018. The number of degree-seeking students had increased from 11,400 in 1998 to 258,100 in 2018, an increase of about 22 times. The average annual growth rate of degree-seeking students was 16.9%. Between 2010 and 2018, the annual growth rate of degree-seeking students was 11.6%. This is much higher than that of the total number of international students in China. During this period, the annual growth rate of undergraduate students, master's students, and doctoral students was 9.9%, 15.3%, and 20.3% respectively. In 2018, there were 258,122 degree-seeking students, accounting for 52.44% of the total number of international students in China, revealing an increase of 16,579 when compared to 2017, or a year-on-year increase of 6.89%. There were 85,062 master's and doctoral students in total, i.e. an increase of 12.28% when compared to 2017, including 25,618 doctoral students and 59,444 master's students.

152 *From a peripheral player to a major hosting country*

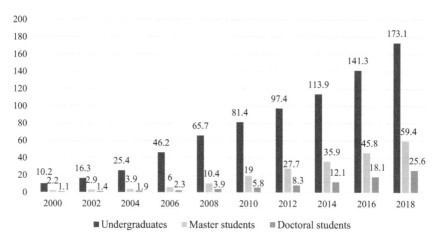

Figure 6.2 Number of international degree-seeking students in China, 2000–2018 (unit: Thousands).

Data Sources: Ministry of Education (2018). *Concise Statistics of International Students in China: 1998-2016*. Beijing: Department of International Cooperation and Exchanges, Ministry of Education; Ministry of Education (2019, April 12). 2018 Statistics on International Students in China. Retrieved June 25, 2019, from http://www.moe.gov.cn/ jyb_xwfb/gzdt_gzdt s5987/ 201904 /t20190412_377692.html.

The majors of international students in China were mainly liberal arts and specializations with Chinese characteristics. As shown in Table 6.4, the number of international students from different disciplines in China has shown a continuous growth trend. The top five disciplines were liberal arts, medicine (including Western medicine and traditional Chinese medicine), economics, management, and engineering. Among them, liberal arts mainly focused on the Chinese language. For example,

Table 6.4 Distribution of disciplines for international students in China, 2002–2016

Subjects	2002	2004	2006	2008	2010	2012	2014	2016
Arts	68,438	83,266	114,846	143,344	165,761	196,136	212,121	211,244
Medicine	6,713	10,971	20,355	28,651	36,165	43,516	52,090	62,357
Economics	2,723	4,525	7,308	11,335	16,863	20,819	27,799	37,315
Management	1,036	2,838	5,954	10,728	14,920	21,873	26,951	32,876
Engineering	2,442	3,519	5,803	9,128	15,130	22,596	34,134	48,394
Law	1,287	2,438	3,667	4,688	6,147	7,296	9,118	11,187
Education	948	992	1,730	3,395	4,473	5,361	6,664	27,900
Science	393	555	1,007	9,978	2,535	2,670	3,927	6,210
History	1,375	742	904	968	1,301	1,380	1,335	1,176
Agriculture	267	298	681	699	1,063	1,538	2,368	3,471
Philosophy	207	700	440	585	732	674	547	543

Source: Ministry of Education (2002–2016). *Concise Statistics on International Students Coming to China: 2002–2016*, Beijing: Department of International Cooperation and Exchanges, Ministry of Education.

among 211,244 liberal arts students in 2016, 169,093 majored in Chinese and only 5,369 majored in arts; 47.7% of students majored in liberal arts, 14.1% in medicine (including traditional Chinese medicine and Western medicine), 8.4% in economics, 7.4% in management, 10.9% in engineering, 1.4% in science, and 10.1% in other disciplines (MoE, Department of International Cooperation and Exchange, 2016, p. 31).

The vast majority of foreign students in China were self-financed. Since the 1980s, policies regarding international students around the world have shifted from focusing on educational aid to focusing on educational service (Peng, 2006). Accordingly, China's focus has also shifted from providing education exchanges and aid, to the recruitment of self-financed students and the expansion of the higher education service. Table 6.5 shows that between 1999 and 2018, the number of self-financed international students increased yearly, reaching 429,144 in 2018, accounting for 87.2% of international students in China. Over the past 20 years, self-financed international students have always accounted for more than 87% of international students in the country.

The regional distribution of foreign students in China is uneven. Most of them are concentrated in coastal areas as well as areas with rich higher education resources. Eastern coastal areas, and municipalities directly under the control of the central government, were still the main destinations for international students in 2018, while the number of international students in all provinces has also increased. The top provinces

Table 6.5 The number and proportion of self-financed international students in China, 1999–2018

Year	Total	Self-financed	Accounted for %
1999	44,711	39,500	88.3
2000	52,150	46,788	89.7
2001	61,869	56,028	90.6
2002	85,829	79,755	92.9
2003	77,715	71,562	92.1
2004	110,844	104,129	93.9
2005	141,087	133,869	94.9
2006	162,695	154,211	94.8
2007	195,503	185,352	94.8
2008	223,499	209,983	94.0
2009	238,184	219,939	93.3
2010	265,090	242,700	91.6
2011	292,611	266,924	91.2
2012	328,330	299,562	91.2
2013	356,499	323,177	90.6
2014	377,054	340,111	90.2
2015	397,635	357,035	89.8
2016	442,773	393,751	88.9
2017	489,172	430,600	88.0
2018	492,185	429,144	87.2

Sources:
1. Ministry of Education (1996–2016). *Concise Statistics of International Students in China: 1996–2016*. Beijing: Department of International Cooperation and Exchanges, Ministry of Education.
2. Ministry of Education (April 12, 2019). 2018 Statistics on International Students in China. Retrieved July 20, 2019, from http://www.moe.gov.cn/jyb_xwfb /gzdt_gzdt s5987/ 201904 /t20190412_377692.html.

and cities in terms of the number of international students were 80,786 in Beijing, 61,400 in Shanghai, 45,778 in Jiangsu, 38,190 in Zhejiang, 27,879 in Liaoning, 23,691 in Tianjin, 22,034 in Guangdong, 21,371 in Hubei, 19,311 in Yunnan, 19,078 in Shandong, 15,217 in Guangxi, 13,990 in Sichuan, 13,429 in Heilongjiang, 12,919 in Shaanxi, and 10,340 in Fujian (MoE, 2019). It can be seen that the geographical distribution of international students is closely related to the geographical locations' degrees of socioeconomic development and the concentration of high-quality resources for higher education. Coastal areas, and the areas with a high level of socioeconomic development and a cluster of higher education institutions, have attracted a large number of international students. Moreover, the more prominent universities in these areas have become gathering places for international students.

As mentioned above, the number of international students in China has increased year by year, but the distribution among the countries of origin is disproportionate. The majority of international students originally came from Asian countries. However, the international students from the "Belt and Road" countries have become a new source of growth in recent years. The academic level of foreign students has also been gradually improved, and more than half of them are degree-seeking students, with undergraduates representing the main body, while the proportions of master's and doctoral students are relatively low. About 90% of international students in China are self-financed and they concentrate on liberal arts and medicine majors.

At present, the dominant trends for inbound international student mobility in China are the rapid expansion of scale, the gradual improvement of the academic level of international students, and the increasing number of hosting colleges and universities. The main drawbacks for development include: (a) The academic level of international students in China is relatively low and there is a large gap compared with developed countries; (b) the distribution of majors and countries of origin of international students in China is uneven; (c) the strategic position of studying in China has not been widely valued; and (d) some rules, regulations, and policies do not meet the needs of facilitating foreign education in China. In the future, the following measures can be taken: (a) To increase the scale and value of government scholarships, and to broaden those channels, so as to attract more high-quality international students; (b) to adjust the language system of teaching and establish a preparatory system for studying in China; (c) to establish a quality monitoring and evaluation system for studying in China so as to ensure the quality of foreign education for international students; (d) to improve the rules, regulations, and management system, so as to create a good policy environment for studying in China; and (e) to improve service work and the service system for studying in China (Jiang, 2010, pp. 21–25).

6.2 The policy and developmental characteristics of international student education in Shanghai

The education of international students is an important aspect of the higher education internationalization. As an international metropolis, Shanghai has made great efforts to promote the internationalization of higher education. The number and quality of international students in Shanghai lead the whole country. This section outlines the policies and developmental characteristics of international student education in Shanghai universities, and provides suggestions for the improvement of related policies and systems.

6.2.1 Higher education policies for international students in Shanghai

The quantity and quality of international students at universities in Shanghai have been relatively high-level. This is not only because of Shanghai's advantageous position, municipal function, and access to high-quality higher education resources, but also due to its own policies on recruiting and attracting international students. In 2012, Shanghai promulgated the *12th Five-Year Action Plan for the Internationalization Project of Education in Shanghai* to build the most popular destination city for study in Asia (Shanghai Municipal Government, 2012). In August 2016, the Shanghai Municipal Government issued the *13th Five-Year Plan for the Reform and Development of Education in Shanghai* (Shanghai Fu Fa [2016] No. 61), targeted at attracting 120,000 international students by 2020, of which 50% will be degree-seeking students. Shanghai aims at further expanding the opening-up of its education to the world, enhancing its international influence and competitiveness, and implementing the "Belt and Road" *Educational Action Plan* to encourage and support educational institutions at all levels to carry out various forms of educational exchanges and cooperation with countries or regions along the "Belt and Road". The following section describes Shanghai's international student admission, fees, and scholarship policies, and teaching and curriculum reform, as well as international student employment policy.

6.2.1.1 Recruitment policy

First, in order to further increase the number of international students, the Shanghai Municipal Government has gradually decentralized the admission authority and given more autonomy to colleges and universities. Second, Shanghai has strengthened its evaluation of colleges and universities that have been previously qualified, to recruit international students. On top of that, the number of colleges and universities that can recruit international students has been increased each year, to lay the foundation for the development of education for international students in Shanghai. Third, the Shanghai Municipal Government has issued *Implementation Measures for the Applications of Shanghai Government Scholarships for Foreign Students* to attract foreign students from all over the world to study in Shanghai (Shanghai Municipal Government, 2006). At the same time, universities in Shanghai have also been constantly refining their international student admission policies and systems to ensure the quantity and quality of international students.

6.2.1.2 Fees policy

China has been charging international students lower tuition fees compared to other developed countries. This is evident in Shanghai. Table 6.6 shows that the tuition fees for undergraduate international students in Shanghai universities are lower

156 *From a peripheral player to a major hosting country*

Table 6.6 Tuition fees for international students in Shanghai universities by degree level, 2018

Institution	Undergraduates (yuan/year) RMB	Master's students (yuan/year) RMB	Doctoral students (yuan/year) RMB
Donghua University	22,000	26,000	32,000
East China University of Political Science and Law	24,000	28,000	34,000
East China University of Science and Technology	22,000	28,000	35,000
Shanghai Jiao Tong University School of Medicine	29,000	37,000	45,500
Shanghai Theatre Academy	36,000	36,000	30,000
Shanghai Institute of Foreign Trade	20,000	30,000	—
Shanghai Conservatory of Music	32,000	40,000	48,000
Shanghai University of Engineering and Technology	18,000	25,000	—
Shanghai Maritime University	20,000	23,000	29,000

Source: The author combined data from the prospectus of foreign students and education fee announcement of each university.

Note: "—" in the table indicates missing data.

than those for master's students and the tuition fees for master's students are also lower than those for doctoral students, with annual tuition fees for international undergraduate students ranging from RMB 18,000 to 36,000, while the fees for international master's students range from RMB 23,000 to 40,000, and the fees for international doctoral students range from RMB 29,000 to 48,000 per year.

6.2.1.3 Scholarship policy

In order to further promote Shanghai's education for international students and attract more outstanding foreign students to study there, the Shanghai Municipal Education Commission has established the Shanghai Government Scholarship for Foreign Students since 2005, which is divided into Categories A, B, and C, and is used to subsidize outstanding foreign students to pursue degree education in Shanghai's HEIs. In 2005 and 2006, the Shanghai Municipal Education Commission allocated a total of RMB 24 million worth of scholarship funds for foreign students in these two fiscal years, and issued *Trial Measures for the Application of Shanghai Government Scholarships for Foreign Students* to regulate the awarding of scholarships for foreign students in Shanghai's HEIs.

Since 2011, the Shanghai Municipal Government has increased the scholarship amount for foreign students from RMB 40,000 to RMB 47,200 per year for Category A. Scholarship recipients receive a full scholarship covering tuition fees, living expenses, and comprehensive medical insurance to ensure that they do not have any kind of financial burden during their study in Shanghai.

6.2.1.4 Teaching and curriculum reform

The internationalization of teaching and curriculum is an important means of attracting international students. It also contributes towards the cultivation of domestic students' global competence. In order to further promote the development of education for foreign students, the Shanghai Municipal Education Commission has stepped up the construction of specialized courses for international students that are taught in English and the training of faculty staff for teaching international students. In particular, to strengthen the faculty's proficiency in foreign languages and improve the pedagogy of faculty members, it launched the *Overseas Teacher Training Program for Higher Education International Curriculum Construction in Shanghai HEIs*, in cooperation with the China Scholarship Council. At present, some well-known universities in Shanghai are constructing courses that are taught in English and are encouraging and supporting teachers who are capable of offering courses in English. These measures play an important role in attracting international students and improving their quality of education. For example, Shanghai Jiao Tong University, Fudan University, East China Normal University, and other well-known universities are financially supporting English language programmes to promote the internationalization of teaching and curriculum, so as to improve the quality of education for international students.

6.2.1.5 The employment policy for international students

In September 2016, Shanghai promulgated the *30 Regulations for Talent* and this policy encourages foreign students to undertake innovation and entrepreneurship directly after graduation in Shanghai. According to the policy, foreign students who obtain a bachelor's degree or above from HEIs in Shanghai can be employed in the "double free" areas (China Shanghai Pilot Free Trade Zone, Zhangjiang National Independent Innovation Demonstration Zone, referred to as the "double free" areas) and can directly apply for a work permit in Shanghai. Foreign students with a bachelor's degree or above who start a business in Shanghai can apply for a residence permit for private affairs (with a special annotation of entrepreneurship) valid for up to two years.

6.2.2 The characteristics of international students in HEIs in Shanghai

6.2.2.1 The expanding scale of international students in Shanghai

The average growth rate of international students in Shanghai was 16.5% between 1995 and 2000. The number of international students in Shanghai had grown rapidly since 2002, from 13,091 in 2002 to 60,226 in 2016, with an annual growth rate of 11.5% (Shanghai Municipal Government, 2016). Among them, long-term students (staying for more than half-a-year) account for about two-thirds of the total number of international students, with the number increasing from 8,993 in 2002 to 43,405 in 2016. The annual growth rate of long-term students is 11.9%, while the growth trend for short-term students is relatively moderate.

158 *From a peripheral player to a major hosting country*

6.2.2.2 International students mainly clustering in research universities

Table 6.7 shows that, in 2016, international students of HEIs in Shanghai mainly studied in research universities and municipal universities with advantageous specializations. The top ten universities in terms of the number of international students were Fudan University (6,849), Shanghai Jiao Tong University (6,670), East China Normal University (6,026), Donghua University (4,783), Tongji University (4,750), Shanghai International Studies University (4,576), Shanghai University (4,082), Shanghai University of Finance and Economics (2,877), Shanghai University of Traditional Chinese Medicine (2,760), and Shanghai Normal University (2,501). These ten universities account for 76.17% of the total number of international students in Shanghai. Significant differences exist in the recruitment strategy of international students in Shanghai universities. Some universities, such as The East China University of Science and Technology and The East China University of Political Science and Law, which used to offer a high-quality undergraduate education, do not show any advantage of attracting international students.

6.2.2.3 The origin of international students is increasingly diversified

As shown in Table 6.8, from 2005 to 2016, international students in Shanghai mainly came from Asian regions, accounting for more than 50% of the total number of international students. However, with the growth in the number of international students from Africa and Europe, the proportion of Asian students decreased. The second largest group of international students in Shanghai was from Europe, and the number was constantly growing.

Table 6.7 The institutional distribution of international students in Shanghai, 2004–2016

Institution/year	2004	2006	2008	2010	2012	2014	2016
Fudan University	4,634	6,270	6,468	6,821	6,922	6,276	6,849
Shanghai Jiao Tong University	4,005	4,488	5,502	4,415	5,908	5,980	6,670
East China Normal University	2,346	3,063	3,473	4,705	5,463	5,710	6,026
Donghua University	741	1,845	2,779	3,847	4,295	4,697	4,783
Tongji University	1,842	2,418	2,695	3,720	4,552	4,950	4,750
Shanghai International Studies University	1,680	2,775	3,060	4,117	4,218	4,540	4,576
Shanghai University	1,332	2,037	2,345	2,783	3,307	3,886	4,082
Shanghai University of Finance and Economics	1,206	2,110	2,253	2,178	2,294	2,625	2,877
Shanghai University of Traditional Chinese Medicine	1,377	1,647	1,882	1,942	1,958	2,449	2,760
Shanghai Normal University	1,280	2,505	2,107	2,023	2,193	2,337	2,501

Source: Ministry of Education (2004–2016). *Concise Statistics on International Students in China: 2004–2016*, Beijing: Department of International Cooperation and Exchanges, Ministry of Education.

Table 6.8 The number of international students in Shanghai's HEIs by place of origin, 2005–2016

Place of origin	Number and percentage	2005	2006	2008	2009	2012	2014	2016
Asia	Number	10,490	10,207	9,748	10,508	12,079	13,463	16,580
	Percentage	76.6	72.4	68.3	68.0	62.3	56.8	52.8
Africa	Number	289	353	647	860	1,366	1,641	2,515
	Percentage	2.1	2.5	4.5	5.6	7.1	6.9	8.0
Europe	Number	1,927	2,253	2,479	2,520	4,201	5,718	8,224
	Percentage	14.1	16.0	17.4	16.3	21.7	24.1	26.2
North America	Number	766	984	949	1,102	1,138	2,075	3,000
	Percentage	5.6	7.0	6.6	7.1	5.9	8.8	9.5
South America	Number	129	191	328	289	389	525	670
	Percentage	0.9	1.3	2.3	1.9	2.0	2.2	2.1
Oceania	Number	90	112	122	168	194	280	427
	Percentage	0.7	0.8	0.9	1.1	1.0	1.2	1.4
Total	Number	13,691	14,100	14,273	15,447	19,367	23,702	31,416

Source: Shanghai Statistics (June 26, 2019). Shanghai Statistical Yearbook (2005–2016). Retrieved July 23, 2019, from http://www.stats-sh.gov.cn/html/sjfb/tjnj/.

6.2.2.4 Changing trends of degree-seeking students and non–degree-seeking students

Table 6.9 shows that the proportion of degree-seeking and long-term students in Shanghai had been increasing between 2006 and 2016. The proportion of degree-seeking students increased from 25.15% in 2006 to 32% in 2016, and the proportion of long-term students increased from 68.7% in 2006 to 72.07% in 2016.

Table 6.9 The proportion of various types of international students in HEIs in Shanghai

Year	Percentage of degree-seeking students (%)	Percentage of non–degree-seeking students (%)	Percentage of long-term students (%)	Percentage of short-term students (%)
2006	25.15	74.85	68.0	31.30
2008	28.83	71.17	70.37	29.63
2010	30.59	69.41	70.97	29.03
2012	27.88	72.12	71.8	28.24
2014	30.18	69.82	70.27	29.73
2016	32.0	68.0	72.07	27.93

Source: Shanghai Local Records Office (June 26, 2019). Shanghai Yearbook (2006–2016). Retrieved July 21, 2019, from http://www.shtong.gov. cn/Newsite/ node2/ node 1982/index.htmL.

Note: "Long-term students" refer to international students who have studied in China for half-a-year or more; while "short-term students" refer to international students who have studied in China for less than half-a-year.

6.2.2.5 International students in Shanghai are mainly self-funded

As shown in Table 6.10, the proportion of self-funded international students enrolled in Shanghai in relation to total enrolment remained above 62% between 2006 and 2016. The proportion of international students sponsored by the Chinese government and institutions had increased.

In addition to the above characteristics, the distribution of international students in Shanghai HEIs were mainly concentrated in the humanities and social sciences. The top five disciplines in terms of the number of students were literature, management, economics, medicine, and engineering. International students that have majored in literature mainly focused on Chinese literature. In 2010, the number of international students majoring in literature accounted for 64.46% of the total number of international students. This is closely related to the fact that China's advantageous disciplines and special disciplines are in the field of liberal arts.

In summary, the characteristics of international students in Shanghai are similar to those of international students in China, but the educational level and diversity of international students in Shanghai is significantly higher than the national average. HEIs in Shanghai have significant potential and advantages in cultivating international students. With the increasing consolidation of Shanghai's status as an international metropolis, the HEIs located in Shanghai will make new breakthroughs, including those related to the education for international students.

6.3 A survey on international students in research universities in Shanghai

In order to examine the characteristics and perceptions of international students in research universities in Shanghai, a questionnaire survey was conducted on international students at Fudan University (FU), Shanghai Jiao Tong University (SJTU),

Table 6.10 Enrolment of international students in Shanghai's HEIs by funding source, 2006–2016

Year	Number and percentage	2006	2008	2010	2012	2014	2016
Total admission	Number	14,100	14,273	17,340	19,367	23,702	31,416
Self-financed	Number	10,741	11,718	12,838	13,425	15,883	19,683
	Percentage	76.2	82.1	74.0	69.3	67.0	62.7
China government funding	Number	815	1,442	2,585	3,424	4,555	6,848
	Percentage	5.8	10.1	14.9	17.7	19.2	21.8
Sending country government funding	Number	153	219	347	286	193	118
	Percentage	1.1	1.5	2.0	1.5	0.8	0.4
Exchanges between HEIs	Number	2,255	894	1,570	2,227	3,070	4,767
	Percentage	16.0	6.3	9.1	11.5	13.0	15.2

Source: Shanghai Statistics (June 26, 2019). Shanghai Statistical Yearbook (2005–2016). Retrieved July 22, 2019, from http://www.stats-sh.gov.cn/html/sjfb/tjnj/.

and East China Normal University (ECNU). The reasons for choosing these universities are: First, each of the three universities has its own characteristics, different development history, and educational resources, while all of them are research universities directly supervised by the MoE, and are also the most internationally competitive HEIs in Shanghai. Second, the three universities have hosted the largest number of international students in Shanghai and have taken the lead in the education for international students among the city's universities. Their education and competent management functions for international students are sufficient enough to illustrate the achievements of Shanghai HEIs in international student education, while the corresponding problems are also common to all Shanghai HEIs.

6.3.1 Research questions and research method

6.3.1.1 Research questions

The main research questions are: Why do international students choose to study in China? Why do they choose to study in Shanghai? What factors influence international students' choice of institutions in Shanghai? How well do international students adapt to the academic environment? How well do international students adapt to life here?

6.3.1.2 Research method

The study adopted a questionnaire survey for data collection. The questionnaire was designed based on the research questions. It includes the respondents' personal background, rationales, and motivations for pursuing studies in China, the factors influencing the choice of a HEI, and their levels of academic and way of life adaptation. The last two open-ended questions were designed to find out the international students' opinions on the institutional administration and education that they received.

The questionnaires were administered among the international students at Fudan University and East China Normal University from May to November 2009 and among the international students at Shanghai Jiao Tong University from October to November 2009. Considering that international students are most accustomed to thinking and answering questions in their native language, the questionnaires were presented in English, Chinese, Korean, and Japanese, depending on the preference of the respondents. South Korean students completed the questionnaires in Korean, Japanese students did so in Japanese, students from English-speaking countries did it in English, while international students from other countries answered the questionnaires in English or Chinese.

Basic information of the survey sample is shown in Table 6.11. A total of 420 questionnaires were distributed in Fudan University, Shanghai Jiao Tong University, and East China Normal University. A total of 307 questionnaires were returned, with a return rate of 73%. In terms of the sampling method, since international students in the three universities are scattered and it was difficult to conduct strict random sampling, this study adopted non-random sampling.

Table 6.11 Sample information of international students from FU, SJTU, and ECNU (N = 307)

Variable	Fudan University (n = 92)	Shanghai Jiao Tong University (n = 123)	East China Normal University (n = 92)
Gender	Male 56.7%	Female 43.3%	
Programme studied	PhD 0.3%	Master 3.6%	Undergraduate 38.1%
Funding sources	All self-financed 73%	Partially self-financed 8.8%	Chinese scholarship 8.5%
			Language student 43.3%
			National scholarship 8.1%
			Other 14.7%
			Other scholarships 1.6%
Age	Under 20 19.9%	20–30 73.2%	31–40 5.9%
			Over 40 1%

From a peripheral player to a major hosting country 163

However, proper consideration was given to the degree level, major, and country of origin of international students. The study only adopted descriptive statistics such as percentages and means to illustrate the characteristics and perceptions of international students in the sample and there was no intention to generalize the findings.

Among the three universities, 120 questionnaires were distributed to East China Normal University, and 92 of which were valid, with a return rate of 77%. Among them, 43.5% of the sample students were male, and 74.7% were fully self-funded. One-hundred-and-fifty questionnaires were distributed to Fudan University, and 92 of which were valid, with a return rate of 61%. Among them, 57.6% of the sample students were male, and 80.4% were fully self-funded. There were 123 out of 150 questionnaires that were retrieved from Shanghai Jiao Tong University, with a return rate of 82%. Among them, 64.2% of the sample students were male, and 67.5% were fully self-financed.

6.3.2 Analysis of the survey results

6.3.2.1 Rationales and motivations for studying in China

The rationales of international students for studying in Shanghai can be classified into three main categories: Economic rationales, cultural and social rationales, and academic rationales. Economic rationales include engagement in the economic and trade activities related to China and concerns the impact of studying in China on prospective employment and jobs, as well as the recognition of degree in the job market. Cultural and social rationales include learning the Chinese language and culture and becoming a cultural bridge connecting China and their home country. Academic rationales involve professional development and academic advancement.

Table 6.12 shows that the main reasons for international students at the three universities to study in China are: (a) To improve their Chinese language skills and learn Chinese culture ($M = 4.28$); (b) to improve their professional and academic level ($M = 4.0$); (c) to gain credits for the study experience in Chinese universities in terms of job seeking ($M = 3.86$); (d) to become a bridge for cultural and educational exchanges between their home countries and China ($M = 3.72$); and (e) to engage in China-related economic and trade activities ($M = 3.65$). It can be seen that international students' reasons for studying in China are driven by various factors and they make decisions according to their cultural and social, academic, and economic rationales.

The survey has explored the international students' reasons for choosing Shanghai as their destination of study and their plans upon graduation. As shown in Table 6.13, Shanghai is attractive to international students mainly because it is an open cosmopolitan city (36.2%) and a window for the cultural exchange between China and Western countries (24.4%). The attractiveness of more employment opportunities being available in Shanghai is not significant, and that of higher education level is low. Only 12.4% of international students considered high levels of higher education as one of the reasons for studying in Shanghai, with Fudan

Table 6.12 Reasons for international students to study in China (mean values)

Sort by	The reason for me to study in China	Fudan University	Shanghai Jiao Tong University	East China Normal University	Total
	Sample number	92	123	92	307
1	To improve my Chinese language skills and learn Chinese culture	4.23	4.28	4.35	4.28
2	To enhance my professional and academic level	3.99	412	3.85	4.0
3	My learning experience at a Chinese university helps in finding a job	3.89	4.0	3.65	3.86
4	To become a bridge for the cultural and educational exchanges between my home country and China in the future	3.66	3.89	3.64	3.72
5	To engage in economic and trade activities related to China in the future	3.57	3.76	3.58	3.65
6	To learn Chinese expertise, such as painting, music, Chinese medicine, martial arts	2.93	3.09	3.2	3.07
7	The tuition fees of Chinese universities are lower than those of other countries	3.35	2.86	3.15	3.09
8	The international academic status of Chinese universities in this field is higher than that of domestic universities	2.78	3.15	2.58	2.87
9	There are Chinese scholarships/academic exchange programmes available	2.33	2.39	2.39	2.37
10	The learning conditions (e.g., libraries) in Chinese universities are better than those in domestic universities	2.62	2.76	2.2	2.55

Note: 1 = completely disagree, 2 = disagree, 3 = neither agree nor disagree, 4 = agree, 5 = completely agree.

From a peripheral player to a major hosting country 165

Table 6.13 Reasons for international students from FU, SJTU, and ECNU to study in Shanghai

The reason for me to study in Shanghai	Fudan University Number	Percentage (%)	Shanghai Jiao Tong University Number	Percentage (%)	East China Normal University Number	Percentage (%)	Total Number	Percentage (%)
It's a window for the cultural exchange between East and West	15	16.3	34	27.6	26	28.3	75	24.4
It's an open cosmopolitan city	30	32.6	43	35.0	38	41.3	111	36.2
More employment opportunities	14	15.2	30	24.4	18	19.6	62	20.2
High levels of higher education	13	14.1	13	10.6	12	13	38	12.4
Intercollegiate exchanges	16	17.4	17	13.8	13	14.1	46	15.0
Others	19	20.7	11	8.9	13	14.1	43	14.0

Table 6.14 Plans of international students upon graduation from Shanghai (%)

Where to go upon graduation	Fudan University	Shanghai Jiao Tong University	East China Normal University	Total
Sample number	92	123	92	307
Stay and study in Shanghai	6.5	4.9	12.0	7.5
Stay and work in Shanghai	16.3	20.3	17.4	18.2
Study in other cities in China	8.7	1.6	4.3	4.6
Work in other cities in China	3.3	1.6	2.2	2.3
Return to the motherland	33.7	18.7	29.3	26.4
Go to other countries	9.8	19.5	12.0	14.3
Uncertain	21.7	33.3	22.8	26.7

University, Shanghai Jiao Tong University, and East China Normal University accounting for 14.1%, 10.6%, and 13%, respectively.

As shown in Table 6.14, after graduation, 26.4% of international students want to return to their home countries, while 14.3% intend to head to other countries. The percentage of international students who prefer to leave China is 40.7%, while 18.2% of international students want to stay and work in Shanghai, and 7.5% want to continue their studies in Shanghai. The percentage of international students who prefer to stay in China is 32.6%, which is about one-third of the total.

6.3.2.2 Influencing factors for choosing a host HEI

In view of the intensified competition for recruiting international students in the globalized higher education market, what are the important factors for international students in choosing their host institutions? Table 6.15 shows the importance of 13 factors that influenced international students to choose Fudan University, Shanghai Jiao Tong University, and East China Normal University. Among the top five most important influencing factors for choosing to enter Fudan University, Shanghai Jiao Tong University, and East China Normal University, four are commonly shared by the three universities, i.e. high-quality education, good institutional reputation, high-quality faculty, rich and extensive curricula, and teaching contents, as well as rich educational resources and advanced facilities.

6.3.2.3 Academic adaptation of international students

Academic adaptation includes course scheduling, teaching language, pedagogical model, student-teacher relationships, peer relationships, and school administration. Table 6.16 shows that international students in the three universities rated their adaptation to the teaching language ($M = 3.67$), pedagogy ($M = 3.57$), and

Table 6.15 Factors influencing international students' choice of FU, SJTU, and ECNU

The reasons for me to choose this university	Mean rating in FU	Mean rating in SJTU	Mean rating in ECNU
Has a reputation for quality and expert staff	4.7	5.04	4.87
Has a reputation for quality education	5.33	5.53	4.73
Offers a broad range of courses and programmes	4.36	4.67	4.52
Rich educational resources and advanced facilities	4.4	4.73	4.51
Has a large number of international students	3.76	3.78	4.41
Has a reputation for being responsive to students' needs	3.84	4.52	4.37
Offers qualifications that will be recognized by employers	4.93	5.03	4.35
Well known for innovation in research and teaching	4.17	4.77	4.24
Well known to me or its alumni/acquaintances refer to me	4.13	4.25	4.13
Standardized, orderly, and efficient administration	4.1	4.52	4.07
Efficient advertising and promotional activities	3.73	3.96	3.97
Willing to recognize my previous qualifications	3.96	4.37	3.82
Provides scholarships for financial assistance	3.35	3.74	3.42

Note: 1 = completely disagree, 2 = disagree, 3 = neither agree nor disagree, 4 = agree, 5 = completely agree.

Table 6.16 Adaptation of international students at FU, SJTU, and ECNU

How are you adapting to each of the following areas?	Mean rating in FU	Mean rating in SJTU	Mean rating in ECNU	Mean rating in three universities
Sample number	92	123	92	307
Ability to adapt to the teaching language of this university	3.58	3.67	3.76	3.67
Ability to adapt to the teaching methods of this university	3.47	3.60	3.62	3.57
Able to adapt to the management style of this university	3.26	3.61	3.47	3.46
Management and teaching staff care and support for international students	3.05	3.66	3.32	3.37
Appropriate course placement for international students	2.99	3.29	3.32	3.21
It is easy to interact with Chinese students at school	3.0	3.05	2.78	2.95
In favour of the campus culture here	3.18	3.42	3.32	3.32

Note: 1 = completely disagree, 2 = disagree, 3 = neither agree nor disagree, 4 = agree, 5 = completely agree.

administration ($M = 3.46$) in a descending order. International students also rated the caring and support of administration and teaching staff, campus culture, course scheduling, and interactions with Chinese students in a descending order.

The survey on international students shows that they encounter various problems in their studies, including the pressure of studying, the use of Chinese language, getting support for their studies, and communication and cooperation with teachers. The extent to which the international students are accustomed to the educational concept, administrative mode, and interpersonal relationship model affect their academic adaptation in Shanghai universities.

6.3.2.4 Life adaptation of international students

Life adaptation includes language, accommodation, food, and interpersonal factors. The survey shows that the major cultural and life adaptation problems for international students are as follows: First, the difficulties in intercultural interpersonal communication and the difficulties in making friends with Chinese people/students; second, the economic pressure, including tuition fees and living expenses; and third, dealing with daily-life problems, such as accommodation, transportation, and food.

6.3.3 Main conclusions

Overall, education for international students in China is still under development and the quality of education needs to be improved. Since the reform and opening-up, education for international students has undergone a transformation from emphasizing the expansion of scale to the development of connotation and the improvement of quality and efficiency aspects, with a sustained expanding scale of international students, the gradually optimized structure, the continuously improved education level, and more diversified sources and types of students.

In accordance with the general policy of the central government of "expanding the scale, improving the education level, ensuring the quality and standardizing the administration", the scale of education for international students is expanding, the structure for international students is being gradually optimized, and the proportion of degree-seeking students is increasing, especially that of graduate students. Shanghai continues to explore the new model of socialization and informatization of the macro administration for international students in order to cope with the pressure brought about by the greatly expanded scale of international students on their comprehensive management. Shanghai tends to continue to give full play to and stimulate the enthusiasm and creativity of all kinds of HEIs, so that the universities at different stages of development can establish effective management systems and development models suitable for their own stages of development, and jointly promote a new pattern of diversified development. According to the survey, the characteristics of international students in Shanghai universities can be summarized as follows.

First, the motivation for studying in China is a combination of multiple factors. To learn about the Chinese culture and language, and the rationales for academic and professional development, as well as economic rationales, are all emphasized in terms of the rationales of international students for studying in Shanghai. It can be seen that the influence of the Chinese language and culture, as an element of China's soft power, is constantly increasing. This has become an important factor attracting the majority of international students to study in China. Additionally, the improvement of education and academic quality in China's "Project 985" universities is also attractive to overseas students who are studying in China. At the same time, some international students also value the comparative advantage of a degree from a Chinese university in the job market, and the fact that it will help them to engage in China-related economic and trade activities in the future.

Second, the role of Shanghai as an international metropolis is prominent among the city's factors. The main reason for international students to choose Shanghai is that Shanghai is an international metropolis and a window of cultural exchange between China and Western countries. The academic level of universities is the third most important factor, which indicates that the attractiveness of Shanghai as an international metropolis for international students is prioritized, while the function of HEIs has not yet been fully manifested.

Third, the quality of education is one the important influencing factors of international students' choice of HEIs. The most important factors influencing the choice of universities in Shanghai are the faculty members, quality and reputation of education, curricula and teaching content, educational resources, and facilities, as well as the recognition of degrees in employment, the satisfaction of meeting students' needs, and the degree of innovation associated with their qualifications.

Fourth, the educational and academic attractiveness of Shanghai universities towards international students has yet to be improved.

Fifth, academic adaptation is still acceptable, but some difficulties in learning exist. The differences in pedagogical models, examination concepts, teacher–student relationships between Chinese and foreigners, as well as the contradiction between the single pedagogical model in Chinese universities and the developmental needs of international students with a multicultural background, may cause some academic adaptation problems. International students' difficulties in learning mainly come from academic pressure, language learning, the difficulties associated with getting academic support, and insufficient communication with teachers. The self-evaluation of international students' adaptation status in respect to the teaching language, pedagogy, administrative model, attitudes of administrative and faculty staff, and curriculum scheduling at the three research universities in Shanghai are relatively positive.

Last, interpersonal adaptability and economic pressure become the main challenges. Due to the distinctiveness of education for international students, some universities have separated the teaching, housing, and administration for international students from local students. This makes it difficult for international students to integrate into the overall culture of the university and to interact with, and learn from, the local students. Hence, the most important problem in life and cultural adaptation lies in intercultural and interpersonal communication. International students face such problems as having limited interactions with Chinese students, difficulties in integrating with local students, high financial pressure, and daily-life adaptation.

6.4 The problems and suggestions in terms of education for international students

Since studying in Shanghai reflects the problems of studying in China, this section focuses on the problems of studying in China based on the survey of studying in Shanghai. Countermeasures are then proposed.

HEIs do not only have national characteristics and contribute to the social, economic, political, and cultural aspects of a country, but also maintain an international nature. They are an integral part of the world's knowledge system. Policies on international students involve multiple levels of philosophy and interactions between the state, institutions, and individuals of the society. At the national level, there are political, economic, cultural, and social, as well as academic rationales for recruiting international students. Recruiting international students can enhance a country's political and cultural influence, gain economic benefits through charging tuition fees and living expenses, improve the academic and talent cultivation capacity of HEIs, and facilitate and deepen the internationalization of education. The developed countries have formulated policies to encourage HEIs to expand the recruitment of international students. The recruitment and cultivation of international students in China can expand the influence of Chinese culture, language, and teaching, achieve cultural diplomacy, and enhance China's participation and competitiveness in the international market. However, the recruitment, education, and administration of international students involve very complex aspects of governmental administration and higher education. How should this enterprise be developed in an organized way to gradually improve the ability of Chinese HEIs to attract and train international students? It raises a series of new questions in terms of HEIs' curriculum and teaching, faculty, foreign language proficiency, and administration.

6.4.1 Problems in the education of international students

6.4.1.1 The management and system construction problems at the macro level

Problems such as structural defects, and low quality and poor ability of international students exist in international student education in China. However, a bigger problem is that the institutional construction and administration related to international student education are seriously lagging behind. If the problem of institutional construction is not effectively solved, with the expansion of international students, more serious administration and quality problems related to international student education are bound to appear. The main problems are as follows.

First, the policies and regulations at the macro level need to be improved. Specifically, the following problems need to be solved: (a) The policy development lags behind the needs of practical development. It is urgent to formulate relevant policies and regulations to solve problems, such as immigration and employment issues, during and after the graduation of foreign students. (b) There is no mechanism to guarantee the quality of international student education. With the gradual expansion of the scale of international students in the future, if the quality of faculty, curriculum, resources, and management cannot be improved, educational problems for international students, especially regarding the quality of education for degree-seeking students, will be increasingly prominent. (c) At both the national and local government levels, the tracking system concerning provision for detailed information regarding international students from different institutions has not yet been established. This would not be conducive to the effective management and planning of education for international students, and the dynamic development of the international student group cannot be systematically analyzed. (d) The resource investment is insufficient. The funding channel for international students is unitary, and funding mainly comes from government support. It is urgent to establish a funding system in various forms and with multiple channels, and increase the amount and scope of scholarship funding, to attract and retain outstanding and high-level international students, especially postgraduates. (e) The macro-management means are relatively unitary, which mainly concerns administrative management. A management system combining legislation, finance, information service, policy guidance, data monitoring, and appropriate administrative means should be gradually established. (f) The overall strategic thinking at the central government and local government levels is still insufficient (Jiang, 2010, pp. 21–25).

Second, social problems that are encountered, such as off-campus accommodation and part-time jobs for international students, are prominent. It is necessary to create a favourable environment and atmosphere for society, enterprises, and professional organizations to support the education of international students. In addition, the differences in treating international students and domestic students in terms of university support have caused widespread social controversies and need rational guidance.

6.4.1.2 Problems at the institutional level

The management, teaching and service system, and quality have been improved. However, there are still major problems, including: (a) The lag of quality management policies and systems for international students. The collaborative mechanism and collaborative ability among departments within the university needs to be improved. (b) There are insufficient investments regarding the development of faculty's competence on teaching and supporting international students. The hardware facilities need to be improved, as well as the scholarship system, considering that the amount of scholarship is low, the coverage is small, and the role of scholarships in improving the level and quality of international degree-seeking students has not yet been manifested. (c) The proportion of international students in terms of disciplines and countries of origin is unbalanced, and both the academic level of international students and the proportion of degree-seeking students, especially graduate students, are low. (d) There is a lag of various supporting policies and systems, such as work-study programmes, off-campus housing management, etc.

The management is too bureaucratic and the service consciousness and service ability need to be enhanced. The number of international students in colleges and universities is increasing rapidly, but there are problems such as the lack of personnel in international student management, the slow improvement of the quality of international student management, the emphasis on teaching and learning management, and a lack of service consciousness among management personnel, which are in stark contrast with the service-oriented awareness towards student affairs promoted by first-class universities abroad. Chinese universities should strengthen the services for international students in terms of both their study and living. The services for international students should not only include visa procedures, enrolment, academic registration, the arrangement of extracurricular activities, accommodations, and scholarships. They should also consider the adaptation of international students. Universities should offer international students more opportunities to communicate with Chinese students and provide sufficient services, such as offering appropriate language courses, psychological counselling, academic support, and career guidance (Li, 2009).

The scholarships for international students are insufficient. Although Fudan University, Shanghai Jiao Tong University, and East China Normal University have established university-level scholarships, investment in funding is still relatively small and the amount and coverage of the funding is very limited. Thus, it is challenging for them to attract outstanding students in substantial numbers. Efforts should be made to increase the support for international student education and raise funds through various channels to attract outstanding international students from all over the world to study in China and improve China's international influence.

The English curriculum and teaching cannot fully meet the needs of increasing numbers of international students. The overall situation of using English language as a medium of instruction (EMI) is not satisfactory in Chinese HEIs. Few specializations offer courses completely in EMI. Effective measures need to be taken in many aspects, such as the faculty, curricula, management, and resource allocation, so as to ensure the quality of international student education, especially the education for degree-seeking students, and to facilitate the academic and cultural adaptation of international students. It is necessary to increase the number of curriculum categories and offer more elective courses to meet students' needs; divide the students and teach them separately according to their language proficiency in Chinese; improve public facilities such as libraries; and arrange more extracurricular activities.

China's higher education as a whole need to enhance its international reputation and recognition in the global higher education market. At present, there is a lack of prominent disciplines that can attract international students, except for traditional predominant disciplines such as Chinese language and Chinese medicine (Tang, 2005).

6.4.2 Suggestions on improving the quality of education for International Students

Based on the surveys on studying in Shanghai, this section proposes related suggestions on education for inbound international students in China in light of the HEIs in Shanghai.

6.4.2.1 Suggestions at the government and societal levels

First, it is suggested to formulate medium- and long-term development strategies and plans for the internationalization of education and promote the brand of Chinese higher education through expanding international student education. Regarding internationalization of higher education in Shanghai, the long-term goal should be to make its internationalization level as competitive as that of Hong Kong (China) and Singapore. The HEIs in Shanghai should focus on enhancing the attractiveness of Shanghai's higher education brand, build an international education hub, and lay the foundation of human resources, education, and management for constructing a comprehensive education pilot reform zone in the Shanghai Pilot Free Trade Zone, thus making educational development, and talent training and recruitment compatible and synergistic with economic and social development. International student education and international talent training and recruitment policies should be given overall consideration, so as to contribute to transforming Shanghai into a "world-class city" with "world-class education" and accelerating the pace of its opening-up regarding education.

Second, it is recommended that the rules, regulations, and management systems be improved in order to create a favourable policy environment for studying in China. Based on the spirit of laws and regulations such as the *Law of the People's Republic of China on Higher Education* and the *Law of the People's Republic of China on the Administration of Entry and Exit of Foreigners*, and with reference to the *Regulations on the Administration of Acceptance of Foreign Students by HEIs* in China, the local *Regulations on the Administration of Acceptance of Foreign Students by HEIs*, policies that meet the needs of international development of higher education in Shanghai should be formulated to clarify the responsibilities, rights, and obligations of the government, HEIs, and foreign students, and to ensure the development of international students in Shanghai by law. HEIs in Shanghai should align their rules, regulations, and management systems in relation to international student education to make the management and cultivation of international students in Shanghai more standardized, scientific, and transparent. This would ensure the interconnection of the work on international students' enrolment, visas, cultivation, graduations, and employment.

Third, it is expected to establish a government-led, socially engaged, and university-based management system for international student education. To increase the power of all stakeholders to participate in the formulation of higher education opening-up policies, the formulation and implementation of HEI policies need to achieve the combination of both the "top-down" and "bottom-up" approaches, and bring into play the initiative of different organizations, including governmental and non-governmental organizations, foundations and intermediary organizations, HEIs, research institutions, and individuals, as well as the role of market mechanisms. It is expected to form a government-led, socially engaged, university-based system for the management of international student education.

Last, it is suggested that an international student education network platform and a related management and service system be established. Both the services and environment for studying in China need to be optimized. More policies should be implemented, such as formulating enrolment standards, guaranteeing enrolment funds, and establishing an enrolment system for studying in China with a clear division of labour, information sharing, resource sharing, and an appropriate level of coordination and interaction. With the premise of fully safeguarding national security, the autonomy of HEIs in managing studying in China can be appropriately expanded, and hence, efficiency can also be improved. Making full use of the functions of the national information management system for international students in China, and incorporating degree-seeking international students into the national electronic registration system for academic qualifications and student registrations are also suggested.

6.4.2.2 Suggestions at the institutional level

HEIs, as the main agents of foreign education, should strengthen the publicity of international student recruitment, accelerate the construction of foreign language websites of HEIs, provide informative and accurate information, and improve management and service level functions. In addition, they should promote the learning and living conditions, facilitate improvement of the quality of education for international students, and strengthen the procedure for follow-up contact with graduated international students.

First, it is suggested to effectively improve the quality of international student education in HEIs in Shanghai and build an international reputation of higher education. According to the survey data, it can be seen that the faculty, education quality, and reputation, social recognition of degrees, scholarships, and curricula, as well as the educational resources and facilities are all important factors in attracting international students. The level and quality of higher education in a region determines the competitiveness and attractiveness of its higher education offerings. Improving the educational level and quality of regional HEIs is a fundamental way to attract international students. HEIs should expand and enhance exchanges and cooperation with overseas reputable universities, learn from experience from those universities, and improve their own educational strength. A few strategies could also be implemented, such as increasing the number of exchange opportunities between international students and Chinese students; increasing the types of courses and offering more elective courses; grouping the international students into different classes according to their language proficiency in Chinese; improving public facilities such as libraries; and arranging richer extracurricular activities.

Second, it is recommended to increase the scale of government scholarships, broaden scholarship channels, and establish various named and institutional-level scholarships. It is a common practice worldwide to provide scholarships for outstanding foreign students, which is conducive to enhancing foreign students' willingness to study abroad, attract and recruit more outstanding foreign students, and improve the level and quality of foreign education. In addition to government scholarships, the channels of scholarships should be broadened, and a scholarship structure with central government scholarships as the main financial support, supplemented by scholarships from local governments, HEIs, enterprises and institutions, and individuals, should be built. The types of scholarships should be gradually increased.

For HEIs, they should not only make full advantage of all kinds of government scholarships, but also explore other sources of scholarship funds and raise scholarships through multiple channels. For instance, a certain amount can be allocated from alumni funds and social and corporate donations. Academic PhD and master's students should enjoy full or half scholarships, and priority should be given to supporting excellent undergraduate, master's, and doctoral students.

Third, for improving the quality of foreign students' educational, it is necessary to adjust the teaching language system, establish the preparatory system for studying in China, and try the teaching model of mixed classes for both international and local students in some specializations. Language is an important factor affecting the mobility of international students. The English language system is currently dominant in the world. In order to attract more outstanding international students to study in China, it is crucial to break through the language barrier. We can enhance the attractiveness of higher education from the following three aspects: (a) We can adjust the teaching language system and offer more English language courses and bilingual courses, to reduce the language barrier for international students. (b) We should establish a preparatory system for international students to study in China, so that they can have a preparatory period of about one year to learn Chinese; promote the examination system for teaching Chinese as a foreign language; and improve the Chinese language level of foreign students before they come to study in China. Moreover, the teaching arrangement of mixed classes for international students and domestic students could be put into trial in some specializations. Foreign students would then be encouraged to use Chinese to study together with Chinese students and participate in teaching, experiments, and internships, to improve their Chinese language proficiency, deepen their understanding of Chinese culture, and facilitate their adaptation to cultural and academic life in China.

Fourth, research universities should expand the scale of international student recruitment, upgrade the educational level of students, and increase the scale of degree-seeking students. The expansion of degree-seeking students and the upgrading of their level requires a series of policies and management support. This includes improving the internationalization of faculty members, increasing the number of English and bilingual courses, increasing investment in the funding, launching more scholarships, improving management measures and functions of management departments, improving the quality of services for international students and scholars, and renovating and expanding international student housing centres.

Last, it is needed to elevate entrance requirements, ensure strict academic standards, guarantee the quality of education and teaching for international students, and establish a good reputation. Fudan University, Shanghai Jiao Tong University, and East China Normal University all require a certificate of Chinese Language Proficiency Test (HSK) level 3 or higher for admission to their Chinese language programmes (external), and there is no written test. The requirements for admission to other programmes are higher than those for Chinese language programmes, requiring a certificate of HSK level 5 or 6 or even higher, plus a written test. However, some international students still have trouble in understanding the courses. Therefore, while increasing the number of international students, we also need to consider how to ensure the quality of education for those students. In order to attract more international students to study in China, Chinese HEIs need to improve their admission criteria and academic requirements, ensure the quality of education and teaching, and establish a good educational reputation (Li, 2009).

Note

1 The Belt and the Road Initiative (it is also called China's One Belt and One Road Initiative) has been proposed in 2013 by President Xi Jinping during his visit to countries of Central- and South-East Asia, it consists of two routes or branches; one is a sea route that is known as the Maritime Silk Road or One Road Initiative and the second is a land route that is known as One Belt Road that connects China's western part with the regions of Central-Asia, the Middle-East, Africa, and Europe through road, railway, and oil and gas pipeline projects.

References

Institute of International Education. (2016). New 2016 project atlas trends and global data factsheet. Retrieved October 9, 2017, from https://www.iie.org/Researchand-Insights/Project-Atlas/Tools/Current-Infographics

Jiang, K. (2010). Laihua liuxuesheng jiaoyu de pingjing wenti ji jiejue [Study in China: Bottleneck problems and solving measures]. *Daxue Jiaoyu Kexue [University Education Science]*, *2*(2), 21–25.

Li, X. H., & Fang, X. T. (2018). Jinshinian gaodeng jiaoyu zhi laihua liuxue jiaoyu: Chengji yu tiaozhan [International students' study in Chinese higher education institutions in recent ten years: Achievements and challenges]. *Guojia Xingzheng Xueyuan Xuebao [Journal of National Academy of Education Administration]*, *4*, 58–64.

Li, X. Z. (2009). *Laihua hanguo liuxuesheng xuexi shiying de yingxiang yinsu yanjiu [Research on influencing factors of academic adjustment of Korean students in Chinese universities]* [Unpublished master's dissertation]. East China Normal University.

Ma, J. N., & Zhou, Z. Y. (2018). Yidaiyilu yanxian gaoduan liuxuesheng jiaoyu mianlin de tiaozhan ji duice [Challenges and strategies of high-level international student education along the belt and road]. *Gaodeng Jiaoyu Yanju [Journal of Higher Education]*, *39*(1), 100–106.

Ministry of Education. (2004). 2003–2007 nian jiaoyu zhenxing xingdong jihua [2003–2007 education revitalization action plan]. Retrieved June 15, 2019, from http://old.moe.gov.cn/publicfiles/business/htmlfiles/moe/moe_177/200407/2488.html

Ministry of Education. (2016). *Laihua Liuxuesheng Jianming Tongji 2016 [Concise statistics on international students coming to China 2016]*. Department of International Cooperation and Exchanges, MoE.

Ministry of Education. (2019). *2018 Laihua liuxuesheng qingkuang [2018 statistics on international students in China]*. Retrieved June 25, 2019, from http://www.moe.gov.cn/jyb_xwfb/gzdt_gzdt s5987/201904/t20190412_377692.html

Peng, Y. F. (2006). Jiaoyu fuwu maoyi zouchuqu [Education service trade going global]. *Liaowang Xinwen Zhoukan [Outlook Weekly]*, *41*, 64.

People's Daily Online. (2012) (n.d.). Xi Jinping dui quanguo liuxue gongzuo huiyi zuochu zhongyao zhishi qiangdiao [Xi Jinping gives important instructions to the national conference on study abroad]. Retrieved June 26, 2019, from http://politics.people.com.cn/n/2014/1214/c1024-26202991.html

Shanghai Local Records Office (June 26, 2019). Shanghai Yearbook (2006–2016). Retrieved July 21, 2019, from http://www.shtong.gov. cn/Newsite/ node2/ node 1982/ index.htmL.

Shanghai Municipal Government. (2006) (n.d.). Shijiaowei guanyu yinfa 《Shanghaishi waiguo liuxuesheng zhengfu jiangxuejin shixing banfa》 de tongzhi [Notice of the municipal education commission on the application of foreign students for Shanghai government scholarship (Trial)]. Retrieved June 26, 2019, from http://www.shanghai.gov.cn/nw2/nw2314/nw2319/nw12344/u26aw9708.html

Shanghai Municipal Government. (2012) (n.d.). Shanghaishi jiaoyu guojihua gongcheng "shierwu" xingdong jihua [Shanghai education internationalization project "Twelfth Five-Year" action plan]. Retrieved June 19, 2019, from http://www.shanghai.gov.cn/shanghai/node2314/node25307/node25455/node25459/u21ai652056.html

Shanghai Municipal Government. (2016). Shanghai Nianjian (2002–2016) [Shanghai yearbook (2002–2016)]. Retrieved June 26, 2019, from http://www.shanghai.gov.cn/nw2/nw2314/nw24651/nw45010/index.html.

Shanghai Statistics (June 26, 2019). Shanghai Statistical Yearbook (2005–2016). Retrieved July 23, 2019, from http://www.stats-sh.gov.cn/html/sjfb/tjnj/.

Tang, A. G. (2005). *Shanghai jiji tuijin laihua liuxuesheng jiaoyu de xianzhuang, wenti ji fazhan duice yanjiu [Study on the status quo, problems and development countermeasures of Shanghai's active promotion of international students' education].* Research Report on Key Issues of Shanghai Municipal Committee of Democratic Parties and Federation of Industry and Commerce, Shanghai Municipal Committee of China Democratic League.

7 From expansion to quality enhancement

Sino-foreign joint venture institutions and programmes

Sino-foreign joint venture education has developed as a third type of higher education model alongside public and private colleges and universities. As an important dimension of the internationalization of higher education (IHE) with Chinese characteristics and an integral part of China's higher education generally, this model of operation, management systems, and development characteristics is in urgent need of study regarding the experience acquired and challenges encountered in its application. The focus in this chapter is, accordingly, on the development of Sino-foreign joint venture institutions and programmes. The discussion starts with an in-depth account of the development, characteristics, and quality assurance measures of three Sino-foreign joint venture institutions based on case analysis and comparison. There follows an overall analysis of the assembly of teaching staff for the Sino-foreign joint venture programmes at undergraduate and postgraduate levels, especially the development of the international teaching staff.

7.1 The development of Sino-foreign joint venture education

7.1.1 Overview

Since China's accession to the WTO in 2001, along with enhancement of the IHE, Sino-foreign joint venture education has developed rapidly, with an expanding scale, a gradual increase in levels, and the utilization of diversified models. Presently, there are three main types of Sino-foreign joint venture education: Sino-foreign joint venture education programmes, non-independent Sino-foreign joint venture institutions, and independent Sino-foreign joint venture institutions, with the first two accounting for the vast majority. As of June 2018, there were 2,342 Sino-foreign cooperative institutions and programmes, of which 1,090 offered undergraduate education and above (Lin, 2018). Most of the Sino-foreign cooperative institutions are colleges within public universities without independent legal status. Only nine Sino-foreign joint venture institutions have such status: The University of Nottingham Ningbo China (UNNC, established in 2004), Xi'an Jiaotong-Liverpool University (XJTLU, established in 2006), New York University Shanghai (NYUS, established in 2012), Duke Kunshan University (established in 2013), Wenzhou-Kean University (established in 2012), The Chinese University of Hong Kong (Shenzhen) (established in 2014), Beijing Normal University – Hong Kong Baptist University United International College (established in 2005),

DOI: 10.4324/9781003424611-7

Shenzhen Moscow State University-Beijing Institute of Technology University (established in 2016), and Guangdong Technion-Israel Institute of Technology (established in 2016) (MoE, 2018a).

7.1.2 Gradual improvement in the policies and managements system

The development of Sino-foreign joint venture institutions and programmes has resulted in improvements in the associated policies and management systems in China. In 1995, what was then the State Education Commission promulgated and implemented the *Provisional Regulations on Sino-foreign Joint Venture Education*, which facilitated the legalization and standardization of Sino-foreign joint venture education activities. After China's accession to the WTO in 2001, the State Council promulgated and implemented the *Regulations of the People's Republic of China on Sino-foreign Joint Venture Education* in 2003 to better meet the development needs of IHE. In this regard, the MoE also issued the *Measures for the Implementation of the Regulations of the People's Republic of China on Sino-foreign Joint Venture Education* in 2004, which further promoted improvement in the Sino-foreign joint venture education system. Subsequently, Sino-foreign joint venture education has entered a period of rapid development, its scale expanding consistently, and has, in the process, encountered numerous problems. Hence, the MoE issued the *Notice on the Review of Sino-foreign Joint Venture Institutions and Projects* (2005), *Opinions on Several Issues of Current Sino-foreign Joint Venture Education* (2006), and *Notice on Further Regulating the Order of Sino-foreign Joint Venture Education* (2007) in succession to regulate this form of education.

With the further development of Sino-foreign joint venture institutions and programmes, the Chinese government has highlighted quality assurance. In 2009, the MoE issued the *Notice on the Evaluation of Sino-foreign Joint Venture Education* requiring the regular evaluation of Sino-foreign cooperative institutions and programmes to ensure their quality and facilitate sustainable development. In 2018, the MoE (2018b) intensified this scrutiny and terminated 243 Sino-foreign joint venture programmes and institutions in a move that reflected the state's attitude and determination to strengthen quality supervision. For quality assurance, the state not only takes active measures but also regulates the construction of the system. The State Council promulgated the *Outline of National Medium- and Long-term Education Reform and Development Plan* (2010–2020) as early as 2010, which emphasized the importance of quality in Sino-foreign joint venture education and directed attention to "strengthening international exchange and cooperation", "introducing high-quality educational resources", and "improving the level of exchange and cooperation". The government's emphasis on the quality of Sino-foreign joint venture education can be seen in the MoE's recent annual work highlights, such as the emphasis on "strengthening industry self-regulation, establishing and improving the quality assurance system, and carrying out evaluation and quality certification" in 2012 and "introducing a number of high-level universities from abroad" in 2013. In 2014, the MoE emphasized that "the categories, discipline structure and regional layout of Sino-foreign joint venture education should be optimized". In 2015, the ministry reiterated that "the supervision of Sino-foreign joint venture institutions should be strengthened". In 2017 and 2018, the ministry expressed its commitment to "accelerating the revision of the *Regulations of the People's Republic of China on Sino-foreign Joint Venture Education*" and its "measures for implementation", revealing the need to change the model from the extensible development of scale to quality improvement.

7.1.3 Quality assurance for Sino-foreign joint venture education

Quality assurance must, then, be addressed in the process of implementing transnational higher education, especially regarding the host countries. In other words, China, as a major importer of transnational higher education, must pay close attention to quality. Huang Futao (2006) found that the quality assurance of Sino-foreign joint venture education depended mainly on the institutions themselves, with neither national supervision nor a rationalized system being in place, and predicted that it would be a prominent issue in the future. Anne Chapman and David Pyvis (2013) argued that a quality assurance system for Sino-foreign joint venture education should be an important part of the design of the project and should maximize the role of scholars. In 2012, an evaluation study by the Quality Assurance Agency for Higher Education (QAA) in the UK on the British multinational higher education activities in Mainland China revealed a lack of effective internal quality assurance in Sino-foreign joint venture education. Some institutions and programmes have not yet established a sound quality assurance system, and some of the quality assurance systems that have been established have been ineffective (QAA, 2013).

Existing studies of the quality of Sino-foreign joint venture education have focused mainly on the provision of high-quality educational resources and the implementation of quality assessment and assurance systems. Lin Jinhui and Liu Zhiping (2010, pp. 20–28) found that the problems encountered in providing high-quality resources to Sino-foreign joint venture education included the uneven qualifications of foreign partner institutions and the lower number of quality educational resources that have been introduced; the lack of macro-control and guidance, unbalanced regional development, and the low-level duplication of disciplines and specialties; the "emphasis on approval but not management", and the unsound monitoring and evaluating system of the education and teaching quality; the unbalanced qualifications of foreign teachers and the lack of effective management; the prominent contradiction between "public welfare" and "profit-making", and the difficulties in implementing the "public satisfaction principle" of cooperative education; the loopholes in enrolment management and the incomplete degree certification system. Ye Lin (2012) conducted an empirical study of transnational degree programmes from the perspective of the students' study experience and found problems in the teaching and evaluation of foreign teachers, the participation of Chinese teachers, and the use of foreign language materials. In a case study of the teaching quality assurance system of the UNNC, Zhao Fengbo (2014) found the "academic evaluation mechanism, curriculum implementation mechanism, and teacher-student interaction mechanism" to be important components for ensuring the quality of university teaching, these also being characteristics of the university.

Over more than ten years of development, then, Sino-foreign joint venture universities have made achievements in the model of operation, institutional management, and talent cultivation, gained wide social recognition, and played a special role in Chinese higher education. However, the regulations and policies governing the issues just discussed still require improvement and in-depth empirical research.

7.2 A comparison of the University of Nottingham Ningbo China and New York University Shanghai

Sino-foreign joint venture universities are important channels for bringing high-quality foreign educational resources to China, and their models of operation have injected new vitality into Chinese higher education and provided experience useful in the reform of higher education in China. In the following discussion, a comparison of the developmental characteristics of UNNC and NYUS serves to exemplify these developments. These universities share certain similarities. In terms of organization, both Sino-foreign cooperative institutions were established as and remain independent legal entities. In terms of education level, both mainly offer four-year undergraduate education. In terms of orientation, both adhere to the value of public satisfaction. Last, in terms of management authority, both operate autonomously, maintaining independent campuses, enrolments, faculty recruitment systems, fund management systems, and so on.

7.2.1 Orientation: Precise orientation with distinctive characteristics

The founding of these outstanding representatives of Sino-foreign joint venture universities represents milestones in terms of distinct phases in the development of these ventures. The UNNC was the first university founded through a cooperative effort of foreign and Chinese institutions and the first Sino-British cooperative entity to offer independent undergraduate education. NYUS, as the first high-level international university founded through a cooperative effort of US and Chinese universities in Shanghai, marked a new stage in the development of Sino-foreign cooperative universities.

In terms of orientation, the UNNC is a high-standard Sino-foreign cooperative university with status as, again, an independent legal entity, having an independent campus and distinctive Chinese and British strengths. NYUS is a non-profit, world-class research university with degree-granting authority and, once more, the status of an independent legal entity (Zhao & Chen, 2012). The mission of the UNNC is to nurture students' development into high-level talent familiar with Chinese and Western cultures, proficient in Chinese and English, capable of independent thinking and innovation, endowed with team spirit and an international mindset and vision, and capable of performing at the professional level and capacity expected by the University of Nottingham.[1] The mission of NYUS is to cultivate international innovative talent with a global, contemporary perspective to excel as global citizens thanks to cross-cultural understanding, communication, and cooperation.

Both the UNNC and NYUS follow the two main principles of their discipline and specialty settings, that is, offering coursework in the dominant disciplines of the parent university and focusing on the specialties that pertain to China's socio-economic development. The main academic units of the UNNC are the Faculty of Science and Engineering, the Faculty of Social Sciences, and the Faculty of Humanities and Education. Since 2009, the UNNC and the University of Nottingham have been jointly recruiting doctoral students, with 22 postgraduate specialties and 18 undergraduate specialties (UNNC, 2019a). NYUS offers specialties in finance, economics, biological sciences, neuroscience, physics, chemistry, electronic information engineering, computer science and technology, digital media, mathematics and applied mathematics, and integrated humanities.

The universities differ in terms of the proportion of their resources that they direct to international students and their strategies for recruiting. More specifically, in the first place, they have distinct admission criteria. NYUS not only takes into account the results of the *Gaokao*, China's national university entrance examination but also applies non-unitary admission criteria depending on the prospective students. Thus, for domestic students, the criteria include, along with the *Gaokao* results, high school academic examination results and a comprehensive quality assessment (in the form of an interview). For international students, NYUS applies the common admissions criteria of New York University in the US. The UNNC, in line with other universities in Mainland China, uses the *Gaokao* results as the sole admission criterion, and its admission quota has been incorporated into China's national admission programme. It has adopted two methods, *Gaokao* selection admission and early admission. The former mainly takes into account prospective students' *Gaokao* results and sets a clear requirement for English language scores. In 2016, the national average admissions scores for liberal arts and science were 40.14 points and 60.21 points, respectively, above the admission score thresholds for the first-tier universities.

Second, NYUS and the UNNC differ with respect to enrolment scale and the proportion of international students. NYUS enrolled about 300 students each year between 2013 and 2017, about half were Mainland Chinese students and half foreign students. Its annual enrolment in Mainland China is very small, only 151 students. At the same time, it has established several research centres and bases jointly with East China Normal University (ECNU) and enrolled a small number of graduate students, with a total enrolment of about 4,000 undergraduate and graduate students (Zhao & Chen, 2012). The UNNC has a much larger enrolment, and the majority of its students are from Mainland China, with a very small proportion of international students and students from Hong Kong, Macao, and Taiwan. The UNNC hosted about 8,000 students in 2018, of whom only 13 were from outside the mainland (UNNC, 2019b).

7.2.2 Management innovation: A balance of domestic and foreign sides, flat structure, and efficient management

7.2.2.1 Leadership balancing domestic and foreign powers

Currently, Sino-foreign joint venture universities in China, including the UNNC and NYUS, have in place a president and hierarchical system under the leadership

Table 7.1 The leadership of the Sino-foreign joint venture institutions

Universities	University of Nottingham Ningbo China	New York University Shanghai
Date of establishment	May 2004	August 2012
Leadership	Executive president hierarchical system under the leadership of a board of governors.	Executive vice-president hierarchical system under the leadership of a board of governors.
Assignment of authority and responsibility	The chairman of the board of Wanli Group chairs the board of governors. The board consists of eight Chinese and seven foreign members, with the president being Chinese and the executive president a foreigner.	The board of governors is the highest decision-making body, which consists of four Chinese and four US members. The president is nominated by East China Normal University and the executive vice-president by New York University.

Source: The authored collected information from field trips to UNNC in June 2014 and NYUS in December 2018.

of a board of governors (see Table 7.1). The board consists of leaders of Chinese and foreign partner universities, educational authorities in the cities where the institutions are located, and the investors. It is responsible for major decisions and the formulation of development policies. The president is usually a Chinese national while the executive president or executive vice-president is assigned by the foreign partner university. The president is mainly responsible for the policy-making relating to institutional operations and obtaining external resources and the foreign president for supervising education, quality assurance, and management of daily operations.

In terms of leadership, the two universities are similar in being under the leadership of a board of governors, with the Chinese and the foreign leaders having distinct duties. The UNNC has adopted the leadership system of British universities, with the chancellor being an honorary position and the vice chancellor exercising power. NYUS is co-directed by two presidents, a Chinese president who concentrates on macro-level management, including external affairs, and a US president who is responsible for academic affairs. As President Yu Lizhong (Personal Communication on December 29, 2018) said, "I am the Chinese president and Jeff is the American president; we should act with 'two bodies and one head'", with the development of the university thus depending on open communication and mutual understanding between the two. In the management and operation of academic affairs and quality assurance regarding education and teaching, the foreign partner universities, the University of Nottingham, and New York University, are in the leading position while the Chinese partner universities coordinate and share resources.

7.2.2.2 Flat management systems

Both universities have adopted a lean, flat structure with a focus on management efficiency. The UNNC has gradually built up an organizational structure with "three levels and two systems" over more than 10 years of operation. The three levels correspond to the institutional decision-making organization, management organization, and implementation team, and the two systems involve executive decision-making on the one hand and the committee's supervision on the other. Regarding the structure and operation of the administration, the university's board of governors is the highest decision-making body, being responsible for formulating the development plan, the financing of education, approving the budget and final accounts of the partner university, managing the funds and assets of the partner university, and appointing (and, if necessary, dismissing) the head of the university. The university also has a council responsible for implementing and enforcing the decisions of the board of governors and various management bodies with distinct functions as executive teams that are responsible for various issues relating to the operation of the university. This supervision ensures that the university operates in accordance with Chinese laws and regulations and adheres to its mission, and quality assurance supports the university's teaching, research, and services. The university transmits Chinese culture to students and faculty, and actively coordinates operations between China and the UK and relations between the university and the local community.

In order to improve efforts to cultivate talent and improve its status, NYUS emphasizes streamlining and efficiency in its organizational structure, with its management organization consisting of an academic management sector and an administrative management sector (Jin, 2012). The academic management sector is responsible for teaching and research, including academic registration, curricula, managing the faculty, providing resources, services, and support to students, and generally promoting the university's academic development. The administrative management sector is responsible for daily operations. Its oversight of internal affairs includes administration, logistics, public services, personnel management, and campus construction projects, and its oversight of external affairs includes cooperation and exchange, fund-raising, and portfolio promotion.

Unlike domestic universities, which have a hierarchical structure, these universities have mainly adopted a flat organizational structure and follow the principles of streamlining, efficiency, and service orientation in their operations. Both are organized so that all of the departments are parallel, having no strict hierarchy or subordination. In terms of their organizational functions, most of the departments serve the goal of talent cultivation in keeping with the concept of "serving students". The organizational system of the UNNC is very mature and well-established, having a party committee guarantee system with localized characteristics. The organizational structure and system of NYUS are improving, having been in operation for only a relatively short time, but its student-centred educational philosophy and management organization can serve as a model for other universities.

7.2.2.3 Student management and service networks centred on student development

The UNNC focuses on moral education in terms of student management, employing a pedagogical model consistent with the actual development of the university and based on the traditional Chinese model into which the classical Western paradigm has been integrated. Its approach consists, first, of selecting the appropriate starting point, following the growth process of young students, and finding ways to combine Chinese and Western higher education, thereby promoting the development of good students and good citizens. Second, the university promotes the realization of individual value, motivating students to be independent and self-disciplined and improve themselves. Third, it uses Chinese and Western approaches in complementary ways to teach students to learn to live together, think critically, and make appropriate choices.

NYUS attaches great importance to student management, services, and support and has established a strong system for their security, academic development, and daily lives. This support includes the establishment of an Academic Resource Management Center at which professional staff offer one-on-one, face-to-face professional counselling to help students overcome academic challenges and to fill the gaps in communication between students and teachers after class. In terms of daily life, the university provides a variety of customized services to meet the needs of students. For example, international and Chinese students live in integrated dormitories so as to enhance cross-cultural communication and stimulate their initiative and self-management. In terms of health and hygiene, professional medical services, including mental health counselling, are available to students. The campus environment was built without walls to enhance the students' engagement with the outside world. The internal facilities include public activity spaces for barrier-free communication and brainstorming.

Regarding the management of students, both universities uphold the "student-centred" management concept, closely follow the institutional construction goals of talent training, and have made some achievements. On the other hand, owing to differences in the training objectives and orientation of the universities, the two HEIs show distinct characteristics in the concrete implementation of student management. The UNNC pays more attention to localized development while introducing high-level foreign educational resources, innovating a series of characteristic management models, and taking into account the current situation of domestic education. NYUS has a clear orientation to serve students, taking their needs as the primary starting point in its management practices, which have laid a solid foundation for the realization of its talent-cultivation goals.

7.2.3 Major stakeholders and conditions: Tripartite cooperation among local governments, universities, and the market

The UNNC and NYUS differ in terms of their parent institutions, host cities and investment mechanisms, and founding dates and institutional environments.

7.2.3.1 Parent universities

The Chinese partner of the UNNC, Zhejiang Wanli College, is an average HEI that offers undergraduate education. The Chinese partner of NYUS, ECNU, is "Double-first-class" university under the supervision of the MoE. The mission of Wanli College is to cultivate application-oriented talent in Zhejiang Province, while that of ECNU is to cultivate comprehensive high-level talent from across the country while playing a role in research and social services as a research university. The difference between the universities in terms of the Chinese cooperative institution affects the extent to which the Chinese partner participates in the teaching and talent-cultivation aspects of cooperative education as well as the role of high-quality educational resources. For example, the strengths and faculty of ECNU in the humanities facilitate the successful integration of Chinese and Western culture into the general education provided by NYUS. In addition, a former president of ECNU went on to serve as the president of NYUS, further transferring the characteristics of the latter to the former and making good use of the parent university's resources. The main advantage of Wanli College is its market-oriented rationale, its investment in the partner university being reflected in its financial support and market financing mechanism totalling more than RMB 700 million in the construction of the UNNC.[2]

The foreign partner universities of the Sino-foreign cooperative universities also have similarities and differences. Both the University of Nottingham and New York University are world-class universities, in the UK and US, respectively, with long histories. The former is a public university founded in 1881, and the latter, one of the largest private universities in the US, was founded in 1831. Both have established multiple campuses around the world and amassed extensive multinational and multi-campus education experience. The University of Nottingham has, in addition to several campuses in the UK, a campus in Kuala Lumpur, Malaysia, as well as the campus in Ningbo, while New York University has, in addition to campuses in New York, a campus in Abu Dhabi in the United Arab Emirates as well as the campus in Shanghai. Their respective foreign partner universities play a leading role in determining the teaching resources, talent training, and quality assurance at NYUS and UNNC.

7.2.3.2 The host cities and investment in universities

The local governments play an important role in the establishment and development of Sino-foreign cooperative universities through policies, laws and regulations, the provision of resources, and so on. The differences between Ningbo and Shanghai affect the level of local support that the universities receive. Both Zhejiang Province and Ningbo City provide strong policy and financial support to the UNNC. In terms of policies, Ningbo promulgated the *Regulations on the Promotion of Private Education in Ningbo* in 2006 to support and regulate private education, including Sino-foreign joint venture education, and the regulations treat the teachers and students of various types of universities equally in many respects. In terms of funding, the Zhejiang government allocated RMB 50 million to support the construction of the UNNC. The city of Ningbo prioritized the UNNC as its "No. 1 Project" ("Project of Revitalizing the City through Science and Education"), allocating RMB 100 million in special funding and facilitating land acquisition and construction. To bolster the science and engineering disciplines at the UNNC, the city provides special subsidies, including an annual RMB 18,000 per student, from its financial education fund, spending a total of RMB 36.71 million from 2011 to 2012.[3] The Shanghai Municipal Government has made NYUS one of the beneficiaries of special funding for academic construction, faculty development, and internationalization of local universities in the city. Since 2013, the Shanghai Municipal Education Commission has provided a certain amount of start-up funding for NYUS every year. The Shanghai Municipal Government and Pudong New Area Government have identified the construction of NYUS as an important pilot project for comprehensive educational reform and offered strong support for the construction of infrastructure (i.e. university buildings and dormitories) for its operation. During the early stages of NYUS, ECNU and the *Lujiazui* Group of Companies provided an excellent campus environment and space to operate.

7.2.3.3 The establishment of the universities and their institutional environment

From the establishment of the UNNC in 2004 to the official enrolment in NYUS in 2013, the IHE and Sino-foreign joint venture education in China underwent nearly ten years of development, during which the institutional environment changed. Thus, the two universities were established at different stages in the development of Sino-foreign joint venture education. The UNNC was founded only three years after China's accession to the WTO and in the early stages of the IHE, when the primary goal for transnational education was to provide quality resources to meet the demand of Chinese students for international higher education and to relieve the pressure to study abroad by making it possible for students to enjoy foreign educational resources without leaving China. In terms of the management system, the *Regulations of the People's Republic of China on Sino-foreign Joint Venture Education*, promulgated in 2003, defined Sino-foreign joint venture education as "foreign educational institutions and Chinese educational institutions in China must cooperate in educational institution activities with Chinese citizens as the main target market". Accordingly, the UNNC recruits students from Mainland China.

By the time NYUS was established, with China's deepening reform and opening-up as well as further internationalization, Sino-foreign joint venture education was entering a stage of rapid development and standardized management. The universities in Mainland China recognized the competitive nature of the international student market, and the government formulated strategic plans to enhance their internationalization and competitiveness. The central government formulated the strategy of "Study in China Program" and planned to make China the largest destination country in Asia for international students by attracting 500,000 students to China by 2020. Shanghai formulated the *Twelfth Five-Year Plan for Shanghai's Education Internationalization Project* to vigorously promote the internationalization of education and development of Sino-foreign joint venture education.

At this stage, although the introduction of high-quality resources remains one of the main objectives of Sino-foreign joint venture education, the development of Sino-foreign joint venture institutions involves a new mission and contemporary objectives. These objectives are, first, to achieve innovation in the management system and provide a template for the construction of a modern university system in China; second, to explore and experiment with the cultivation of high-level innovative talent and guide public universities in the reform of their models for cultivating talent; and, third, to play the crucial role in the IHE of recruiting and retaining international students and cultivating high-level international talent for urban development. The new round of development of Sino-foreign joint venture educational entities carries forward the historical mission of reforming China's higher education and furthering its internationalization. In this context, the establishment of NYUS has new connotations for the Sino-foreign cooperative model and has involved the incorporation of new mechanisms. Moreover, NYUS has received unprecedented support in terms of policies, resources, and campus construction.

7.2.4 Conclusions: Development experience, challenges, and prospects

Through the comparison of the two universities, it can be seen that China's Sino-foreign joint venture education has entered a new period of development, introduced new elements, and gained momentum for Chinese higher education through the vigorous promotion of a diversified model for university operations. At the same time, the accumulated management experience provides an excellent example for domestic universities of how to construct a modern university system. The leadership and management systems of these institutions differ from those of public universities. The leadership system reflects the interests of multiple stakeholders and ensures the independence and autonomy of universities as academic institutions and organizations. The management system and structure are flat and efficient, avoiding the bloat that characterizes functional departments and complex bureaucratic structures. In Sino-foreign joint venture institutions, the ponderous administrative departments of public universities are streamlined into one organizational department, while students have easy access to academic affairs, services, and teaching, these having become the core functions and tasks of university management. Regarding investment in the university, diversified funds and resources confer complementary advantages. Thus, the Chinese and foreign governments, together with the universities, students, and Chinese society, guarantee the sustainability of an institution rather than government or tuition fees alone serving to maintain its needs. Moreover, the advantages and strengths of the Chinese and foreign partners are complementary with respect to the leadership, management, and investment systems. For example, the composition and roles of the board of governors are equal. The Chinese partner is more involved in the management of student affairs and administration while the foreign partner is more responsible for the management of academic affairs and academic quality assurance. Returning to the topic of investment, the Chinese government provides support in terms of land, infrastructure, and special funds, and the foreign partner provides for the operation of the university, being concerned with curricula, faculty, educational branding, and, again, quality assurance, especially in the form of intellectual property rights.

At present, although the development of Sino-foreign cooperative institutions is stable, some challenges to sustainable development persist. The UNNC has essentially broken even and entered a period of stable development thanks to the financial support of Zhejiang Province and Ningbo City, the *Wanli* Education Group, and the scale effect of its enrolment. In the future, it is necessary to give further thought to the orientation of development, operational characteristics, and competitive advantages of universities in addition to the dilemmas that they face. The competitive advantages are based on the development characteristics, which are reflected in the advantages and disadvantages of the UNNC compared with foreign universities as well as other Chinese and foreign cooperative institutions in China. In particular, in terms of improving the cultivation of master's and doctoral students, increasing the scale of international enrolments, and cultivating science and technology and high-quality international talent, it is necessary to explore and reflect constantly on ways to give full play to the advantages of the cooperative parent bodies, that is, China and Britain, so as to achieve new breakthroughs.

In the initial founding period of NYUS, the first class of students, the class of 2017, went on to well-known enterprises and famous universities at home and abroad for employment and further education. The academic reputation of the university has been consolidated and enhanced. The immediate goals of NYUS are fairly clear, but its medium and long-term goals are still developing, and its social image, brand effect, and institutional status remain to be determined. The dilemmas faced by NYUS include, first, maintaining sufficient financial and resource investment required for sustainable development. The tuition revenue cannot cover the average education cost of each student, and, if positioned as a small, high-level, world-class university, the institution will find it difficult to take advantage of the scale effect given its limited enrolment and, therefore, tuition revenue, leaving the unit cost high. Second, regarding school space and campus construction, NYUS relied, for its first year of operation, on the campus of ECNU, and most of the current facilities are provided by the Shanghai Municipal Government, Pudong New Area, and *Lujiazui* Group. Since it is located in the prosperous *Lujiazui* Finance and Trade Zone, the operating costs are very high. NYUS announced in June 2019 that it would establish a new campus in the *Qiantan* of Pudong, thereby solving the problem of school space and resource investment and laying the foundations for future development. However, the institution's long-term development and sustainability may continue to depend on local government support in terms of hardware facilities and similar needs. Third, regarding the mobility and stability of the faculty, NYUS has tried to build a high-level, international faculty, relying on that of New York University, recruiting full-time faculty worldwide while also employing the faculty of ECNU for certain courses and specialties. However, the high level of faculty required brings the problem of high salaries. Building a high-level and international full-time faculty will remain an important task for the university.

190　*From expansion to quality enhancement*

7.3 The quality assurance system of Xi'an Jiaotong-Liverpool University

At present, the operation of Sino-foreign joint venture education has resulted in positive outcomes with regard to quality assurance, but here also some problems persist. In terms of the external environment of its development, the concept of quality assurance has not been adequately popularized, and some Sino-foreign joint venture institutions and programmes have yet to establish an effective quality assurance system. To provide further insight into the quality assurance system of Sino-foreign joint venture institutions, the following discussion considers the successes and shortcomings of Xi'an Jiaotong-Liverpool University over its relatively long history.

7.3.1 Overview of Xi'an Jiaotong-Liverpool University

Xi'an Jiaotong-Liverpool University is a Sino-foreign joint venture university established by the University of Liverpool (UOL) in the UK and Xi'an Jiaotong University in China and headquartered in Suzhou. UOL is a member of the Russell Group of universities and a famous "red brick university" in the UK with a long history of distinguished teaching and research. In 2003, with the promulgation of the *Regulations of the People's Republic of China on Sino-foreign Joint Venture Education*, the policy environment became favourable for the two universities to establish a Sino-foreign joint venture university.

In September 2004, the University of Liverpool and Xi'an Jiaotong University signed a cooperation agreement to establish an independent, international higher education institution utilizing a joint venture approach. In 2006, XJTLU obtained the necessary licence from the MoE and recruited 168 undergraduates majoring in financial mathematics, information and computing science, communication engineering, computer science and technology, electronic science and technology, and information management and information systems. Over more than ten years of development, the number of students enrolled at XJTLU has increased annually. The university has been improving its talent training and management system and developing a distinctive character. By 2018, it had hosted more than 15,000 registered students (of whom more than 3,000 were studying at the UOL in the UK), including some 1,000 international students, 900 master's students, and 200 doctoral students (XJTLU, 2018a). XJTLU offers more than 70 undergraduate and graduate programmes in the fields of science, technology, engineering, design, management, economics, culture, and art, with 17 faculties and departments and three teaching centres. In early 2018, the XJTLU Entrepreneur Academy was established in Taicang in Jiangsu Province to explore human resources and new models of education in the era of artificial intelligence as well as the modalities of the universities of the future.

For more than a decade, XJTLU has been committed to realizing its role as "a research-oriented, unique, world-recognized Chinese university and an international university in the land of China". In order to ensure the effectiveness of its operations and maintain high quality standards in training talent, XJTLU has

From expansion to quality enhancement 191

established a system based on the multi-subject collaborative governance system with external mechanisms exercising control over internal quality management processes (XJTLU, 2018b).

7.3.2 *Multi-subject collaborative governance: The external quality governance system at XJTLU*

Since XJTLU grants bachelor's degrees from both Chinese regular universities and the University of Liverpool in the UK, the quality of the education that it delivers is subject to both Chinese and British supervision. This joint oversight constitutes XJTLU's external quality assurance system with multiple subjects, while the accreditation of its degrees by professional organizations in the UK enhances its international profile and attractiveness to international students. Figure 7.1 illustrates this external quality governance and internal quality assurance system.

7.3.2.1 *Quality supervision of XJTLU in the UK*

In the UK, the QAA and the University of Liverpool oversee the quality of education at XJTLU. All programmes and institutions that grant British higher education degrees are subject to regular quality assessment by the QAA (Ma, 2014). In order to meet the demands associated with the internationalization of UK higher education, "to protect the interests of everyone studying for a UK higher education degree" and "to maintain academic standards and improve the quality of UK higher education", the QAA also assesses UK education programmes overseas (QAA, 2017). Therefore, the QAA (2018) has set out, in the second part of the UK Quality Code for Higher Education, the criteria for assessing collaborative

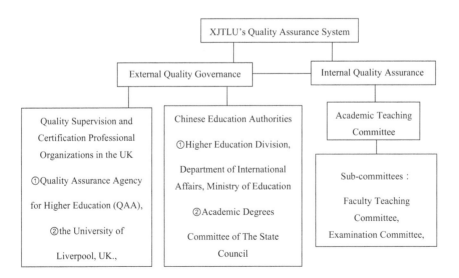

Figure 7.1 XJTLU's external quality governance and internal quality assurance systems.

192 *From expansion to quality enhancement*

education programmes (Managing the Provision of Higher Education with Others). The QAA's assessment of XJTLU is, then, part of its assessment of cross-border higher education, conducted every six years, which consists mainly of an examination of the operation and management of universities, the quality of the education that they deliver, and the information and resources that they provide to their students (QAA, 2013). The QAA first requires universities to conduct an internal self-assessment based on the content that it specifies and then assesses the effectiveness of the internal quality assurance mechanism based on the initial self-assessment materials that they provide. The assessment process consists of four main steps. First, the QAA distributes questionnaires to the administrators of Sino-foreign joint venture universities to gather information about the current state of transnational education activities and then selects universities with certain characteristics based on the results of the questionnaires. Second, it collects and analyzes the data on cooperative education and asks the selected universities to provide relevant data and information and then further assesses the operations of specific institutions and programmes. Third, the QAA sets up an evaluation team consisting of senior administrators from other universities in the UK and QAA staff to conduct an on-site inspection that involves reviewing the self-assessment report and detailed information on the operation of institutions and programmes, asking administrators for relevant evidence, and interviewing staff members and students. Finally, the evaluation reports are written up and published that includes an overview, independent evaluations of the operations of each institution, and special case studies (QAA, 2017).

Since XJTLU grants degrees from the UOL, the latter university requires that the quality of education at XJTLU be up to the same standards as that of the parent university and subject to its supervision and evaluation. For the purpose, the UOL conducts an Accreditation and Re-accreditation Visit, an Annual Monitor Visit, and a Validation Visit (University of Liverpool, 2018a).

The Accreditation and Re-accreditation Visit is usually conducted every five years, its purpose being to determine whether XJTLU should continue to grant UOL degree. The evaluation takes into account the academic structure, quality assurance and enhancement system, administrative and technical infrastructure, management structure, selection of faculty, post-service development system, learning resources and facilities, student support services, academic standards, rules and regulations, professional management, and so on (University of Liverpool, 2018b).

The Annual Monitor Visit supplements the Accreditation and Re-accreditation Visit, serving to ensure that the quality of education at XJTLU remains consistent afterward and to track the university's development. The focus is fairly narrow, remaining mainly on the students, specifically, the specialty setting, learning environment, support, performance, achievements, and so on and touching as well on faculty development and the quality assurance system (University of Liverpool, 2018c).

The Validation Visit focuses mainly on the specialty and curriculum designs but also includes some aspects of the specialties and curricula, such as the revision of syllabi and correction and review of examination papers. The general process consists of (1) submission of an application to offer a new specialty to the

XJTLU Planning and Policy Committee in early September, (2) internal review in December, after which approved applications are forwarded to the UOL's Collaborative Provisional Sub-Committee for further review, (3) a request by the UOL later that month or in January of the following year that XJTLU provide more information for assessment by external advisers at the UOL in the appropriate academic subject area, (4) approval or disapproval of the application by the Liverpool Collaborative Provision Sub-Committee in March based on the assessment results, (5) submission by the XJTLU of the complete application and assessment report to the UOL's Academic Quality and Standards Committee in June, and (6) completion by XJTLU of the processes necessary for the admission of students to begin studying the approved specialty in September (University of Liverpool, 2018d).

7.3.2.2 Supervision by Chinese education authorities

The Chinese authorities are mainly responsible for supervising the quality of the education at XJTLU. The MoE handles the review of degree-granting authority and maintains the overall quality of education. In addition, the Jiangsu Provincial Education Department is responsible for periodic evaluation of the quality of the education at XJTLU.

The relevant provisions of *Principles and Measures of the Academic Degrees Office on the Accreditation of Degree Conferring Units* stipulate that any university that has been approved by national education authorities, offers specialties in accordance with the national undergraduate teaching plan, and meets the other relevant requirements can apply to be listed as a bachelor-degree–conferring unit beginning the year in which the first cohort of undergraduates' graduates. Accordingly, XJTLU received the authority to confer undergraduate degrees in 2010. The review process includes two parts. The preliminary review combines peer review with examination by the education authorities with the assistance of local education departments. The MoE and the Academic Degrees Committee of the State Council conduct the second-round review of the universities and specialties applying for bachelor's-degree-conferring authority based on the results of the preliminary review. In addition, after being granted this authority, the MoE will evaluate XJTLU every six years to determine whether the quality of the education has remained consistent with certain standards.

At the same time, as a Sino-foreign joint venture institution, XJTLU is also subject to the Quality Assessment of Sino-foreign Joint Venture Education organized by the Department of International Cooperation and Exchange Department of the MoE, which includes self-assessment and random assessment. In the former case, the target of evaluation will complete self-evaluations, submit self-evaluation reports and relevant data and information, and organize educational and teaching management documents and materials for inspection, within a specified period of time in accordance with the "evaluation index system for Sino-foreign joint venture institutions (or programs)". In random assessments, on the other hand, experts review the self-evaluation results and conduct an on-site inspection, taking into account the management system, operating funds and their use, training objectives and programmes, training conditions, the faculty, the organization of teaching, the quality of the training, social reputation, and operating characteristics (MoE, 2018a).

Assisting the national education authorities, the Jiangsu Provincial Department of Education also routinely assesses the quality of the education that XJTLU provides along with that of the other universities in the province. The provincial assessment emphasizes the overall situation of university education, faculty team-building, teaching infrastructure, teaching design and reform, quality assurance systems, and student learning. The final report will be published on the official website of the Jiangsu Provincial Education Department.

7.3.2.3 Accreditation by international professional organizations

XJTLU actively participates in the quality certification provided by international professional organizations, with external specialized industry organizations fully evaluating and certifying its programmes. When this research was conducted, the undergraduate programme in architecture and the master's programme in architectural design offered by the Department of Architecture had been accredited by the Royal Institute of British Architects (RIBA); all of the undergraduate and master's programmes in the School of Business had been accredited by the Association to Advance Collegiate Schools of Business International (AACSB), the Association of Chartered Certified Accountants (ACCA), and the Institute of Chartered Accountants in England and Wales (ICAEW); the Joint Board of Moderators (JBM) had fully accredited all of the specialties offered by the Department of Civil Engineering; all of the undergraduate programmes in the Department of Electrical and Electronic Engineering as well as the Master of Science in Sustainable Energy Technologies and the Master of Science in Multimedia Communications programmes, had been accredited by the Institution of Engineering and Technology (IET); the undergraduate programme in Applied Chemistry had been accredited by the Royal Society of Chemistry (RSC); and the undergraduate programme in Biological Sciences had been accredited by the Royal Society of Biology (RSB).

7.3.3 Self-regulation and autonomy: XJTLU's internal quality assurance system

In addition to external quality control and professional accreditation, XJTLU seeks to achieve self-regulation and autonomy in quality management and, for this purpose, has built a comprehensive system to ensure the quality of teaching and learning from the perspectives of the university, colleges or departments, specialties, curricula, and student academic assessment.

7.3.3.1 Building a sound university-level organizational system and regulatory framework

At the university level, XJTLU has established an organizational system and regulatory framework for academic quality assurance. In the organizational system, the Academic Committee of XJTLU coordinates all of the work, formulates the university's academic strategic development plan, and reviews the resolutions of all of the subcommittees regarding major programmes and proposals. These subcommittees are responsible for the work related to various fields. For instance, the Development Advisory Committee and Industrial Advisory Committee receive feedback from prominent members of the community and industry, and the Examination Committee appoints external examiners as needed to determine the teaching quality regarding such issues as curriculum design, examination methods, and course content. The Faculty Teaching Committee, which mainly involves faculty members, is responsible for peer review and sharing teachers' experiences and improvement efforts (XJTLU, 2018c). In terms of the regulatory framework, the university has implemented a series of management systems to clarify the quality standards of each link, including the Four-Year Undergraduate Degree Grading System, Undergraduate Bachelor's Degree Cultivation Model, Teaching Management Policy and Policies of XJTLU, Undergraduate Teaching Standards and Quality Policy, Rules and Regulations for the Implementation of Examination Evaluation, Code of Conduct for Examinations, and other documents.

7.3.3.2 Establishing faculty-level teaching and professional management guarantee mechanisms

A teaching quality management system has been set up and quality assurance implemented at the faculty level. The Faculty Academic Teaching Committee is the highest authority, overseeing all teaching and learning affairs at this level. The faculty also has a student-staff liaison committee composed of both students and faculty members for which student representatives collect general student opinions about their education to inform the discussion of solutions and strategies with faculty representatives. The faculty members conduct regular self-evaluation on a four-year cycle, comprehensively reviewing the teaching and student training in all degree programmes and monitoring whether training goals are being met. The faculties are responsible for quality assurance at the programme level and are required to submit an annual self-assessment report at the beginning of each academic year to assess the effectiveness and overall relevance of the degree programmes offered from the perspective of disciplinary development and industrial applicability and evaluate the educational quality of the programmes and the overall learning experience of the students (XJTLU, 2018c).

At the curriculum level, the applications for new courses and adjustments to existing syllabi are subject to a rigorous process of funding application, programme review, departmental review, university review, external review, and accreditation by the UOL. The quality of curriculum delivery is also assessed regularly, mainly through peer review, student assessment, and internal and external examiners. The faculty members in a programme assess each other; the student assessment is conducted through questionnaires and interviews; and the internal and external examination is conducted by the faculty members and third-party experts in the preparation and marking of examination papers, respectively.

XJTLU also has a well-established system for academic evaluation at the individual student level. To begin with, students are offered special training regarding academic standards, and all are taught about the serious consequences of academic misconduct in their English for Academic Purposes (EAP) courses. Second, all students' course papers and research reports are subject to inspection by the international "academic misconduct detection system" (using Turnitin software). When academic misconduct is discovered, the university imposes the appropriate penalties in view of the severity of the situation, such as the annulment of grades or expulsion. Students, for their part, have the right to defend their rights and interests by appealing any charge of misconduct in their courses and filing complaints about perceived injustice in their courses or examinations. They may also elect student representatives to participate in university management activities; for instance, the student representative participates the Student-Faculty Liaison Committee, which regularly reviews the majors that departments offer. And the student interviews provide feedback on all of the university's external evaluation activities.

XJTLU's quality assurance system effectively integrates the best educational and management practices followed in both China and the UK. The system is characterized by, first, a multi-layered structure, with both external supervisions, mainly from the government and professional bodies, and internal assurance measures distributed across all levels of the university, faculties, and majors. Second, the system includes multiple collaborative subjects, including teachers, students, administrators, external examiners, and members of the community. Third, the concept of being student-centred has been implemented throughout the system to improve the quality of education and, ultimately, contribute to the overall development of students, who have opportunities to assess themselves and the right to participate in quality assurance activities at all levels.

7.3.4 Challenges of quality assurance at XJTLU

Having been in operation for more than ten years, XJTLU has made some noteworthy achievements, and its positive influence on Chinese higher education deserves recognition. However, its development has entailed some problems regarding its capacity to maintain the quality of the education that it delivers that also merit consideration. Practical measures need to be taken to improve the quality assurance system continually and highlight the characteristics of Sino-foreign joint venture universities.

7.3.4.1 Synchronization and coordination of the scale, efficiency, and quality of development

Continued expansion has placed additional pressures on the faculty and learning resources. The student body increased nearly 20-fold over XJTLU's first 12 years, from the initial cohort of 168 undergraduates in 2006 to the 3,500 undergraduates enrolled in 2018. The university's development plan for the next five years predicts that the number of students will increase to 14,000–15,000, with a proportionate demand for additional faculty and resources. Currently, with more than 12,000 students and nearly 700 educators, the student-teacher ratio is 17:1 (XJTLU, 2018b), which is still far from the international first-class standard. Further expansion of the faculty is thus necessary to achieve the goal of building a "world-recognized international university". The student-teacher ratio is only one important indicator of the quality of talent cultivation, though; effective talent cultivation also depends on the teaching level and skill of the faculty. Hence, the stability and quality of the faculty team need to be guaranteed by recruiting more faculty with stronger teaching and research records. Regarding the need for new investment in learning resources created by the increase in student enrolment, the existing library materials, electronic resources and databases, and learning facilities are simply insufficient.

7.3.4.2 The effectiveness of the quality assurance system

The above analysis shows that XJTLU has established a fairly complete internal quality assurance system but needs to optimize its operations. The results of the 2012 QAA assessment show that the university's annual self-assessment activities, tied to the UOL's annual assessment, provide insufficient internal oversight for quality assurance (QAA, 2013). XJTLU's internal quality assurance system is based in large part on those of British universities, especially the UOL, such as in its use of external examiners and degree grading. However, as an independent university, XJTLU should not be satisfied with merely drawing on the experience of its foreign partners but should take measures on its own to bolster quality assurance.

7.3.5 Building a quality assurance system for Sino-foreign joint venture institutions with multiple-subject collaborative governance

The policy and institutional environment for the development of the Sino-foreign joint venture education programmes into an important component of China's higher education has gradually improved as the internal management system has matured. A distinctive education educational environment has also gradually emerged, but challenges remain to the future development of this approach to cultivating talent in China.

7.3.5.1 Coordinating scale and quality to ensure sustainable development

The increasing public demand for higher education is creating favourable conditions for expansion of the scale of Sino-foreign joint venture institutions. During this process of expansion, ensuring the quality of education always remains the primary challenge for Chinese and foreign institutions alike. The national education authorities and institutions must cooperate, so the MoE should provide additional supervision and guidance to Sino-foreign joint venture institutions, including regular evaluation and improvements to the regulatory system. Presently, the ministry is improving its monitoring in this regard. In 2010, a pilot assessment was

198 *From expansion to quality enhancement*

conducted in four provinces and cities (Liaoning, Tianjin, Suzhou, and Henan), with nationwide quality assessments conducted in 2013, 2014, and 2015 (Center for Development of Academic Degrees and Postgraduate Education, Ministry of Education, 2018c). Chinese universities need to improve the facilities for scale expansion, the investment in the faculty, campus facilities, teaching resources need to be increased. At the same time, rationalize their approach to university quality by building a more comprehensive internal quality assurance system that features regular evaluation and real-time supervision.

7.3.5.2 Effectively combining multi-subject collaborative governance and third-party quality-assessment mechanisms

Sino-foreign joint venture education involves multiple stakeholders, including Chinese education authorities, local governments, and universities as well as foreign universities, education authorities, and even third-party evaluation agencies and other quality assurance organizations. Effective quality assurance requires the support, recognition, and participation of all of these stakeholders (Lin & Liu, 2014). Sino-foreign joint venture education, as a non-traditional approach that combines the advantages of Chinese and foreign education rather than merely catering to the interests of Chinese and foreign stakeholders, can serve as a model for traditional approaches to higher education. As for accreditation by third-party educational evaluation agencies, cooperative institutions have the natural advantage of maintaining close ties with several of them. These institutions thus need to use third-party evaluations to improve the quality of education. In the case of XJTLU, these stakeholders effectively constitute the quality assurance system, but, in practice, they function independently and are not well-integrated. The Chinese educational administration department only controls the macro level of supervision relating to the day-to-day operations of XJTLU while the UOL is more concerned with academic quality and the validity of the foreign degrees awarded by XJTLU. The QAA serves to assess the quality standards of British higher education, and other professional bodies accredit activities within their purview. However, for the Sino-foreign joint venture institutions, a sound internal quality assurance system is fundamental, so their internal autonomy and self-regulation should be the starting point for all quality assurance discussions and measures. The effective integration of these bodies so as to promote the quality of university operations jointly will be an important aspect of the development of XJTLU going forward.

7.3.5.3 Improving the unique quality-assurance system of Sino-foreign joint venture institutions

The quality assurance system of Sino-foreign joint venture institutions has been established, but improvement is needed in several respects. From the perspective of the various authorities, the roles of education administration departments, Chinese and foreign universities, and third-party evaluation agencies should be given full play, and their integration should be accelerated. Educational administrative departments should monitor the situation to ensure the quality of the introduced resources, change perceptions of the notion of "emphasizing approval but not management", develop the concept of whole-process supervision, and establish an independent evaluation and supervision system that is applicable to Sino-foreign joint venture education. The institutions that offer this form of education should achieve balanced development in quality assurance, establishing a system that integrates the characteristics of both parties cooperatively rather than using external educational quality standards as the sole criterion. Third-party assessment organizations have a role to play as social intermediaries in terms of reducing the intervention of administrative forces in quality assessment, ensuring the impartiality and objectivity of the assessment results, and strengthening cooperation with international assessment organizations to promote continuous improvement in and development of China's social assessment system. By following these recommendations, the quality of Sino-foreign joint venture education can be ensured, Chinese higher education can earn recognition for high quality, and a model for other regular universities can be established.

7.4 Faculty team-building in Sino-foreign joint venture education programmes

The descriptive analysis presented here begins with the data retrieved from the faculty members in 876 Sino-foreign joint venture education programmes that were offering undergraduate or graduate degrees in 2016 and includes demographic characteristics, quality status, specialty, and regional distribution. An analysis of the international faculty reveals their structural characteristics and quality level and traces the recruiting of quality teachers from abroad during the development of Sino-foreign joint venture education programmes. After a summary of the characteristics of the faculty in Sino-foreign joint venture education programmes, some measures for improving the teaching staff are discussed.

7.4.1 Structure and quality of the faculty in the Sino-foreign joint venture education programmes in 2016

In keeping with the statistics provided by the MoE, the present statistical analysis of the information about the faculty in 876 Sino-foreign joint venture undergraduate and graduate programmes excludes invalid data. Thus, because some faculty members did not fill in all of the personal information, the total number of samples in the charts varies.

7.4.1.1 Gender ratio of the faculty

In 2016, the gender ratio of the faculty members in Sino-foreign joint venture education programmes was fairly balanced, with the number of male faculty members only slightly surpassing that of female faculty members, accounting for 54.31% of the total. From the perspective of the various levels of education, though the proportion of male and female faculty members in undergraduate programmes is

200 *From expansion to quality enhancement*

balanced, there is a significant difference in the proportion of male and female faculty members in graduate programmes: The proportion of male faculty members in master's programmes was 72.42% and in doctoral programmes reached 79.74%. In other words, the level of the programme correlated with the proportion of male faculty members, with men being dominant at the graduate level of Sino-foreign joint venture education.

7.4.1.2 Academic backgrounds and professional titles of the faculty

In general, the academic background of the faculty members in the Sino-foreign joint venture education programme is extensive. As Table 7.2 shows, 87.47% held graduate degrees, 45.6% having master's degrees and 41.87% having doctoral or associate doctoral degrees. Only 12.25% of teachers had earned only a bachelor's degree. So, while most of the teachers have graduate degrees, to improve the quality of the programmes, the proportion with doctoral degrees, especially in the undergraduate programmes, can still be increased and should be considering the core position of undergraduate programmes in Sino-foreign joint venture education.

The professional title structure of the teachers in Sino-foreign joint venture education programmes is fairly impressive. As Table 7.3 shows, in 2016, 39.02% of the faculty members in Sino-foreign joint venture education programmes had intermediate professional titles, followed by 33.6% with associate senior professional titles, 17.91% with senior professional titles, and 9.47% with junior or other professional titles. Thus, a relatively large portion of the faculty in Sino-foreign joint venture education had professional titles. However, the proportion with senior professional titles was less than one-third and lower in undergraduate than graduate programmes, so there is room for improvement in this respect.

Table 7.2 Academic levels of teachers in Sino-foreign joint venture education programmes in 2016

Academic qualifications	Level of educational programme			Total (%)
	Number of staff members in undergraduate programmes	Number of staff members in master's programmes	Number of staff members in doctoral programmes	
Below Bachelor's	44	0	0	44 (0.15)
Bachelor's	3,459	45	5	3,509 (12.10)
Master's	12,822	370	25	13,217 (45.59)
PhD	10,346	1,467	207	12,020 (41.46)
Associate Doctoral	120	0	0	120 (0.41)
Other	80	1	1	82 (0.28)
Total	26,871	1,883	238	28,992

Note: These statistics exclude 242 invalid (missing) pieces of data.

Table 7.3 The professional title structure of the teachers in Sino-foreign joint venture education programmes in 2016

Title	Level of educational programme			Total (%)
	Number of staff members in undergraduate programmes	Number of staff members in master's programmes	Number of staff members in doctoral programmes	
Junior	1,217	16	2	1,235 (4.27)
Intermediate	11,024	231	29	11,284 (39.02)
Associate Senior	9,044	609	63	9,716 (33.60)
Senior	4,240	806	133	5,179 (17.91)
Other	1,275	216	10	1,501 (5.19)
Total	26,800	1,878	237	28,915

Notes:
1. These statistics exclude 319 surveys that were invalid (missing data).
2. Professional title classification: Senior professional titles: Professor and full senior engineer, etc.; associate senior professional titles: associate professor and senior engineer and other titles; intermediate professional titles: lecturer, assistant professor, engineer, etc.; junior professional titles: assistant professor, post-doctoral, etc.

7.4.1.3 Disciplinary structure and regional distribution of teachers

The disciplinary structure of the faculty members in Sino-foreign joint venture education programmes is also significantly unbalanced because of the disciplinary structure of the programmes. As Table 7.4 shows, the 876 Sino-foreign undergraduate and graduate cooperative programmes in 2016 were distributed into ten major disciplinary categories, the top five of which were engineering (37.9%), management (19.06%), economics (13.7%), art (10.73%), and science (4.91%). Many faculty members are in these programmes, the largest number in engineering, representing more than one-third of the total and comparable to the management,

Table 7.4 Disciplinary distribution of the teachers in Sino-foreign joint venture programmes in 2016

Disciplinary category	Number of programmes (%)	Number of teachers (%)
Engineering	332 (37.90)	11,672 (39.93)
Management	167 (19.06)	4,384 (15.00)
Economics	120 (13.70)	4,502 (15.40)
Fine Arts	94 (10.73)	3,111 (10.64)
Science	43 (4.91)	1,314 (4.49)
Medicine	38 (4.43)	2,125 (7.27)
Literature	34 (3.88)	822 (2.81)
Education	22 (2.51)	529 (1.81)
Law	13 (1.48)	351 (1.20)
Agriculture	13 (1.48)	424 (1.45)
Total	876 (100%)	29,234 (100%)

economics, and arts faculties combined. A balanced arrangement of disciplines should be considered going forward.

In 2016, 28 provinces, cities, and autonomous regions in China had launched Sino-foreign joint venture education programmes, across which the number of teachers employed varies. The ten provinces and cities with the most were Henan (3,293), Jiangsu (2,934), Heilongjiang (2,692), Shanghai (2,640), Shandong (2,324), Hubei (2,076), Jilin (1,988), Beijing (1,818), Zhejiang (1,267), and Tianjin (969). In terms of regional variation, a decreasing trend was evident moving from east to west, with 54.11% (15,819) in the eastern region, 41.34% (12,085) in the central region, and only 4.55% (1,330) in the western region.

7.4.2 Characteristics of the international faculty in Sino-foreign joint venture programmes in 2016

Overseas teachers[4] are an important part of the faculty of Sino-foreign joint venture education programmes, naturally playing a key role in educational activities. First of all, as the facilitators of these activities, overseas teachers have the potential to provide cutting-edge disciplinary knowledge, pedagogical models, and educational concepts and introduce high-quality foreign educational resources. These teachers play a unique role in Sino-foreign exchanges in terms of cooperating with local teachers and using their extensive international academic networks to promote Sino-foreign teaching and academic exchanges as well as communicating with them and their students regularly to better understand Chinese culture and help the locals people broaden their perceptions of foreign cultures. They thus contribute to the exchange between and integration of Chinese and foreign cultures. The overseas teachers are, therefore, important not only for the development of Sino-foreign joint venture education but also for the ongoing internationalization of China's higher education.

7.4.2.1 The number and proportion of overseas teachers

The analysis presented here is of the 808 Sino-foreign joint venture education programmes that provided information on 6,893 overseas teachers in 2016. The actual sampling related to certain indicators was calculated based on the valid sample statistics. In 2016, then, there were 808 Sino-foreign cooperative programmes (including those between the mainland and Hong Kong, Macao, and Taiwan) that submitted information about overseas teachers (including the teachers from Hong Kong, Macao, and Taiwan). A total of 29,142 teachers were engaged in Sino-foreign cooperative programmes in 2016, of which 22,249 (76.35%) were local teachers from the mainland and 6,893 (23.65%) were from overseas. As Table 7.5 shows, 679 undergraduate programmes submitted information on 5,828 overseas teachers, 115 master's programmes submitted information on 988 overseas teachers, and 14 doctoral programmes submitted information on 77 overseas teachers. The average number of foreign faculty members was lowest in the doctoral programmes while the average number of offshore faculty members in undergraduate and master's programmes

Table 7.5 The number of overseas faculty members by level of educational programme in 2016

Number of programmes and teachers	Level of educational programme			Total
	Undergraduate programmes	Master's programmes	Doctoral programmes	
Number of programmes	679	115	14	808
Number of overseas teachers (%)	5,828 (84.55%)	988 (14.33%)	77 (1.12%)	6,893
Average number of overseas teachers per programme	8.58	8.59	5.5	8.53

Table 7.6 Academic degree distribution of overseas teachers in Sino-foreign joint venture education programmes by level of programme in 2016

Teacher's academic degree	Level of educational programme			Total number (%)
	Number of overseas staff members in undergraduate programmes	Number of overseas staff members in master's programmes	Number of overseas staff members in doctoral programmes	
PhD	2,847	787	66	3,700 (54.65)
Associate Doctor	115	—	—	115 (1.70)
Master's	1,802	179	8	1,989 (29.38)
Bachelor's	925	18	2	945 (13.96)
Below Bachelor's	3	—	—	3 (0.04)
Other	17	—	1	18 (0.27)
Total	5,709	984	77	6,770

Note: "—" indicates that data were missing or not available.

was about the same, with more than eight per programme, so there is an urgent need to increase the portion of overseas faculty members in the doctoral programmes.

With the development of Sino-foreign joint venture education programmes in China, the nationality distribution of overseas teachers has become increasingly wide. Currently, teachers from 87 countries and regions are engaged in education and teaching in Sino-foreign joint venture education programmes. The ten countries that sent the most teachers to China have been the US, UK, Australia, Russia, Canada, South Korea, Germany, France, Ireland, and Japan, which, except for Russia, are developed countries and major exporters of education.

7.4.2.2 Academic qualifications and professional titles of overseas teachers

As Table 7.6 shows, in 2016, 3,700 of the overseas teachers held doctoral degrees, accounting for 54.65% of the total. The proportion of teachers with doctoral degrees, correlated with the level of Sino-foreign cooperative programmes, has increased.

204 *From expansion to quality enhancement*

Table 7.7 shows the distribution of professional titles of the overseas faculty. Most of the faculty members in undergraduate programmes held intermediate professional titles, while most of the teachers in master's and doctoral programmes held senior professional titles (more than 70% and 80%, respectively). In general, about half of the faculty members in China's Sino-foreign cooperative programmes held senior professional titles. The proportion of faculty members with senior professional titles correlated with the level of educational programme increases.

7.4.2.3 Rich professional experience of overseas teachers

The distribution of the length of the teaching experience of the overseas teachers correlated with the teachers' age; that is, the older teachers tended to have more years of teaching experience. The working experience of the teachers varied depending on the levels of educational programmes, with those in undergraduate programmes tending to have fewer years of teaching experience; specifically, more than one-third had been teaching for less than ten years. The overseas teachers in master's and doctoral programmes had more years of professional teaching experience.

The qualification status of overseas teachers has raised concerns. Overall, about 40% of overseas teachers had no teaching qualifications (see Table 7.8), and it is unclear whether the teachers without teaching qualifications were sufficiently competent to teach in a cooperative education programme. Chinese partner institutions need to scrutinize the qualifications of teachers and the reasons for overseas teachers' lack of qualifications to ensure that those who teach specialized courses and core language courses are qualified to do so.

7.4.2.4 Disciplinary distribution of overseas teachers

Since China's Sino-foreign cooperative programmes have been offered in all professional disciplines except military science, the professional backgrounds of overseas teachers also show diverse distribution characteristics and a strong correlation

Table 7.7 Distribution of overseas teacher's professional titles in Sino-foreign joint venture education programmes by level of programme in 2016

Teacher's professional title	Level of educational programme			Total number (%)
	Number of overseas staff members in undergraduate programmes	Number of overseas staff members in master's programmes	Number of overseas staff members in doctoral programmes	
Professor	1,376	426	40	1,842 (27.23)
Associate Professor	1,302	285	22	1,609 (23.79)
Intermediate level	1,922	99	6	2,027 (29.97)
Primary level	185	2	1	188 (2.78)
Other	915	175	8	1,098 (16.23)
Total	5,700	987	77	6,764

Table 7.8 Qualifications of the overseas teachers in Sino-foreign joint venture education programmes in 2016

Whether the teacher has teacher qualifications	Level of educational programme			Total
	Number of overseas staff members in undergraduate programmes	Number of overseas staff members in master's programmes	Number of overseas staff members in doctoral programmes	
Yes	3,584	568	49	4,201
No	2,135	408	20	2,563
Percentage of overseas teachers with teaching qualifications (%)	62.67	58.20	71.01	62.11

with the distribution of specialties in the programmes (see Table 7.9). In 2016, large numbers of faculty members were teaching courses in engineering, management, literature, science, and economics, with the largest number teaching literature in the undergraduate programme. This distribution was mainly due to the fact that most of the undergraduate programmes employed a large number of teachers to improve the students' foreign language proficiency, thus reflecting the teaching characteristics of cooperative programmes and the requirements for students.

Table 7.9 Disciplinary distribution for overseas teachers in Sino-foreign joint venture education programmes in 2016

Faculty professional background	Level of educational programme			Total (%)
	Number of overseas staff members in undergraduate programmes	Number of overseas staff members in master's programmes	Number of overseas staff members in doctoral programmes	
Philosophy	75	13	1	89 (1.32)
Economics	363	152	13	528 (7.84)
Law	214	75	1	290 (4.31)
Education	310	42	2	354 (5.26)
Literature	887	28	4	919 (13.65)
History	69	5	—	74 (1.10)
Science	575	52	6	633 (9.40)
Engineering	1,549	143	7	1,699 (25.23)
Agriculture	78	1	10	88 (1.31)
Medicine	255	23	11	289 (4.29)
Management	765	414	22	1,201 (17.83)
Fine Arts	538	33	—	571 (8.48)
Total	5,678	980	77	6,735

Note: "—" indicates that data were missing or not available.

206 *From expansion to quality enhancement*

7.4.2.5 Distribution of overseas teachers across provinces and municipalities

At present, Sino-foreign joint venture education programmes are available at universities in all 28 provinces and municipalities directly under the central government as well as in China's autonomous regions except for Qinghai, Ningxia, and Tibet. As Table 7.10 shows, the largest numbers of programmes and teachers in 2016 were in Shanghai, Henan, and Beijing. These locations with relatively high average numbers of overseas teachers per programme demonstrated fairly effective recruitment in this respect. By contrast, the number of overseas teachers in many central and western provinces has generally been low. For example, the average number of overseas teachers per programme was less than five in Inner Mongolia and Gansu.

7.4.3 Problems with and developmental characteristics of the faculty in Sino-foreign joint venture education programmes

The analysis presented above of the 2016 data indicates that the overall development of the faculty in China's Sino-foreign joint venture education programmes has been stable and characterized by a reasonable and balanced structure and high quality. However, significant variations persist across the disciplinary, programme, and regional levels on which government authorities and institutions should focus. In the case of the foreign faculty, a disparity is apparent in the introduction of high-quality international education resources. Thus, there is room for improvement in terms of the number, qualifications, teaching level, and research ability of the overseas teachers on the faculty teams for these programmes. Increasing efforts to recruit high-level teachers is, accordingly, a key consideration in the development of the international teaching staff. At the same time, the management of overseas teachers

Table 7.10 Distribution of overseas teachers in Sino-foreign joint venture education programmes by province/municipality in 2016

Province	Number of programmes	Number of overseas teachers	Province	Number of programmes	Number of overseas teachers
Shanghai	77	770	Hebei	21	120
Henan	73	701	Hunan	23	119
Beijing	56	673	Shaanxi	12	114
Jiangsu	82	632	Jiangxi	14	102
Heilongjiang	66	556	Sichuan	14	95
Shandong	65	485	Anhui	13	93
Zhejiang	50	421	Yunnan	10	83
Hubei	49	404	Guangxi	12	71
Jilin	42	309	Inner Mongolia	7	30
Guangdong	24	271	Guizhou	3	21
Liaoning	26	253	Hainan	4	21
Tianjin	30	212	Xinjiang	1	6
Fujian	15	182	Shanxi	1	5
Chongqing	19	141	Gansu	1	3

From expansion to quality enhancement 207

can be improved through the establishment of a targeted corresponding management system to motivate the teachers to play their special role in cooperative education more effectively, improve the teaching effect, and promote the overall improvement of education quality in Sino-foreign joint venture education programmes.

7.4.3.1 Scale of the faculty and proportion to be optimized

In 2016, the characteristics of the faculty in national Sino-foreign joint venture education programmes were reasonable and balanced, particularly with respect to gender, education level, and professional titles. However, certain problems persist. First, the proportion of teachers with high-level professional titles and academic qualifications was still less than 20%, so there is still a need to recruit high-level teachers. Second, the specialties of the faculty have continued to be concentrated in engineering, management, and economics; these applied disciplines account for more than 70% of the total number of teachers. Further efforts are needed to maintain balanced disciplinary development. Third, regional differences have remained significant, with more faculty members in the eastern and central regions and fewer in the west. Fourth, there has also been variation at the programme level correlated with the level of faculty members such that the quality of the faculty in the undergraduate programmes with the largest number of projects was much lower than that in the other two levels of programmes. Attention to these problems can promote the balanced development of the faculty in Sino-foreign joint venture programmes and, thereby, gradually improve the quality of the education that they provide.

7.4.3.2 Recruitment of high-quality teachers from abroad

In 2016, the overall quality of overseas faculty remained stable and relatively high. More than half of the faculty members held doctoral degrees and senior professional titles. As the self-assessment report shows, most were senior faculty with the foreign partner universities and had rich teaching experience. Many foreign faculty members were also distinguished scholars and leading experts in their fields with strong research capabilities. They have facilitated the development of many collaborative research projects during their teaching careers. In addition, using flexible recruitment channels, many programmes have hired foreigners with practical experience as part-time teachers to provide practical teaching and guidance to students. At the same time, the Chinese partners have been actively recruiting teachers from abroad, beginning with language teachers and gradually expanding to those able to offer professional courses. The overseas teachers recruited in this way have gradually come to play an important role in the cooperative education programmes.

7.4.3.3 Scale and management of overseas teachers

Regarding the improvements needed in the overseas faculty, first, the scale of quality teachers needs to be expanded. In 2016, teachers from foreign countries represented about one-quarter of the total in Sino-foreign joint venture education programmes.

Increasing the proportion can further the goal of enhancing the quality of the educational resources. Also beneficial in this regard would be increases in the proportion of teachers with high-level academic degrees and professional titles, especially the latter since only one-third of the teachers from abroad had senior professional titles. At the same time, the qualifications of overseas teachers must continue to be strictly controlled given that, in 2016, some 40% had no teaching qualifications. Therefore, the recruitment of quality teachers from abroad should be the focus of efforts to increase the proportion of teachers with high-level titles and qualifications.

Second, the management system needs to be strengthened and optimized in Sino-foreign joint venture education programmes. The management of overseas teachers usually involves two main aspects. First, there is personnel management, which involves integrating teachers in cooperative education into the unified management of teachers in the Chinese partner university. Second, teaching activity management is coordinated by the host institution of the programme in the same way that it is for the Chinese teachers in the programme. So, a special management system has not been established for overseas teachers in cooperative education programmes. In view of the distinct position of overseas teachers in these programmes, a specific management system should be established to motivate their work, improve the quality of their teaching, and increase the effectiveness of university operations generally.

Third, the stability and sustainability of faculty team-building need improvement. In 2016, about 80–90% of the overseas teachers in Sino-foreign joint venture education programmes were selected by the foreign partner institutions while relatively few overseas teachers were recruited by the Chinese partners. The teachers selected and dispatched by the foreign partner universities usually choose the short-term teaching model because they have to fulfil their responsibilities at their home universities. In 2016, 80% of the teachers from abroad finished all of their teaching tasks within one semester. This "flight teaching" model is not consistent with the fundamental rules of pedagogy, for it can greatly reduce the quality of teaching and increase the learning burden on students, thereby affecting the learning effect (Lin & Liu, 2014). Other surveys show that the time that the teachers recruited by Chinese institutions or programme agencies spend in their positions has not been stable: Language teachers usually work for one academic year and, even when offered long-term employment, have rarely remained for more than two consecutive years (Feng, 2007).

7.4.4 Suggestions for improving the faculty teams in Sino-foreign joint venture education programmes

7.4.4.1 Optimizing policies and regulations related to the foreign faculty team

The policies and regulations for the management of teachers in Sino-foreign joint venture education programmes, such as the *Regulations of the People's Republic of China on Sino-foreign Joint Venture Education* and the *Measures for the Implementation of the Regulations of the People's Republic of China on Sino-foreign Joint Venture Education*, were formulated some 20 years ago. The recent policy document *Opinions of the MoE on Further Strengthening the Quality Assurance of Sino-foreign Joint Venture Education in Higher Education* was also issued seven years ago. In view of the rapid development of Sino-foreign joint venture education, these policies and regulations may be out of step with the reality of development from the perspective of timeliness. In addition, these policy documents only offer regulations for administering faculty members at the macro level. Thus, "faculty management" often appears in only a section of a chapter in these policies and regulations and is addressed only in general terms. Even less is said about the management of overseas teachers, so the need to develop detailed descriptions of specific practices remains.

Therefore, the policies and regulations of Sino-foreign joint venture education should follow the practical development of the programmes, adapt to their development needs, and make timely adjustments and revisions according to the actual conditions. In this way, they can play the macro-guiding role in the implementation of policies and regulations effectively. At the same time, the issuance of targeted special policies and regulations can improve and guide the management of the programmes' faculty teams. Such clarification of the regulations and requirements for the management of special groups can facilitate the effective oversight of educational activities.

7.4.4.2 Further efforts to recruit quality teachers from abroad

As Sino-foreign joint venture education enters a period of rapid development, there is a particular need to strengthen the requirements regarding its quality. Overseas teachers are, as has been seen, important human resources for this type of education; thus, their number and quality greatly influence its actual impact. Sino-foreign joint venture universities have recruited a large number of overseas teachers, but they can do more in this regard.

First, the number of teachers from abroad should be expanded. At present, about one-quarter of all teachers are from overseas, a proportion insufficient to meet the basic requirement that "teachers from abroad should be responsible for at least 1/3 of the core courses". This ratio can be increased to one-third or one-half to meet the needs of curriculum implementation. Second, the number of full-time teachers employed by the programmes should continue to increase in order to maintain the stability of the faculty, ensure the quality of teaching, and reduce the adverse effects of short-term and flight teaching. Both partner institutions should reach an agreement on teacher recruitment at the beginning of the programme and jointly implement teacher recruitment standards that meet the needs of the programme, and recruit practical talent who truly meet the standards.

7.4.4.3 Establishing a long-term management mechanism for overseas faculty

Presently, the responsibilities for managing overseas teachers in Sino-foreign joint venture education programmes are not clear. The partner institutions take on some of these responsibilities at the university level while the colleges that host cooperative programmes take on others. The lack of distinction in the administration of foreign and local faculty seems appropriate in light of the peculiarities of the former.

Therefore, a targeted management mechanism should be established to administer the international faculty. First, in terms of personnel management, the overseas teachers should be integrated into the routine management of a programme's affiliated institutions so as to facilitate day-to-day communication and practical operations. Second, in terms of educational management, overseas teachers usually adopt international teaching and assessment methods and should be given the right to develop and implement their own teaching plans, designs, content, and activities. Third, in terms of evaluation, the focus should be on the teaching effect and student feedback on the courses taught rather than simply on the number of courses that teachers teach. A corresponding incentive mechanism should be established to reward teachers who achieve a good teaching effect and deliver high-quality instruction. Last, overseas teachers should be provided with all-around support for addressing the problems and obstacles that they encounter.

Sino-foreign joint venture education will continue to play an irreplaceable role in the internationalization of China's higher education. The participating institutions have as their main goals maintaining smooth operations and training of high-level international talent, and prestigious foreign universities are the main target for their efforts to attract high-quality educational resources. Sino-foreign joint venture education, as a way to "study without going abroad", will continue to appeal to some Chinese students if it continues to develop in a stable manner. The quantity and quality of the education received by students who study in China will improve as larger numbers of international students enrol in Sino-foreign joint venture institutions. Thus, the government, society, and the higher education sector alike need to study and promote the sustainable development of this new type of higher education institution in terms of theory, policy, and practice.

Notes

1 The data are from the author's fieldwork at the University of Nottingham Ningbo China on June 26, 2014.
2 The data are from the author's fieldwork at the University of Nottingham Ningbo China on June 26, 2014.
3 The data are from the author's fieldwork at the University of Nottingham Ningbo China on June 26, 2014.
4 In this chapter, "overseas teachers" include teachers from foreign countries as well as Hong Kong, Macau, and Taiwan.

References

Chapman, A., & Pyvis, D. (2013). *Enhancing quality in transnational higher education: Experiences of teaching and learning in Australian offshore programs*. Lexington Books.
Feng, F. M. (2007). Zhongwai hezuo banxue de shizi wenti ji duice tanxi [Exploring the issues and countermeasures surrounding faculty team of Sino-foreign cooperative education]. *Jiaoyu Yu Zhiye [Education and Vocation]*, 6, 33–34.

Huang, F. (2006). Transnational higher education in mainland China: A focus on foreign degree-conferring programs. *Transnational Higher Education in Asia and the Pacific Region, 10*, 21–24.

Jin, Z. M. (2012). Guanyu zhongwai hezuo banxue yuxing jizhi de sikao: Yi Shanghai Niuyue daxue weili [To improve the operation mechanism of Chinese-foreign cooperation universities: A case study of New York University in Shanghai]. *Jiaoyu Fazhan Yanjiu [Research in Educational Development], 32*(7), 1–6.

Lin, J. (2018). Zhongwai hezuo banxue de zhengce mubiao ji qi shixian tiaojian [On the policy goal and its implementation conditions of Chines-foreign cooperation in running schools]. *Jiaoyu Yanjiu [Educational Research], 39*(10), 70–75.

Lin, J. H., & Liu, M. J. (2014). Gaoxiao zhongwai hezuo banxue xiangmu neibu jiaoxue zhiliang baozhang jiben yaosu ji lujing [On the policy goal and its implementation conditions of Chines-foreign cooperation in running schools]. *Zhongguo Daxue Jiaoxue [China University Teaching], 5*, 62–66.

Lin, J. H., & Liu, Z. P. (2010). *Gaodeng Jiaoyu Zhongwai Hezuo Banxue Yanjiu [The study on the Sino-foreign cooperative higher education]*. Guangdong Gaodeng Jiaoyu Chubanshe [Guangdong Higher Education Press].

Ma, J. P. (2014). Yingguo de xuewei shouyuquan shenhe zhidu ji qishi [The audit system of degree granting authority in the UK and its inspiration]. *Gaodeng Nongye Jiaoyu [Higher Agricultural Education], 7*, 125–127.

Ministry of Education, Sino-foreign Cooperation Supervision Work Information Platform. (2018a). Zhongwai hezuo banxue zhiliang pinggu jieshao [Introduction on quality assurance of Sino-foreign joint venture education]. Retrieved September 15, 2018, from http://www.crs.jsj.edu.cn/index.php/default/index/sort/5

Ministry of Education, The General Office. (2018b). Jiaoyubu bangongting guanyu zhongzhi bufen zhongwai hezuo banxue jigou he xiangmu de tongzhi [Notice of the general office of the ministry of education on the termination of some Chinese-foreign cooperative education institutions and programs]. Retrieved June 21, 2018, from http://www.moe.gov.cn/srcsite/A20/moe_862/201807/t20180705342056.html

Ministry of Education, Center for Development of Academic Degrees and Postgraduate Education. (2018c). Zhongwai hezuo banxue pinggu [Evaluation of Sino-foreign cooperative education]. Retrieved September 15, 2018, from http://www.chinadegrees.cn/xwyyjsjyxx/zlpj/zwhzbxpg/

The Quality Assurance for Higher Education. (2013). *Review of UK transnational education in China: University of Liverpool and Xi'an Jiaotong-Liverpool University*. QAA.

The Quality Assurance Agency for Higher Education. (2017). *Transnational education (TNE) review handbook*. QAA.

The Quality Assurance Agency for Higher Education. (2018). Assuring standards and quality. Retrieved September 15, 2018, from https://www.qaa.ac.uk/quality-code/the-existing-uk-quality-code/part-b-assuring-and-enhancing-academic-quality

The University of Nottingham Ningbo. (2019a). Nottingham Ningbo daxue 2015–2016 xuenian zhiliang baogao [Quality report of University of Nottingham Ningbo 2015–2016 academic year]. Retrieved June 20, 2019, from http://www.nottingham.edu.cn/cn/about/documents/2017new-Chinese-version.pdf

The University of Nottingham Ningbo. (2019b). Nottingham Ningbo daxue jieshao [Introduction to the University of Nottingham Ningbo]. Retrieved July 17, 2019, from https://www.nottingham.edu.cn/cn/About/index.aspx

University of Liverpool. (2018a). Partner approval process guidance. Retrieved September 15, 2018, from https://www.liverpool.ac.uk/media/livacuk/tqsd/collaborative-provision/policies-and-procedures/Partner-Approval-Process-Guidance.pdf

University of Liverpool. (2018b). Taxonomy of teaching and learning collaborative provision. Retrieved September 15, 2018, from https://www.liverpool.ac.uk/media/livacuk/tqsd/collaborative-provision/policies-and-procedures/TandL-Taxonomy.pdf

University of Liverpool. (2018c). Guidance for annual monitoring visits. Retrieved September 15, 2018, from https://www.liverpool.ac.uk/media/livacuk/tqsd/collaborative-provision/policies-and-procedures/Taught-Annual-Monitoring-Guidelines.pdf

University of Liverpool. (2018d). XJTLU validation and modification process. Retrieved September 15, 2018, from https://www.liverpool.ac.uk/media/livacuk/tqsd/collaborative-provision/xjtlu/validation-modification-xjtlu-processes.pdf

Xi'an Jiaotong-Liverpool University. (2018a). Niandu zhaosheng shuju [Enrollment data by year]. Retrieved September 15, 2018, from http://www.xjtlu.edu.cn/zh/study-with-us/admissions/admission-data

Xi'an Jiaotong-Liverpool University. (2018b). Xi'an jiaotong liwupu daxue 2017 zhongwai hezuo banxue niandu ziping baogao [Annual self-evaluation report of 2017 Sino-foreign cooperative education of Xi'an Jiaotong-Liverpool University]. Retrieved September 15, 2018, from http://www.xjtlu.edu.cn/zh/about/policies-and-regulations/self-evaluation-report

Xi'an Jiaotong-Liverpool University. (2018c). Xijiaoliwupu 2016–2017 xuenian benke jiaoxue zhiliang baogao [Xi'an Jiaotong-Liverpool University 2016–2017 undergraduate education quality report]. Retrieved September 15, 2018, from http://www.xjtlu.edu.cn/assets/files/policies/Online%20publicity/2016-17-UG-Education-Quality-Report-XJTLU.pdf

Ye, L. (2012). *Kuaguo Xuewei Xiangmu de Zhiliang Baozhang [The quality assurance of transnational degree programs]*. Zhejiang University Press.

Zhao, F. B. (2014). Zhongwai hezuo daxue de jiaoxue zhiliang baozhang jizhi tanxi—Jiyu ningbo nuodinghan daxue de fenxi [Research on assurance mechanism of teaching quality-at the university of Nottingham Ningbo]. *Zhongguo Gaojiao Yanjiu [China Higher Education Research]*, 6, 79–84.

Zhao, F., & Chen, T. (2012). Yu Lizhong: New York University Shanghai shi yikuai shiyantian [Yu Lizhong: New York University Shanghai is an experimental plot]. *Shanghai Jiaoyu [Shanghai Education]*, 30, 17–19.

8 A comparative study on internationalization of higher education in international Asian metropolitan cities

This chapter first examines the internationalization of students and faculty members, curriculum, and cooperative education in the National University of Singapore (NUS) and Nanyang Technological University (NTU) in Singapore, the University of Hong Kong (HKU) and Hong Kong University of Science and Technology (HKUST), as well as Fudan University (FU) and Shanghai Jiao Tong University (SJTU) in Shanghai. Then, it compares the features, approaches, and models of higher education internationalization in Singapore, Hong Kong, and Shanghai. Finally, it proposes suggestion for enhancing the internationalization of higher education in Shanghai.

An interdependent and interactive relationship exists between the internationalization of higher education institutions and that of the cities. International metropolises are large platforms that gather talent, information, capital and technology, and often develop and invest in higher education as a pillar industry. The linkage between the two forms of internationalization is reflected in the functions of universities, including the training of international talent, the development of knowledge-intensive industries, and industries with a high international dependency. The industrial transformation and upgrading of cities as well as the development of the knowledge-based economy depends on higher education to provide intellectual support in terms of supplying talent, knowledge, and technology, while the development of higher education requires cities to offer capital, provide a social institutional environment for talent development, and absorb their technology transfer and graduates. There are abundant studies on the internationalization of higher education, but few of them were conducted to explore both higher education and the internationalization of the research universities in international metropolises in Mainland China with reference to Asian international metropolises.

8.1 Comparison of the internationalization of research universities in Singapore, Hong Kong, and Shanghai

The three Asian cosmopolitan cities of Singapore, Hong Kong, and Shanghai are selected for comparison in this chapter based on the comparability of their urban functions and internationalization, the internationalization of higher education, and the equal importance of the interrelationship between the internationalization of their cities and the internationalization of higher education. Singapore and Hong

DOI: 10.4324/9781003424611-8

Kong, as small economies, former British colonies, and places where Chinese and Western cultures have integrated, have an industrial structure that is dominated by tertiary industries. The two regions have adopted a highly outward-oriented and knowledge-intensive economic development path, as well as comprehensive internationalization strategies in various aspects. While Shanghai, as the economic and financial centre of China, relies on the resources and institutions of the entire country to give full play to its functions and advantages of serving it. The internationalization of higher education in Singapore, Hong Kong, and Shanghai takes on different characteristics, approaches, and models, while all three cities are Asian financial centres, talent hubs, and high-quality higher education hubs. The development of a knowledge economy and science and technology leads industrial upgrading and development, and the development of cities and higher education is very dependent on the development strategy of internationalization. However, Singapore is a city-state, Hong Kong is a special administrative region of China, and Shanghai is a coastal city in Mainland China opening to the world, so the three cities exhibit differences in terms of their location advantages and development strategies. If the internationalization of higher education systems is investigated, it is bound to have certain pertinence. Therefore, this section selects two research universities respectively in the three cities as comparative cases, to compare their internationalization regarding different dimensions. Then, combining with existing literature and policy analysis, the chapter summarizes the development characteristics, paths, and modes of the internationalization of higher education in the three aforementioned cities. The six case universities are all public research universities, representing the highest level of higher education development and internationalization in their regions. The overall degree of internationalization of the case universities in Hong Kong and Singapore is higher than that in Shanghai, but the degree of internationalization of the case universities varies in different dimensions, which are described in the following four aspects: Student internationalization, faculty internationalization, curriculum internationalization, and international cooperation.

8.1.1 *The share of international students is higher in universities in Singapore and Hong Kong than in Shanghai*

Student internationalization is the most fundamental dimension of internationalization, and it is also an area of internationalization that all six research universities attach great importance to. This section uses data from "Quacquarelli Symonds" International University Rankings 2016 to compare the number of international students and their proportion in the total student population in these universities. Table 8.1 shows that the two universities in Singapore have a relatively large number of international degree-seeking students, accounting for about 30% of the total number of students enrolled. NUS has presented a global and multicultural character. It has 16 schools and departments in 3 campuses, with 37,000 students from more than 100 countries. More than 20% of its undergraduate students and 60% of its postgraduate students are international students (Ma, 2014).

A comparative study on internationalization of higher education 215

Table 8.1 The number and proportion of international (non-local) students at the six research universities in 2016 QS Ranking.

Institution	Total number of students	Number of international (non-local) students	International (non-local) undergraduate students as a percentage of international (non-local) students	International (non-local) graduate students as a percentage of international (non-local) students	International (non-local) students as a percentage of student population
National University of Singapore	32,705	9,443	53%	47%	28.9%
Nanyang Technological University	25,367	7,845	57%	43%	30.9%
University of Hong Kong	20,797	8,194	47%	53%	39.4%
Hong Kong University of Science and Technology	12,154	4,532	35%	65%	37.3%
Fudan University	28,159	4,400	65%	35%	15.6%
Shanghai Jiao Tong University	38,931	2,858	67%	33%	7.3%

Source: The data were collected from: QS (Quacquarelli Symonds) international university rankings (http://www.topuniversities.com/ universities/ region/ asia) by the author in June, 2018.

The degree of diversity between students is high in universities in Hong Kong as well. Both the HKU and the HKUST have a high proportion of non-local students. In 2016, 39.4% of students in the HKU were non-local, with the majority consisting of Mainland Chinese students and a higher proportion of graduate students than undergraduates. The number of international students in Shanghai's FU and SJTU is increasing year-on-year, but the proportion is relatively low, with international graduate students accounting for 33% and 35% of international students in the two universities, respectively (see Table 8.1). According to the statistics, the proportion of international degree-seeking students in FU was 15.6% in 2009. There were 2,531 international students in FU, including 1,980 undergraduates, 412 graduate students, and 139 doctoral students. In 2012, there were 1,674 international degree-seeking students in SJTU, accounting for 4.83% of the total number, including 55 doctoral students, 271 graduate students, and 1,348 undergraduates. It can be seen that the higher the academic level, the lower the number and proportion of international students in the two universities in Shanghai.

Hong Kong and Singapore share a similar student structure, hosting a large number and high proportion of international students; the number of international students in Shanghai is growing rapidly, but both the proportion and the academic degree that international students seek are lower compared with the other two regions. The proportion of international students indicates, to some degree, the capacity and competitiveness of universities to attract and accommodate international students. The research universities in Singapore and Hong Kong are more attractive to international degree-seeking students than the research universities in Shanghai.

8.1.2 Universities in Singapore and Hong Kong have a more internationalized faculty composition than that of Shanghai

The internationalization of faculty teams in Shanghai is mainly reflected in the proportion and academic level of international faculty members (Ren, 2016). The difference in the proportion of international faculty is more prominent in each university, mainly reflected in the number of foreign teachers and the number of teachers with overseas studies experience. The scale of foreign teachers in Hong Kong and Singapore is relatively larger than that in Shanghai. Foreign teachers in Shanghai account for a lower percentage of the overall faculty members. One of the greatest strengths of universities in Hong Kong is their faculty members, almost all of whom have studied abroad. To be specific, most of the faculty members of the HKU and the HKUST have graduated from well-known overseas universities (Zhang et al., 2009). However, in recent years, universities in Shanghai have quickened their pace to attract and recruit overseas academic talent. As of 2011, the quality of foreign academics has increased in Fudan University, given the disciplinary demand and research projects of the university. A total of 103 long-term experts (working for more than three months) and 608 short-term experts (working for less than three months) have been employed. In 2012, among the 2,873 full-time faculty members of SJTU, 2,125 of them hold doctoral degrees, 473 hold overseas doctoral degrees, accounting for 16.5% of the whole faculty, and 88 are foreigners.

A comparative study on internationalization of higher education 217

As of 2017, the total number of faculty members in SJTU is 3,126, including 154 foreign faculty members.

Table 8.2 shows that, according to the 2016 QS (QuacquarelliSymonds) data on the internationalization of university faculty members, the university faculty in Hong Kong and Singapore share similar characteristics, i.e. having a large scale and a high proportion (more than 60%) of faculty members with international education background. The number and proportion of faculty members with overseas academic credentials in Fudan University and Shanghai Jiao Tong University are growing rapidly, accounting for about one-quarter.

8.1.3 The internationalization of curriculum in research universities in Shanghai is being steadily facilitated

The internationalization of curriculum and teaching is an important dimension of the internationalization at home and internationalization of talent training. Different definitions of internationalization of curriculum exist. This section adopts the scale of English curriculum to assess the extent of curriculum internationalization. The four case universities in Hong Kong and Singapore have a high degree of internationalization of their curricula, as English is the official language in both Hong Kong and Singapore due to their colonial histories. While Shanghai has a lower degree of internationalization of its curriculum, it is accelerating the development of English curricula and programmes. The internationalization of curriculum at FU and SJTU is progressing steadily, with an increasing number of foreign and returned faculty introduced to the universities. According to statistics, in 2010, FU offered 98 English courses, forming a four-module English curriculum system of history and culture (36.3%), politics and law (21.2%), economics and management (15.2%), and science

Table 8.2 Number and proportion of international (non-local) faculty at the six research universities in the 2016 QS Rankings

Research university	Total number of faculty members	Number of international (non-local) faculty members	Number of international (non-local) faculty as a percentage of total faculty members
National University of Singapore	5,062	3,174	62.7%
Nanyang Technological University	4,334	3,000	69.2%
University of Hong Kong*	3,054	2,018	66.1%
Hong Kong University of Science and Technology*	1,092	834	76.4%
Fudan University	3,705	878	23.7%
Shanghai Jiao Tong University	3,544	887	25%

Source: The data were collected from: QS (Quacquarelli Symonds) international university ranking data (http://www.topuniversities.com/universities/region/asia) by the author in June, 2018.

Note: The numbers at HKU and HKUST refer to non-local faculty numbers, while the numbers at all other universities refer to international faculty numbers.

and technology (27.3%). In 2011, FU offered 165 English courses. SJTU attaches importance to the construction of English courses, and the *Phase III of the "985 Project" – The Interim Evaluation Report on the Construction of the Undergraduate Innovative Talent Cultivation System at Shanghai Jiao Tong University* proposed to build seven English teaching majors and 236 English teaching courses in order to improve the internationalization of undergraduate programmes.

8.1.4 A comparison on international cooperative education in the three regions

International cooperative education plays an important role in strengthening cooperation in higher education. It includes two directions of "going out" and "bringing in", covering cooperative institutions and programmes. The main international cooperative education of the case universities is shown in Table 8.3, in which Singaporean universities emphasize both "bringing in" and "going out" models of cooperative education. On the one hand, they are vigorously bringing in famous overseas education brands and building branch campuses, while on the other hand, they actively participate in cooperative education programmes in Asian countries and regions. Hong Kong has a relatively high quality of higher education, so the demand for bringing in overseas universities is not very strong. It emphasizes more on bringing in international courses rather than international programmes and institutions, as well as exporting education programmes and courses. Universities in Hong Kong actively run cooperative programmes with universities in Mainland China. For instance, the Chinese University of Hong Kong has established a branch campus in Shenzhen, the Hong Kong Baptist University has established a joint college with Beijing Normal University, and the Hong Kong University of Science and Technology set up a research institute in Shenzhen. Both HKU and HKUST have strategic plans to build up branch campuses in Mainland China. Universities in Shanghai are mainly in the "bringing in" model, introducing a large number of overseas programmes at sub-school and project level. As of January 2016, there are 89 Sino-foreign cooperative programmes above the undergraduate level, including 62 undergraduate programmes, 25 master's programmes, and 2 doctoral programmes, revealing a stable development mode of Sino-foreign joint venture education. In 2006, Shanghai Jiao Tong University (SJTU) and the University of Michigan (UM) established the Michigan College of SJTU (Zhang, 2011), a non-independent legal entity. In 2012, East China Normal University (ECNU) and New York University (NYU) established New York University Shanghai (NYUS). These cooperative institutions are developing well and have successfully brought in quality education brands, contributing to the internationalization at home in Shanghai.

8.1.5 Comparing the developmental degree of internationalization of case universities in the three regions

From the above dimensions of students, faculty, curriculum, and cooperative education, there are differences in the internationalization degree among research universities in Shanghai, Hong Kong, and Singapore. Among them, Singapore and Hong

Table 8.3 Selected international cooperative institutions/programmes of six research universities

Research university	Cooperation partners	Cooperation institutions (projects)	Year	Specialties
University of Hong Kong	Fudan University	Master's Program of Business Administration	1998	MBA, Executive Master
Hong Kong University of Science and Technology	Shenzhen Government, Peking University	Shenzhen Research Institute of the Hong Kong University of Science and Technology	2001	MBA, Master of Electrical Engineering
National University of Singapore	Johns Hopkins University School of Medicine	Johns Hopkins University Singapore	1998	MD, PhD in Clinical Medicine, Medical Research
	Massachusetts Institute of Technology, USA	Singapore-MIT Alliance	1998	Graduate Education of Engineering Technology
	Georgia Institute of Technology, USA	Asia Pacific Logistics Academy	2001	Master's degree programmes in logistics and supply chain management, research programmes, on-the-job training, etc.
	Eindhoven University of Technology, Netherlands	Design Technology Research Institute	2002	Master's Program of Technical Design
	Technical University of Munich, Germany	German Academy of Science and Technology	2003	Senior professionals in the field of industrial chemistry and chemical engineering
Nanyang Technological University	Shanghai Jiao Tong University	Shanghai Jiao Tong University Graduate School in Singapore	2002	MBA
	Stanford University, USA	Singapore and Stanford Partnership	2003	Environmental Engineering Graduate Education
	Massachusetts Institute of Technology, USA	Singapore-MIT Alliance	1998	Engineering Technology Graduate Education
Fudan University	University College Dublin, Ireland	Bachelor of Science Program in Computer Science and Technology	2003	Undergraduate Education Program in Computer Science and Technology
Shanghai Jiao Tong University	University of Michigan	University of Michigan-Shanghai Jiao Tong University Joint Institute	2005	BS, MS, PhD in engineering, life sciences, medicine, arts, and sciences
	European Management Development Fund	China Europe International Business School	1994	MBA, EMBA

Source: Singapore data from Gong Siyi (2005). Guoji Fenxiao: Xinjiapo de Jingyan Yu Qishi [International branch campuses: Singapore's experience and insights]. *Liaoning Jiaoyu Yanjiu [Liaoning Education Research]*, (10):51–52, 82; other data were collected from the websites of universities by the author in June 2018.

Kong research universities have a higher degree of internationalization, as evidenced by a high proportion of foreign faculty and faculty with overseas degrees, a high proportion of international students, a high degree of integration of international languages and content in their curricula and teaching, and a high degree of strategic and managerial emphasis on the internationalization dimension. The degree of internationalization of research universities in Shanghai is relatively low and still in its early stages, which is reflected in the low degree of integration of international elements into teaching, research, management, and services, and campus environment, and the uneven development of each dimension of internationalization. To be specific, the ratio of international degree-seeking students is low, and the ratio of foreign faculty members and those who have earned their doctoral degrees from renowned universities abroad is relatively low. All the activities and dimensions involved in internationalization are still in the early stages of development, only partially integrating internationalization factors and concepts, with a limited amount of investment and resources at its disposal and limited impact in terms of breadth and depth.

The differences in the degree of higher education internationalization are also caused by the different stages of development. In terms of the strategic orientation of the governments and universities in internationalization, the three cities are at different stages of internationalization of higher education. Singapore and Hong Kong are at the mature and improvement phase of development, and their governments and universities have higher strategies and management capabilities, which accommodates a higher degree of internationalization. Their internationalization of higher education has become one of the core strategies of their cities. However, the internationalization of higher education in Shanghai is still on the rise, and the concept of internationalization is only implemented at the university level, but has not been highlighted as the official government strategy. While the main carriers of internationalization of higher education in Shanghai is mainly its research universities, the government's attention to internationalization needs to be improved.

8.2 Comparison of the characteristics, approaches, and models of higher education internationalization in Singapore, Hong Kong, and Shanghai

8.2.1 Comparison of the characteristics of the internationalization of higher education in three regions

8.2.1.1 Comparison of the interaction between city internationalization and higher education internationalization

The internationalization of higher education in Hong Kong and Singapore is already at a more mature stage of development and they can lead the education industry and education exports, synergize with the development needs of urban internationalization, and even lead the development of urban internationalization. The urban internationalization and higher education internationalization in Hong Kong and Singapore are highly integrated, synergistic, benignly interactive, and intrinsically driven, thus forming the two-way leading and synergistic development and innovation.

The internationalization of higher education in Shanghai is still at the rising phase of development. It has not yet been integrated into the strategic goal of international development of the city, let alone become a supporting industry sector, as it is passively catching up and adapting to the needs of the international development of the city. The relationship between urban internationalization and the internationalization of higher education in Shanghai is still at the stage of relative separation, lack of synergy, limited interaction, low facilitation, and external promotion. As Shanghai is the economic centre of China, and Fudan University and Shanghai Jiao Tong University are both affiliated to the Ministry of Education, the national influence on their internationalization of higher education exceeds the role of the municipal government. The construction of "985 project" and "double first-class" projects in China reflect the important strategic influence at the national level, while at the municipal level, although the role of Shanghai as a city in guiding and promoting the internationalization of research universities is constantly improving, it is still limited in the form of superficial interaction.

In Singapore and Hong Kong, the roles of the government and universities in the internationalization of higher education are clearly defined. The internationalization of higher education is based on the macro coordination of the government and the independent innovation of universities. It is an effective combination of government leadership and university autonomy. The Hong Kong government takes the leading role in coordinating eight public universities to develop their respective strengths and position themselves rationally, to avoid a similar functional positioning and disorderly internal competition.

Unlike Hong Kong and Singapore, where the internationalization of education is a strategic priority at the government level, the Shanghai municipal government does not plan and implement the internationalization of higher education as a strategic policy. The municipal government lacks an overall strategic positioning and promotion mechanism for the internationalization of higher education. The strategies of internationalization of higher education is mainly embodied at the institutional level in Shanghai. Universities have clearly proposed internationalization as an important development strategy in their 12th Five-Year Plan. However, with an accelerated economic transformation and upgrading, the speeding up of the construction of science and technology innovation centres, the Shanghai municipal government has promulgated and implemented such policies as the *Higher Education Peak and Plateau Project* and *30 Articles on Bringing in Overseas Talent* in recent years, which will promote the process of higher education internationalization.

8.2.1.2 Different rationales for the internationalization of higher education in the three regions

Internationalization is one of the key development strategies of the three cities and the six case universities, but the underlying motivation for the internationalization of higher education differs among the three cities, as evidenced by the concept surrounding internationalization adopted by their research universities.

The underlying reason for the internationalization of higher education in Singapore is primarily due to its economic rationale, which is committed to attracting human resources and obtaining tuition fees from international students. Higher education has been regarded as a major industry and the internationalization of higher education is recognized as an export trade by the Singapore government. It has vigorously introduced and built overseas branch campuses to attract international students and faculty with its high-quality education, in order to create an international higher education service port city and international campuses.

The underlying motivation for the internationalization of higher education in Hong Kong is relatively complex, combining academic rationales, economic rationales, and national interests. The academic rationales are embodied in attracting global outstanding faculty and recruiting non-local excellent students based on international academic standards. HK provides high salaries for international high-level faculty and scholarships for non-local graduate students. The eight public universities showcase their strengths to jointly build the regional higher education hub and attach importance to the overall academic competitiveness and influence. At the same time, the Hong Kong government attaches importance to the economic rationales, treating higher education as an important industry, retaining human resources needed for Hong Kong's socioeconomic development, allowing talented human resources, including non-local students, to stay and work in Hong Kong, gradually relaxing the quota for non-local students, and emphasizing the impact of talent on economic development and industrial competitiveness. Its emphasis on national rationales is mainly reflected in the large number of Mainland Chinese students it accepts. Between 2011 and 2012, for example, 72.2% of non-local postgraduate students at the University of Hong Kong were from Mainland China.

The underlying motivation of the internationalization of higher education in Shanghai is to improve the academic competitiveness of local higher education, so that the academic rationale takes priority over economic, political, and cultural development. China is a large country with abundant talent, so the student source of universities in Shanghai is mainly from the Mainland, and the faculty is mainly comprised of Chinese local talent. Shanghai's motivation for the internationalization of higher education is oriented to the capacity building of universities, aiming at improving the higher education quality of Shanghai, building world-class universities and first-class disciplines, and serving for the cultivation of internationalized and high-quality local talent.

As a matter of fact, the dominant rationales for the internationalization of higher education in each city are dynamic, with one or two rationales taking precedence over the others, and the dominant rationale(s) may be different in various dimensions and activities of higher education for different target groups in the same university. For example, the recruitment of undergraduate students may be dominated by the economic rationale and financial benefits; however, the recruitment of international graduate students may be dominated by the academic rationale and the principle of educational quality. Singapore, Hong Kong, and Shanghai all offer scholarships to selected international (non-local) students with a focus on long-term talent competition, research development, and a sustainable mode for world-class university building, rather than just economic benefits.

8.2.2 A comparison of the approaches to the internationalization of higher education in the three regions

8.2.2.1 Different priority rationales and internationalization focus determine their respective development approaches

The specific approach to, and focus of, the internationalization of higher education in the three regions are also different. Singapore focuses more on the industrial value and economic benefits of internationalization of higher education, as well as profit-making through cooperative education (including the introduction of first-class international educational institutions and universities to set up branches in Singapore, and enabling local universities to set up branch campuses abroad), which is an "education-economy-talent" development model, emphasizing economic rationales and the physical building of institutions. Hong Kong focuses on employing global academic talent with high salaries, attracting outstanding students with scholarships, and recruiting a high percentage of non-local graduate students. In cross-border cooperation, more emphasis is placed on project mobility, scientific research cooperation, and cooperative courses. The Hong Kong government and universities do not aim for economic benefits exclusively, but advocate a progressive approach to enhance cross-border economic and cultural exchanges through course offerings and studies, and to cultivate and recruit talent with a global perspective. Its emphasis on academic rationales and focusing on enhancing the international competitiveness of higher education can be described as an "education-academic-talent" model. Compared with Singapore and Hong Kong, Shanghai still lags behind in the depth and breadth of internationalization of higher education, with a limited number of international students and an emphasis on recruiting academic talent, especially overseas Chinese talent, in faculty development. Research universities have made internationalization an important development strategy, aiming to promote internationalization in the aspects of staff exchanges, curriculum and pedagogy, research, and cooperative education. Universities hope to improve their academic quality and international competitiveness, and to expand the cultural exchange and China's influence through the strategy of internationalization. The internationalization of higher education in Shanghai focuses on the improvement of academic capacity and cultural influence, and attaches importance to academic, social, and cultural rationales, thus manifesting itself in a "hybrid" rationale model, i.e. the "education-academic, cultural, political development model". Currently, due to the small number of international self-funded students and low tuition fees charged by universities in Shanghai, the economic rationale for the internationalization of higher education is far less important than that in Singapore and Hong Kong.

8.2.2.2 From transplantation to transcendence: The development approaches of Hong Kong and Singapore

Hong Kong and Singapore have a number of Asian and even world-renowned universities, and their approaches to the internationalization of higher education is to first transplant and then to transcend. During the period of establishing higher education, they relied on historical inheritances and transplanted the UK or US higher education models. Then in the 1980s, they further introduced advanced elements and high-quality educational resources from all over the world by using their own geographical advantages and internationalized institutional environment to promote the internationalization of higher education and build Asian higher education hubs to achieve transcendent development. Both regions have a high degree of dependence on foreign countries for both faculty members and students, and rely mainly on institutional innovation and financial investment to develop a high-end education supply and occupancy in the education market. This "transplant-transcendence" model in both regions has achieved corresponding results and suits their historical and realistic conditions.

8.2.3 Comparison of the models of the internationalization of higher education in the three regions

8.2.3.1 Singapore and Hong Kong follow an outward-oriented internationalization model, while Shanghai undertakes an inward-oriented internationalization model

Both Singapore and Hong Kong are prioritizing economic rationales, aiming to establish educational services trade zones, and to build Asian and even world academic centres and education hubs through the creation of internationalized campuses and world-class higher education institutions. As economies with scarce resources and small internal markets, Hong Kong and Singapore, with their human resources and markets abroad, leverage their institutional advantages to bring in and activate resources, in order to capture as much of the external market as possible. In light of the vast market demand in Asia, both regions attach great importance to establishing friendly cooperation with Mainland China, South Korea, Indonesia, India, etc. to develop their external markets and resources. For example, the University of Hong Kong has obtained more than 200 partners, the Hong Kong University of Science and Technology has built 380 partner institutions and research institutes, the National University of Singapore has established partnerships with more than 30 countries and regions, and Nanyang Technological University has established partnerships with more than 300 institutions. Both regions focus on taking education as a major industrial sector and actively develop educational service trade, by firstly "bringing in" and then "going out" to achieve the rapid development of export of educational services.

The internationalization of higher education in Shanghai tends to be inward-oriented, mainly relying on domestic human resources and the local market, aiming to promote the internationalization of local human resources and recruit overseas talent to build first-class universities. It is driven by the goal of "Project 985" university construction at the national level, aiming to build world-class universities. This is different from the outward-oriented internationalization goals of Singapore and Hong Kong, featuring in exporting high-quality educational resources and operating tertiary education as an industry.

8.2.3.2 Focusing on the internationalization of personnel and curricula

Both Hong Kong and Singapore regard the internationalization of personnel and curricula as the core and key to the development of higher education. The internationalization of personnel includes both faculty members and students, involving the two modes of "bringing in" and "going out". The four case universities in both regions have adopted various policies to bring in outstanding international teaching, research, and administration staff to improve the quality of teaching and research, and their international competitiveness. In terms of student internationalization, on the one hand, they actively attract non-local students, expand the scale of enrolment, focus on the quality of students, and optimize the proportion of students; while on the other hand, through the establishment of partnerships with overseas higher education institutions, students are encouraged to go abroad for academic exchanges. Curricula is the main carrier of the internationalization of education. The four case universities have adopted English as the teaching language and offer a variety of international courses to provide platforms for students to broaden their international horizons. The National University of Singapore has offered more than 70 dual degree courses and 30 joint degree courses with world-renowned universities (Ma, 2014).

Shanghai has taken the internationalization of personnel as a breakthrough opportunity to gradually promote internationalization. The government has implemented a number of programmes to bring in overseas talent. Universities are vigorously working on the internationalization of students and faculty members. It can be seen that the number of international students at the two case universities in Shanghai has been increasing year-on-year, with more degree-seeking international students and an increasingly optimized structure. The number of local students visiting and studying abroad has also been increasing. In terms of the internationalization of the faculty team, more young faculty members have obtained overseas academic credentials or overseas study experience.

8.3 Reflections on the prospect of internationalization of higher education in Shanghai

Through the comparison of the higher education internationalization in Singapore, Hong Kong, and Shanghai, it can be seen that the internationalization of higher education in Shanghai is at a stage of rapid development, with sufficient momentum, great potential, and promising prospects. Shanghai can learn from the experience of Singapore and Hong Kong in higher education internationalization and take the following measures to facilitate its process of internationalization.

8.3.1 Highlighting academic and economic rationales while also taking cultural and political rationales into account

First of all, it should be figured out which rationale(s) dominate(s) the policies and practices on the internationalization of higher education. The rationales for internationalization are the driving forces and value orientation of internationalization policies and behaviours, exerting a profound influence on the developmental direction, model, and approach related to internationalization. At present, although the internationalization of higher education in Shanghai attaches importance to the academic rationale, it has not yet paid attention to establishing their own international academic brands and featured disciplines, as well as the use of scholarships to recruit global outstanding undergraduate and graduate students. In the meantime, it has not yet paid sufficient attention to the economic rationale for internationalization and has not yet regarded higher education as the international talent cultivation and gathering centre in relation to long-term economic development, hence it needs to enable higher education to play its role in developing the education industry, and highlight educational service exports. Only led by academic and economic rationales while taking both the cultural and political rationales into account, can the strategic position of higher education internationalization in the international development of the city be truly obtained.

8.3.2 Shifting from an inward-oriented internationalization model to a balanced model of both inward- and outward-orientation

Compared with the internationalization of higher education in Hong Kong and Singapore, the development model of higher education internationalization in Shanghai is inward-oriented. Both Hong Kong and Singapore adopt the outward-oriented internationalization model, i.e. bringing in overseas high-quality educational resources, enhancing the internationalization capability of universities, cultivating internationalized talent, and improving their internationalized research level. Their student markets and faculty members mainly come from overseas. They recruit and retain Asian or global students and faculty members, establishing internationalized educational service hubs by taking advantage of their own system and geographical advantages. To some extent, higher education is seen as a service industry in Hong Kong and Singapore. They are committed to enhancing their strengths in the higher education industry as well as their ability to trade in educational services (Mok, 2011).

The internationalization development model of higher education practised by Shanghai is still mainly inward-oriented internationalization, i.e. taking Mainland Chinese students as the main target of international talent cultivation, with a small number and proportion of international students, and the international students who are offered scholarships mainly come from developing countries and emerging economies. In terms of the internationalization of higher education, it does not pursue scale and economic benefits, but pursues political and cultural soft power goals, serving the needs of the national strategy for the internationalization of higher education. The international talent needed by Shanghai's knowledge-based economy, export-oriented economy, and science and technology industry development are mainly met in two ways, one is to bring in overseas talent and the other is to cultivate talent locally. Due to the limited capacity of local higher education in terms of internationalization and attracting and retaining international high-quality students, and the importance of cultivating international talent through local education has not yet been fully conceived, the international talent needed for economic development are to a certain extent dependent on the introduction of talent.

In the medium and long term, the strategy for the internationalization of higher education in Shanghai needs to shift from an inward-oriented international development model to an international development model that emphasizes both inward- and outward- orientations, focusing on the internationalization at home and exporting international education resources, in order to enhance the international competitiveness of education. Inward-oriented internationalization cultivates international talent to serve local economic development, shifting from relying mainly on bringing in international talent to cultivating talent locally. Outward-oriented internationalization highlights the export and expansion function of education, requiring the recruitment of a larger scale and higher level of international students, and giving full play to the function of educational exports and the educational service trade.

8.3.3 Improving the international competitiveness of Shanghai's higher education with "Project 985" universities as leadership

As the national spearhead in higher education, Shanghai should not only have certain quantity and scale advantages, but also highlight its quality, brand, and featured advantages. If it only focuses on its scale and quantity, it will not be able to play a leading and dominating role. Drawing on the approach of highlighting "differential positioning and individual strengths" of Hong Kong universities (He, 2005), with FU, SJTU, ECNU, and Tongji University as the pioneers, Shanghai needs to lead the "First-class discipline" universities and other universities to implement differential positioning and competition, and develop comparative advantages, in order to improve the overall internationalization level of more than 60 universities in Shanghai. The internationalization of the three types of higher education institutions, namely, the internationalization of public universities, the internationalization of Sino-foreign joint venture institutions and programmes, and the internationalization of private universities, requires different orientations, objections, and focuses. Public universities are divided into research universities, teaching and research universities, and teaching universities, all of which can adopt different internationalization approaches and formulate different strategies and rationales.

Shanghai should focus on the internationalization of personnel and curricula, improve the international academic level of faculty members, and build a more comprehensive English curriculum system, in order to serve the cultivation of high-quality local talent, improve the internationalization of teaching and research in universities, attract more high-quality international students to study in Shanghai. The faculty, quality and reputation of education, social recognition of degrees, scholarships, curricula, as well as educational resources and facilities are all important factors in attracting international students. The competitiveness and attractiveness of higher education are determined by the level and quality of higher education in a region. Universities in Shanghai should expand cooperation with overseas reputable universities and learn from their experiences to enhance the internationalization and international competitiveness of their advantageous and featured disciplines.

8.3.4 The government needs to enhance the brand of higher education and establish an international education hub in Shanghai.

The long-term goal of higher education internationalization in Shanghai should refer to that in Hong Kong and Singapore, focusing on enhancing the brand of higher education, building an international education hub, laying the foundation of human resources and intellectual support for the construction of a comprehensive education reform pilot zone and Shanghai Pilot Free Trade Zone, as well as accumulating experience in education and management. An overall consideration should be given to the cultivation of both international students and local internationalized talent, recruitment of high-quality international faculty members, and the internationalization of scientific research to enhance the international competitiveness of higher education that matches Shanghai's status as an international metropolis and a science and innovation centre.

The Shanghai municipal government needs to execute scientific, reasonable, and long-term strategic planning for the comprehensive development and the internationalization of the city. It should integrate education, especially higher education, into its economic, scientific, and technological planning as a driving force for development, to strengthen the municipal government's planning, investment, and coordination of the higher education system, and turn a number of research universities into world-class universities that have international competitiveness. On the basis of strengthening the macro coordination, the planning and input of the municipal government and the market mechanism should be used to stimulate all stakeholders to participate in the internationalization of higher education and to establish an administrative system of higher education internationalization adopting governmental guidance, social participation, and university autonomy. The policy formulation and implementation of higher education internationalization need to combine both "top-down" and "bottom-up" models, bring into play the initiative of different operators, including government sectors, NGOs, foundations and intermediary organizations, as well as higher education institutions and research institutes, and make full use of the market mechanism.

Quality educational institutions and projects should be attracted to settle in Shanghai by improving the regulations and policy measures related to the internationalization of education. Taking the construction of New York University Shanghai as an opportunity, Shanghai should bring in more high-quality foreign education brands and launch high-level Sino-foreign joint venture institutions and programmes that rely on higher education institutions. There is still huge market demand for cross-border higher education in China. As a frontier city in facilitating the internationalization of higher education, Shanghai needs to seize this historical opportunity to develop the inward-oriented internationalization of higher education. At the same time, Shanghai needs to properly develop the outward-oriented internationalization of higher education, strengthening the export of the higher education industry, promoting the educational service trade, and improving the economic benefits brought about by higher education internationalization.

References

Gong, S. Y. (2005). Guoji fenxiao: Xinjiapo de jingyan yu qishi [International branch campuses: Singapore's experience and insights]. *Liaoning Jiaoyu Yanjiu [Liaoning Education Research]*, *10*, 51–52, 82.

He, B. (2005). Xianggang gaodeng jiaoyu guojihua xianzhuang fenxi [Analysis of the status quo of the internationalization of higher education in Hong Kong]. *Bijiao Jiaoyu Yanjiu [International and Comparative Education]*, *1*, 16–19.

Ma, H. T. (2014). Quanqiuhua gaoxiao de chuangjian celue tanxi: Yi xinjiapo guoli daxue weili [Exploring the strategies for establishing a globalized higher education institution: The case of National University of Singapore]. *Zhongguo Gaoxiao Keji [Chinese University Science and Technology]*, *4*, 39–41.

Mok, K. H. (2011). The quest for regional hub of education: Growing heterarchies, organizational hybridization, and new governance in Singapore and Malaysia. *Journal of Education Policy*, *26*(1), 61–81.

Ren, Y. Q. (2016). "Shuang yiliu" zhanlue xia gaodeng jiaoyu guojihua de weilai fazhan [The future development of internationalization of higher education under the "double first-class" strategy]. *Zhongguo Gaodeng Jiaoyu [China Higher Education]*, *5*, 15–17.

Zhang, S. S. (2011). Yinjin chuangxin zouxiang yiliu: Shang Hai Jiaoda Mixigen Xueyuan de gongcheng jiaoyu gaige tansuo [Introducing innovation and stepping into the first-class-engineering education reform at UM-SJTU joint institute]. *Gaodeng Gongcheng Jiaoyu Yanjiu [Research in Higher Education of Engineering]*, *2*, 16–26.

Zhang, W. F., Zhong, L. P., & He, B. (2009). Xianggang gaodeng jiaoyu guojihua dui Neidi gaoxiao fazhan de qiashi [Enlightenment from Hong Kong internationalization of higher education to mainland college development]. *Jiaoyu Xueshu Qikan [Education Research Monthly]*, *7*, 38–40, 44.

Index

12th Five-Year Action Plan for the Internationalization Project of Education in Shanghai 155
12th Five-Year Plan for Shanghai's Education Internationalization Project 187
13th Five-Year Plan for the Development of National Education 15
13th Five-Year Plan for the Reform and Development of Education in Shanghai 155
2003-2007 Action Plan for Revitalizing Education 146

AACSB *see* Association to Advance Collegiate Schools of Business International
academic adaptation of international students 166–168
academic backgrounds of faculty, Sino-foreign joint venture education 200–201
academic career development: of returned faculty 102–107; of Thousand Youth Talent Program scholars 130–135; *see also* career development
academic centres 29
academic environment, views of overseas Chinese scholars on 67–69
academic evaluation system 114–115
academic innovation, mini environments 116
academic qualifications of overseas teachers, in Sino-foreign joint venture education 203–204
academic returnees: accumulation and transfer of transnational capital 106–107; institutional environment and situation on professional development 107–119; role and influence of 105–106
academic talent: accumulation of transnational capital 35–36; classification of Chinese academic talent overseas 43–44; *see also* Chinese academic talent in US; outflow of academic talent
academic work characteristics of returned faculty 115–116
Accreditation and Re-accreditation Visit, Xi'an Jiaotong-Liverpool University 192
accreditation by international professional organizations, Xi'an Jiaotong-Liverpool University 194
accumulation of transnational capital by academic talent 35–36
activity-based approach 6
adaptation: academic adaptation of international students 166–168; life adaptation of international students 168; of returned faculty 103–104
Administrative Measures for Overseas Young Scholars' Cooperative Research Fund 83
Administrative Measures for the Approval of Foreigners' Permanent Residence in China 87
Annual Monitor Visit, Xi'an Jiaotong-Liverpool University 192
Association to Advance Collegiate Schools of Business International (AACSB) 194
attracting high-level innovative and entrepreneurial talent (2008-present) 87–88
autonomy, Xi'an Jiaotong-Liverpool University 194–196

banding together 113
Beijing Normal University 178, 218
"Belt and Road" *Educational Action Plan* 10, 15, 17, 21, 147, 155
Belt and Road Initiative (BRI) 15
brain circulation 27, 31–32
brain drain 27, 31–32, 42, 54–55
brain gain 27, 31–32
brain outflow 26

capitalism, globalization 4–5
career development: changing trends of overseas returnees 102–103; reasons for staying in US 60–62; of returned faculty 105, 119; of Thousand Youth Talent Program scholars 123–125, 130–135, 140–141; views of academic career environment 67–69; *see also* academic career development
career development space for Thousand Youth Talent Program scholars 127–130
CAS *see* Chinese Academy of Sciences
CAS Management Measures for Attracting Outstanding Talent from Abroad 86
Center for China and Globalization (CCG) 102
centre-periphery model 11, 110
Certificate of Returned Personnel From Studying Abroad 83
Changjiang Scholars Achievement Award 84
Changjiang Scholars Award Program 84
Changjiang Scholars Program 98
Changjiang Scholars Recruitment Measures 84
characteristics of: academic work of TYTP awardees 135–138; international faculty in Sino-foreign joint venture education (2016) 202–206; international mobility of Chinese students and academics 44–54; international students in China 147–154; international students in Shanghai 157–160; internationalization of higher education 220–225; transnational academic work 38–39; transnational flow of academic talent 37–38
China Scholars Abroad 82
China Scholarship Council (CSC) 13, 47, 79
"China-is-a-threat Philosophy" 18
China's Education Modernization 2035 Blueprint 15
Chinese academic talent in US 54; brain drain 54–55; cooperation with academic counterparts in China 69–73; factors triggering talent to return to China 64–67; reasons for staying in US 60–64; research questions and methods 56–57; to return or not return to China 57–59; views of academic career environment 67–69
Chinese Academy of Sciences, Hundred Talent Program 84
Chinese Government Scholarship Fund 147

Chinese Service Centre for Scholarly Exchange (CSCSE) 81–82
The Chinese University of Hong Kong (Shenzhen) 178, 218
Chunhui Plan 84
circulation of talent in global labour market 138–139
classification of Chinese academic talent overseas 43–44
collaborative objective of Chinese scholars in US **71**
Collaborative Provisional Sub-Committee 193
commercial presence 2
comparison of academic career between China and the US **68**
competency approach 6
Confucius Institutes 15, 22
consumption abroad 2
cooperation with academic counterparts in China 69–73
cooperative scientific research for Thousand Youth Talent Program scholars 130
countries of origin for international students in China 149–150
cross-border supply 2
CSC *see* China Scholarship Council
CSCSE *see* Chinese Service Centre for Scholarly Exchange
cultural capital 106
curriculum, internationalization of curriculum in research universities in Shanghai 217–218
curriculum delivery, Xi'an Jiaotong-Liverpool University 195

Decision on the Reform of the Education System 13
degree of internationalization of case universities, comparing in Singapore, Hong Kong, and Shanghai 218–220
degree-seeking international students 150–152, 159
developed countries 29–30; as destinations for Chinas academic mobility 48–49
development of research teams for Thousand Youth Talent Program scholars 130
developmental degree of internationalization, comparing in Singapore, Hong Kong, and Shanghai research universities 218–220
diaspora 27, 32–34

Index 233

differentiated demand 45
disciplinary distribution of overseas teachers in Sino-foreign joint venture education 204–205
disciplinary structure (for faculty), Sino-foreign joint venture education 201–202
disequilibrium of supply and demand 44
distribution of overseas teachers in Sino-foreign joint venture education 206
domestic research mentality 114
double first-class universities, TYTP awardees 92–93
double free areas 157
Duke Kunshan University 178

East China Normal University (ECNU) 161–162, 166, 218
economic benefits, gap between academic professions between China and US 69
economic factors, reasons for staying in US 62–63
education hubs 10
Education Initiatives in Advancing the Joint Construction of the "Belt and Road" 15
education of international students in China 146–148; improving 172–174; problems with 170–171
educational trade services 2
eligibility for Thousand Youth Talent Program 121–125
employment policy for international students in Shanghai 157
encouraging overseas academic talent to serve China 84–85
English 175; as lingua franca 3
English curriculum for international students in China 172
English for Academic Purposes (EAP) courses, Xi'an Jiaotong-Liverpool University 196
enrollment, UNNC compared to NYUS 182
establishment of: New York University Shanghai (NYUS) 187–188; University of Nottingham Ningbo China (UNNC) 187–188
evaluations, Principles and Measures of the Academic Degrees Office on the Accreditation of Degree Conferring Units 193
evolution of overseas academic talent policies 79–80, 83–85; attracting high-level innovative and entrepreneurial talent (2008-present) 87–88; global competition for talent (2001-2007) 85–87; intensive opening-up (1984-1991) 81–82; market-oriented transformation (1992-2000) 83–85; reform and opening-up (1978-1983) 80–81
Examination Committee, Xi'an Jiaotong-Liverpool University 195
excess demand 45
expansion diffusion 9
export resources 8
exported internationalization 9

factors triggering talent to return to China 64–67
faculty members 43–44; comparing faculty in Singapore, Hong Kong and Shanghai at research universities 216–217; gender ratio of, Sino-foreign joint venture education 199–200
Faculty Teaching Committee, Xi'an Jiaotong-Liverpool University 195
faculty team-building, Sino-foreign joint venture education 199–210
faculty-level teaching, Xi'an Jiaotong-Liverpool University 195–196
family factors: reasons for staying in US 62; triggering talent return to China 65–66
fees policy, higher education policies for international students in Shanghai 155–156
field theory 35
flat management systems, UNNC compared to NYUS 184
flight teaching model 208
forced IHE 8
Fudan University (FU) 160–162, 166, **217, 219**
funding: enrollment of international students in Shanghai by funding source (2006-2016) **160**; for international students in China 171; to support development of returned students 82–84; for Thousand Youth Talent Program scholars 129–130; see also scholarships

Gaokao 182
gender ratio of faculty, Sino-foreign joint venture education 199–200
glass ceiling 19, 66
global campuses 10
global competition for talent (2001-2007) 85–87
global knowledge networks 33

global mobility of Chinese academics 76–77
globalization 1–4, 43; characteristics of 5–6; concepts of 4–5
government scholarship standards for international students in China 147, 174
government-led progressive mode of internationalization 15–16
growth trajectory of Thousand Youth Talent Program (TYTP) scholars 125–126
Guangdong Technion-Israel Institute of Technology 179
Guidance Opinions on Classifying and Promoting the Reform of Talent Evaluation Mechanism 98
Guidelines on Defining Overseas Educated Graduates in the Attraction of Overseas Talent 85

HEIs *see* higher education institutions
higher education, challenges for 1–4
higher education institutions (HEIs) 6–7, 170; centre-periphery model 11; characteristics of international students in Shanghai 157–160; education of international students in China 173–175; enrollment of international students in Shanghai by funding source (2006-2016) **160**; influencing factors for choosing 166–167
higher education internationalization: classification of Chinese academic talent overseas 43–44; comparing in Singapore, Hong Kong, and Shanghai 220–225; limitations of 20; prospects for 20–23; Shanghai 225–228
higher education policies, for international students in Shanghai 155–160
high-level academic talent 26
high-level international talent, cultivating 21
history of internationalization of higher education 12; government-led progressive mode of internationalization 15–16; Stage four post-2012 14–15; Stage one 1978-1991 13; Stage three 13–14; Stage two 1992-2000 13
Hong Kong: comparing higher education internationalization 220–225; comparing internationalization of research universities 213–220
Hong Kong Baptist University United International College 178

Hong Kong University of Science and Technology **217–219**
horizontal correlation 136
host cities, Sino-foreign joint venture education 186–187
human capital 35–36; brain drain 31–32
human capital theory 32
human resources 2; flow of 31–32
Hundred Talent Program 84, 86, 91, 99

ICAEW *see* Institute of Chartered Accountants in England and Wales
identity 33
identity capital 34
identity construction, Thousand Youth Talent Program (TYTP) scholars 127
IET *see* Institution of Engineering and Technology
immigration motives, Chinese academic talent in US 63
impact of overseas study and work on individuals **109**
Imperial College of Science, Technology and Medicine 10
Implementation Measures for the Applications of Shanghai Government Scholarships for Foreign Students 155
importable HE resources 8
imported internationalization 8
improving faculty teams in Sino-foreign joint venture education programmes 208–209
influencing factors for choosing, HEIs 166–167
innovation of Thousand Youth Talent Program scholars 136
Institute of Chartered Accountants in England and Wales (ICAEW) 194
Institution of Engineering and Technology (IET) 194
institutional distribution of awardees, Thousand Youth Talent Program (TYTP) **93**
institutional distribution of international students in Shanghai (2004-2016) **158**
institutional environment, professional development of academic returnees 107–119
Interim Measures for the Attraction of Overseas High-level Talent 87
Interim Measures of the Dispatch of International Graduates 81

Interim Provisions on Self-financed Studying Abroad (Interim Provisions) 80–81
internal drive for work, Thousand Youth Talent Program (TYTP) scholars 136
internal quality assurance system, Xi'an Jiaotong-Liverpool University 194–196
international academic mobility 28; brain circulation 27; brain drain 27, 31–32; brain gain 27; brain outflow 26; high-level academic talent 26; knowledge diaspora 32–34; transnational capital accumulation 34–37; world system theory 28–31
international cooperative education, comparing in Singapore, Hong Kong, and Shanghai 218
international faculty in Sino-foreign joint venture education (2016), characteristics of 202–206
international flow of talent 28; *see also* international academic mobility
International Knowledge Networks 33
international open talent recruitment system, implementation of 94–96
international student education in Shanghai 154–160
international student hub 10
international students in China 43, 146–148; characteristics of 147–154; life adaptation 168; majors of 152–153; mobility 154; number of students between 1996 and 2018 *148*; problems for 169–170; rationales and motivations for studying in China 163–166; regional distribution of 153–154; self-financed 153; share of international students in Singapore and Hong Kong versus Shanghai 214–216; Top 5 countries of origin (1998-2018) **149**; types of (1998-2018) **151**
internationalization 1, 4, 43; concepts of 6–7
internationalization development model, Shanghai 226
internationalization higher education (IHE): forced/spontaneous IHE 8; inward- and outward-oriented 8–9; new forms 9–10; new trends 10; Shanghai 225–228
internationalization of higher education: history of 12–18; limitations of 20
"Internationalization of Personnel" 16
"Internationalization of Projects and Institutions" 16

interpersonal networks, for Thousand Youth Talent Program scholars 130
interpersonal relationship 112–113; in China, reasons talent stays in US 61–62
interviews on Chinese academic talent in US 57–58
investment in universities 188–189; Sino-foreign joint venture education 186–187
inward- and outward-oriented, Shanghai 226
inward-oriented IHE 8–9
inward-oriented internationalization 17; Shanghai 226

Japan, percentage of international students in China 150–151
JBM *see* Joint Board of Moderators
Jiangsu Provincial Department of Education 194
job satisfaction of returned faculty 104–105
Joint Board of Moderators (JBM) 194

knowledge diaspora 27, 32–34, 76–77
knowledge transfer 17; cooperation with academic counterparts in China 72–73
knowledge/innovation hub 10

laboratory and disciplinary platform construction 127
Lao Soochow University 10
leadership, Sino-foreign joint venture education 182–183
level of degree obtained by Chinese scholars staying in US **59**
life adaptation of international students 168
limitations of internationalization of higher education 20
local level, talent recruitment 90
long-term management mechanisms, establishing for overseas faculty 209–210
Long-term Program for Innovative Talent 87

majors of international students in China 152–156
management innovation, UNNC compared to NYUS 182–185
management mechanisms, establishing for overseas faculty 209–210
market globalism 1
market-oriented transformation (1992-2000) 83–85
Matthew effect 97, 99

236 *Index*

Measures for the Administration of Foreign Students 146
Measures for the Implementation of the Regulations of the People's Republic of China on Sino-foreign Joint Venture Education 179
Measures for the Implementation of the Special Fund of the State Education Commission for Sponsoring the Short-term Return of Overseas Students to Work in China 84
Michigan College of SJTU 218
micro-level factors, influencing talent's choice of staying in US 74
micro-spaces 116
migration of human capital 27
mini environments, academic innovation 116
Ministry of Education Chunhui Plan Implementation Measures for Overseas Talent Returning to China on Academic Leave (in Trial) 84
ministry of Education Research Start-up Fund for Returned Overseas Students 82
mobility: characteristics of 39; of international students in China 154; *see also* migration
modes of internationalization 17
motivations for international students to study in China 163–166
multiple-subject collaborative governance, building quality assurance systems for joint venture institutions 197–199
multi-subject collaborative governance, Xi'an Jiaotong-Liverpool University 191
mutual exchange 21–22

Nanyang Technological University **217**, **219**
nation state 1–2
national level, talent recruitment 90
National University of Singapore **217**, **219**
negative factors affecting US Chinese scholars' willingness to return to China **61**
neocolonialism theory 30
new forms of internationalization of higher education 9–10
New York University Shanghai (NYUS) 178, 218; compared to University of Nottingham Ningbo China 181–189; establishment of 187–188; leadership 182–185
Ningbo, investment in universities 186–187

non-degree-seeking international students 150–151, 159
Notice on Adjusting the Standard of Living Expenses of Foreign Students Financed by Scholarships 147
Notice on Carrying Out Preparatory Education for International Undergraduate Students Sponsored by the Chinese Government Scholarship 147
Notice on Further Improving the Chunhui Plan 84
Notice on Further Regulating the Order of Sino-foreign Joint Venture Education 179
Notice on Handling the ID Certificate of High-level Overseas Students 86
Notice on the Evaluation of Sino-foreign Joint Venture Education 179
Notice on the Review of Sino-foreign Joint Venture Institutions and Projects 179
number of international students at research universities in 2016 **215**

opening-up policies, optimizing 22–23
Opinions of the Central Talent Work Coordination Group on the Implementation of the Plan for the Attraction of Overseas High-level Talent see Thousand Talent Program
Opinions of the MoE on Further Strengthening the Quality Assurance of Sino-foreign Joint Venture Education in Higher Education 209
Opinions on Deepening the Reform of Project Evaluation, Talent Evaluation and Institutional Assessment 98
Opinions on Encouraging Overseas High-level Talent to Return to Work in China 84
Opinions on Encouraging Overseas Students to Serve China in Various Forms 85
Opinions on Further Improving the Usage of Chinese Permanent Residency (Green Card) 87
Opinions on Several Issues of Current Sino-Foreign Joint Venture Education 179
Opinions on the Green Channel for Overseas High-level Talent Returning to Work in China 86
opportunities for Thousand Youth Talent Program scholars 137–138

orientation, UNNC compared to NYUS 181–182
origin of international students in Shanghai's HEIs (2005-2016) **159**
outflow of academic talent: developed countries as destinations for China's academic mobility 48–49; post-doctoral fellows 52–54; reasons for return of talent 103; research universities in US 51–52; return rate 47–48; Sino-US educational exchange 49–51; studying abroad 44–46; *see also* brain drain
Outline of National Medium-and Long-term Education Reform and Development Plan (2010-2020) 179
Outstanding Youth Program 99
outward-oriented IHE 8–9
outward-oriented internationalization 17
overseas academic talent policies 79–80; attracting high-level innovative and entrepreneurial talent (2008-present) 87–88; global competition for talent (2001-2007) 85–87; intensive opening-up (1984-1991) 81–82; market-oriented transformation (1992-2000) 83–85; problems with 96–100; reform and opening-up (1978-1983) 80–81
overseas high-level talent program, implementation of 88–96
Overseas Teacher Training Program for Higher Education International Curriculum Construction in Shanghai HEIs 157
overseas teachers, in Sino-foreign joint venture education 202–208

parent universities, Sino-foreign joint venture education 186
permanent residency systems 86–87
"personnel internationalization" 16
perspectives of, Thousand Youth Talent Program (TYTP) scholars 121–125
PhDs, return rate of 50–51
plans for international students upon graduation in Shanghai **166**
policies: on education of international students in China 146–148; to encourage overseas academic talent to serve in China 84–85; to encourage overseas talent to return to work in China 85; for luring overseas academic talent back to China 83–84; for overseas academic talent to serve China 85–86
post-correlation 136

post-doctoral fellows 43–44, 52–54
pre-correlation 136
Principles and Measures of the Academic Degrees Office on the Accreditation of Degree Conferring Units 193
process-based approach 6
professional development 115–116; of academic returnees, institutional environment 107–119; *see also* career development, returned faculty
professional evaluation, tracking talent programmes 100
professional experience of overseas teachers, in Sino-foreign joint venture education 204
professional management guarantee mechanisms, Xi'an Jiaotong-Liverpool University 195–196
professional titles of faculty in Sino-foreign joint venture education 200–204
Program for Entrepreneurial Talent 87
Project 211 111
Project 985 111; Shanghai 227
"project and institutional internationalization" 16
prospects for higher education internationalization 20–23
public-funded study abroad 45–46
push-pull factors: Chinese academic talent in US 54–55; factors triggering talent to return to China 64–66; leading Chinese academic talent to stay in US 74

qualifications of overseas teachers, in Sino-foreign joint venture education **205**
Quality Assessment of Sino-foreign Joint Venture Education 193
quality assurance for: Sino-foreign joint venture education 180–181; Xi'an Jiaotong-Liverpool University 190–199
quality supervision, Xi'an Jiaotong-Liverpool University 191–193
questionnaire survey on Chinese academic talent in US 56–57

rationale/ethos approach 6
reasons for: international students to study in China **164**; international students to study in Shanghai **165**; outflow and return of talent 103; staying, Chinese academic talent in US 60–64
recruitment: of high-quality teachers for Sino-foreign joint venture education 207, 209; of overseas high-level talent 88–96

recruitment policy for international students in Shanghai 155
reform and opening-up 18–19; overseas academic talent policies 80–81
regional distribution of international students in China 153–154
regional internationalization 16
Regulations for the Quality of Higher Education for International Students in China (Trial) 147
Regulations of the People's Republic of China on Sino-foreign Joint Venture Education 179, 187
Regulations on Promotion of Private Education in Ningbo 186
regulatory framework, Xi'an Jiaotong-Liverpool University 195
relocation diffusion 9
Report on the Management of Overseas Students Conference 81
Request for Instructions on Self-financed Studying Abroad ("Request") 80–81
Request for Standards for Hosting Self-financed Foreign Students 146
research projects for Thousand Youth Talent Program scholars 129–130
research questions and methods, on Chinese academic talent in US 56–57
research universities 17; comparison of internationalization in Singapore, Hong Kong and Shanghai 213–220; international students in China 175; share of Chinese talent 51–52; survey of international students in Shanghai 160–169
researchers 43–44
Resolution on Issues Concerning the Establishment of a Socialist Market Economic System 83
return of talent 103
return rate 47; of Chinese academic talent in US 57–59; of PhDs 50–51; from studying abroad 47–48
returned faculty: adaptation of 103–104; career development 105, 119; job satisfaction 104–105; perception of institutional environment of academic career 108–112; professional development and academic work characteristics 115–116
returning academic talent back to China, policies for 83–84
Royal Institute of British Architects (RIBA) 194

scholarship policies for international students in Shanghai **156**
scholarships for international students 147, 172, 174
scientific research teams, building 128–129
self-financed, international students in China 153
self-funded study abroad 45–46; international students in Shanghai 160
self-motivation of Thousand Youth Talent Program scholars 136
self-regulation, Xi'an Jiaotong-Liverpool University 194–196
service networks, UNNC compared to NYUS 185
Several Suggestions on the Opening-up of Education in the New Era 147
Shanghai: comparing higher education internationalization 220–225; comparing internationalization of research universities 213–220; as international education hub 228; international student education 154–160; investment in universities 186–187; Project 985 227; prospect of internationalization of higher education 225–228; survey of international students in research universities 160–169
Shanghai Jiao Tong University (SJTU) 160–162, 166, 217–219
Shanghai Pilot Free Trade Zone 173
Shanghai Thousand Talent Program 90
Shenzhen Moscow State University-Beijing Institute of Technology University 179
Short-term Program for Innovative Talent 87
"Silk Road" Chinese Government Scholarship 147
Singapore: comparing higher education internationalization 220–225; comparing internationalization of research universities 213–220
Sino-foreign joint venture education; establishment of universities and their institutional environment 187–188; faculty team-building 199–210; improvements in 179–180; leadership 182–183; overview 178–179; quality assurance for 180–181; UNNC compared to NYUS 181–189; Xi'an Jiaotong-Liverpool University 190–199
Sino-foreign joint venture higher education 22
Sino-foreign joint venture institutions, building quality assurance systems for 197–199

Sino-US educational exchange 49–51
skilled workforce hub 10
social capital 35–36
social problems for international students in China 171
Soochow University 94
South Korea, percentage of international students in China 150–151
Southern University of Science and Technology 94
spontaneous IHE 8
stakeholders in Sino-foreign joint venture education 185–188
strong state-led development model 17
student development, UNNC compared to NYUS 185
student management, UNNC compared to NYUS 185
student-teacher ratio, Xi'an Jiaotong-Liverpool University 197
Study-Abroad Agreement 82
studying abroad 2–3, 44–45; Chinese students and scholars in US **53**; number of Chinese overseas students in the main recipient countries (1998-2017) *49*; number of Chinese students studying abroad (2000-2018) **46**; public and self-funded study abroad 45–46; reasons for not returning to China upon graduation 47–48; return rate of Chinese overseas students (1978-2018) **48**; Sino-US educational exchange 49–51; *see also* overseas academic talent policies
studying abroad fever 3
Studying in China Program 147
supervision by Chinese education authorities, Xi'an Jiaotong-Liverpool University 193–194
survey of international students in research universities, in Shanghai 160–169
sustainability of talent programs 96–97
Suzhou University, Lao Soochow University 10

talent: circulation of 138–139; cultivating high-level international talent 21; global competition for talent (2001-2007) 85–87; high-level academic talent 26; high-level international talent, cultivating 21; *see also* academic talent; Chinese academic talent in US; outflow of academic talent; overseas academic talent policies

talent mobility 26–27, 42; *see also* migration
talent programmes: Matthew effect 97; optimizing leadership and management systems 97–98; tracking 100
teaching and curriculum reform, for international students in Shanghai 157
technology transfer, cooperation with academic counterparts in China 72–73
Thousand Talent Program 87–88, 90–91, 97–98, 103
Thousand Talent Program for Foreign Experts 87
Thousand Youth Talent Program (TYTP) 37, 87–92; academic career development of scholars 120–121; awardees (2011-2018) 91; classification of policies for awardees *89*; double first-class universities 92–93; higher education and training background **126**; impacts of 92; institutional distribution of awardees **93**; meaning and value of identity of awardee 140; number of shortlisted awardees (2011-2018) **95**; perspectives of TYTP scholars 121–125
Thousand Youth Talent Program (TYTP) scholars; academic career development of 123–125, 140–141; characteristics of academic work of 135–138; construction of career development space 127–130; growth trajectory of 125–126; identity construction 127; opportunities and challenges 137–138; patterns of academic career development 130–135; transnational social capital 127
Tongji University 10
"Topping-of-China Theory" 18
tracking talent programmes 100
trade wars, between US and China 5–6
training background, Thousand Youth Talent Program (TYTP) scholars **126**
transcendence in formation of academic development paths, of Thousand Youth Talent Program scholars 137
transfer of, transnational capital 36–37
transnational academic career development, of Thousand Youth Talent Program scholars 135–136
transnational academic work, characteristics of 38–39
transnational capital 34, 123, 139–140; accumulation and transfer of 106–107; accumulation of 35–36; transfer of 36–37

transnational capital transfer 124; Thousand Youth Talent Program (TYTP) scholars 120–121
transnational education 13
transnational flow of talent 139; characteristics of 37–38
transnational human capital 35–36
transnational social capital, Thousand Youth Talent Program (TYTP) scholars 127
transnational social field 35
transnational space 34
transnationalism 34–35
trends on Chinese scholars' international mobility 75–76
Trial Measures for the Application of Shanghai Government Scholarships for Foreign Students 156
Trial Measures for the Electronic Diploma and Certificate Registration of Foreign Students in Higher Education Institutions 146–147
tripartite cooperation, Sino-foreign joint venture education 185–188
Trump, Donald 5
tuition fees for international students in Shanghai **156**
two-way inward internationalization 17
two-way learning 21–22
Type I domestic education **126**
Type I: rapid career development, Thousand Youth Talent Program (TYTP) 131–133
Type II mixed education background **126**
Type II: steadily upward career development, Thousand Youth Talent Program (TYTP) 132–134
Type III mixed education background **126**
Type III: slow career development/start-up career development **132**, 134–135
TYTP *see* Thousand Youth Talent Program (TYTP)

unilateral internationalization 9
United States: percentage of international students in China 150–151; trade war with China 5–6
universities, Top 20 universities hosting international students in US (2018) **52**
University of California, Los Angeles (UCLA) 56
University of Hong Kong **217**, **219**
University of Michigan 218
University of Nottingham Ningbo China (UNNC) 178; compared to New York University Shanghai 181–189; establishment of 187–188; leadership 182–185
University of Tokyo 127
up-or-out employment system 111

Validation Visit, Xi'an Jiaotong-Liverpool University 192
vertical correlation 136
visas 86
visiting scholars 43

Wenzhou-Kean University 178
world academic system, China's position in 110–111
world system theory 28–31
World Trade Organization (WTO) 2; China's accession to 149; internationalization of higher education 13–14

Xiamen University, Xiamen University Malaysia 10
Xi'an Jiaotong-Liverpool University (XJTLU) 190–199

Yu, Lizhong 183

Zhejiang University, Imperial College of Science, Technology and Medicine 10